D1617327

Yale Historical Publications

Map of South Africa

Manufacturing Apartheid

State

Corporations

in South Africa

Nancy L. Clark

Yale University Press

New Haven and London

Published under the direction of the Department of History of Yale University with assistance from the income of the Frederick John Kingsbury Memorial Fund.

Designed by James J. Johnson and set in Trump Roman type by Marathon Typography Service, Durham, North Carolina. Printed in the United States of America by BookCrafters, Inc., Chelsea, Michigan.

A catalogue record for this book is available from the British Library.

10 9 8 7 6 5 4 3 2 1

Library of Congress Cataloging-in-Publication Data

Clark, Nancy L.
  Manufacturing apartheid : state corporations in South Africa / Nancy L. Clark.
    p.   cm. — (Yale historical publications)
  Includes bibliographical references and index.
  ISBN 0-300-05638-9 (alk. paper)

  1. Corporations, Government—South Africa.   2. Government business enterprises—South Africa.   3. Industry and state—South Africa.   4. Apartheid—South Africa.   I. Title.   II. Series.
HD4350.5.C55 1994
338.6'2'0968—dc20   93-48316

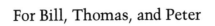

For Bill, Thomas, and Peter

Contents

Illustrations

Frontispiece
Map of South Africa

Preface

This book arose out of a curiosity about the paradox of dominant state enterprise within a country that claimed to be "the last bastion of capitalism" in Africa. In the late 1970s, South Africa's state enterprises were acquiring increasing visibility because of their role in protecting the apartheid government: Armscor helped to quell domestic disturbances in Soweto in 1976 through the local manufacture of weapons, and Sasol eased South Africa's oil demand following the cutoff of Iranian supplies after 1979. Yet at the same time as independence brought socialist governments to power in Angola and Mozambique, the South African government was positioning itself in cold-war politics by loudly proclaiming its place in the "free world" as a capitalist democracy. How did aggressive state enterprise fit into the picture of unfettered capitalism projected by the South African government?

The state corporations were large and increasingly important institutions, with histories going back to the 1920s and origins even further in the past. Moreover, they were some of the largest businesses in Africa; the Electricity Supply Commission (Escom), for example, generated more than 60 percent of all the electricity produced on the African continent. Nevertheless, the corporations have received scant scholarly attention, most of it portraying them unproblematically as creatures of political interests, their policies little more than a barometer of the concerns of Afrikaner nationalists. Otherwise thoughtful scholars have apparently given little thought to the state corporations, briefly describing them only as the "cornerstone of . . . national capitalist development"[1] and symbolic of "attempts to diminish English and foreign control of the economy."[2] They have uncritically used these institutions to support often simplistic descriptions of the links between political and economic power in South Africa.

The one major exception to this generalization is Renfrew Christie's study of Escom and the electricity industry, which concentrates on the economic bases and the larger politico-economic concerns of state electrification. However, Christie's fascinating work contains a basic conceptual flaw. In his introduction Christie describes Escom as essentially a tool of capitalist interests: "The electrical engineer and his industry are the servants of capitalists and the capitalist state, [and] the role of the electrical engineer is to increase capital accumulation." Yet in his conclusion he acknowledges that "the achievements of Escom and the VFTPC [Victoria Falls and Transvaal Power Company] were neither simple nor unimportant. They took place in a highly complex way."[3] Christie never resolves the apparent contradictions between these two interpretive strategies, and thus his attempt to explain the relationship between electrification and capitalism too often declines into a narrative of personal interchange, leaning heavily on the private papers of Bernard Price and the prime minister's archives (the latter no longer open to researchers). The problem with Christie's analysis is that it simplifies the relationship between electrification and capitalism while failing to explain the thoroughgoing and persistent nature of that relationship. The state corporations were influenced by individual politicians and by businessmen; but the corporations also stood at the heart of twentieth-century South Africa's political economy.[4]

At the time that I began my research in the early 1980s, interest in the South African state as a focus of scholarly work had waned. As John Iliffe noted in 1989, "Nothing is more curious about recent South African historiography than its neglect of the state, especially a state so dominating and so profuse in its creation of documents."[5] There had been a flurry of activity in the late 1970s, much of it inspired by Poulantzian Marxists, and although this had produced a number of theoretical studies, no work had been done that was based on thorough research.[6] Yet what seemed needed more than anything else with regard to so complex an issue as the state was archival research. Too often in writings on South Africa stories were repeated until they took on the status of myth. For example, a personal reminiscence by the Simons concerning the training of two hundred Africans as construction workers by the government in 1947 became the statement by Merle Lipton that blacks were trained by the government as operatives in the metal industries, and it then became the basis of the argument by Nicoli Nattrass that black workers were used extensively in factories during World War II.[7] A quick look at the University of Cape Town library would yield a full report in the papers of the Industrial Manpower Commission on the government training scheme used exclusively, but with little success, for whites during the war and encompassing only the two hundred Africans after the war.[8] Nevertheless, it has been conventional wisdom that there are few available sources on government activities, especially as regards the state corporations.

When I began my research, I found myself in the Pretoria archives surrounded by a wealth of material covering every aspect of the interventions of a state that reached directly into the lives of all its citizens. Much of the documentation on which this book is based has never before been used by academics. These documents reveal that the state corporations, rather than embodying narrow political interests, operated on a complex series of political and economic planes. They did not function exclusively as pork barrels, or solely as part of the security apparatus, or, alternatively, as "tools of capital." Their histories reveal that, rather than being monolithic and changeless institutions operating under predetermined objectives, they were ever-changing organizations affected by the personalities of the civil servants and bureaucrats who operated them, by the vicissitudes of South African trade as well as politicians, by the changing technologies of the twentieth century, and by the complex problems of labor (and social) control attendant on enforced racial stratification in South Africa. In short, the state corporations reflected the competing and balancing forces that have shaped modern South Africa.

The result of my inquiry into these state institutions is a wide-ranging study of South Africa in the twentieth century. I have attempted to answer historical questions about why the institutions were established in the first place and how their missions and operations have changed in response both to political and to economic pressures. In the course of answering these questions, many topics needed to be addressed, from the basis of political and economic power in the Zuid Afrikaansche Republiek (ZAR) in the nineteenth century to the size of South Africa's foreign debt at the end of the twentieth. In addition, there are also obvious implications in this study for the future of state economic intervention. South Africa will not be able to resist change as either white rule is redefined and adapted to new situations or as majority rule is finally achieved. In either case, the history of the state corporations suggests that they are institutions that will shape as well as reflect new South African realities.

Numerous people and institutions provided support in the preparation of this book. An award from the Fulbright-Hays Dissertation Research Abroad Program made it possible for me to spend a year in South Africa conducting research, and a California State University Faculty Support Grant allowed me the time for revisions. As every researcher knows, there are numerous librarians and archivists who make our work possible, and I would like to thank Jan Ferreira at the Central Archives in Pretoria, Barbara Conradie and Letitia Theunissen at the Standard Bank Archives in

Johannesburg, Karen Fung at the Hoover Institution Library, Moore Crossey at Yale University, and numerous other archivists and librarians at the Cape Archives, the South African Parliamentary Library, the Institute for Contemporary History in Bloemfontein, Barclays Bank in Johannesburg, and the libraries of the Iron and Steel Corporation (Iscor), the Industrial Development Corporation (IDC), and the universities of the Witwatersrand and Cape Town.

Special thanks are due to the late Alice Jacobs and her family, who shared their homes, hospitality, and memories of H. J. van der Bijl. Those colleagues whose comments over the years have helped me include Phil Bonner, Bill Freund, Alan Mabin, and Richard Roberts, as well as the participants in the Southern Africa Research Program at Yale who were intermittently subjected to reading chapters of the manuscript. In particular, I would like to thank my advisers at Yale: Bill Foltz for his unerring sense of political reality; Bob Harms for encouraging nuanced rather than sledgehammer arguments; Robin Winks for detecting stylistic problems; and Leonard Thompson for leading me through this process and helping me to become a historian.

Last but certainly not least, I would like to thank my family. Over the past decade they have provided support in countless ways through babysitting, computer advice, and even company on an extended visit to Pretoria. My sons, Thomas and Peter, came along halfway through this process; they slowed it down but often provided relief from the world of the state corporations. Most important, I want to thank my husband, Bill, who has always supported but never directed my efforts; whether I needed time, materials, or inspiration, he always found a way to help.

CHAPTER ONE

State Corporations and History

The role governments play in the economies of their nations came under increasing scrutiny toward the end of this century. In countries around the world, social and political stability appeared linked to the successes and failures of government economic intervention. The apparent failure of the Communist economic model was blamed in part for the collapse of the former Soviet Union; the successes of government interventions in various Asian nations were credited with increasing economic stability and affluence. In both cases, state economic intervention was credited with playing a major role in the achievement of significant social transformations. Responding to these perceptions, many governments rushed to "privatize" state enterprise, while others enacted increasing trade barriers and official subsidies, all in attempts to improve economic and social conditions. The economic role of governments was credited with the achievement of national stability and global hegemony in a period of breathtaking historical change.

South Africa also faced possible momentous changes as the twentieth century came to a close. But the country's changes were less the result of sweeping global trends than the possible culmination of centuries-old internal struggles for political and economic control. In 1990 the South African government initiated a process of political reform that President F. W. de Klerk claimed would end apartheid—the country's legal system of racial stratification—and lead to the enfranchisement of Africans for the first time. Making any reform of apartheid a reality, however, will entail far more than granting Africans a vote. As in the rest of the world, political control in South Africa was and will be affected by the economy and the role that the government played and will choose to play in the future. Political apartheid was accompanied by years of government economic intervention that shaped and limited the material opportunities of generations of Africans. Economic privilege for whites was the result not solely

1

of free-market forces but also of intentional government action, including subsidies, regulations, and provisions of services.

One of the most direct methods of government economic intervention in the twentieth century was the use of state corporations, government-owned enterprises producing goods and services directly for public use. As elsewhere, politicians in South Africa need to examine these institutions—can they be blamed for apartheid or will they be useful in the rebuilding of South African society? Are they capable of helping to create an economically and politically stable South Africa (the Asian model), or are they archaic remnants of a politically driven ideology (the Soviet model)?

Judging from the history of state enterprises around the world, they are not institutions that can be easily categorized. State enterprises have existed probably as long as states themselves—for example, the Roman imperial plantations, the Chinese salt monopoly, and the various state firms of the mercantilist period. Since the Industrial Revolution, however, the motivation for government intervention has shifted from the creation of government owned and controlled monopolies to the initiation of broad-based national industrial development. The proliferation of such enterprises in the twentieth century began in parallel but ideologically opposed movements: with the establishment of Communist economies in the Soviet Union, China, and Eastern Europe as well as in former colonies, first in Latin America and later in Asia and Africa, attempting to create their own local industries. In the depths of the Depression, even advanced capitalist states began to turn to state enterprise to subsidize services and products deemed necessary for the survival of society. And in postwar Europe, a number of state enterprises were established to save failing industries formerly under the control of private citizens or fascist dictatorships. In short, state enterprises have been employed by almost every imaginable type of government for a wide variety of purposes.

Even among ostensibly similar cases, state enterprises exhibit great differences. For example, Alice Amsden and Peter Evans have written about state enterprises in two countries that would both fall into the category of "newly industrializing economies"—Korea and Brazil, respectively—yet there are many differences in the behavior of their state corporations.[1] Although facing apparently similar concerns in manufacturing the same product—for example, steel—Korean and Brazilian state managers followed different policies dictated less by the natures of their industries than by their societies and histories. Indeed, any similarities found in state enterprise policies were between those within the same country, not within the same industry. For example, a Brazilian state steel firm operated more like a Brazilian state chemical firm than like a Korean state steel firm. The success of Brazil's state enterprises was built on partnerships with private local and foreign firms (Evans's "triple alliance"), whereas the Korean state firms expanded their expertise less through private assistance than through an attention to shop-floor experience (Amsden's "industrializing through learning").

Instead of operating under one set of rules or conditions as monolithic institutions or solely in reaction to the needs of a specific industry, state enterprises adapt to their specific environment or setting and reveal the particular political and economic constraints on industrialization in their own societies. In judging their usefulness or impact on societies—as in a postapartheid South Africa or in the emerging Asian "minidragons"— state enterprises should be viewed neither as autonomous institutions nor as revolutionary institutions: they reflect, rather than contradict, national social forces.

While from an economist's point of view the differences between state enterprises may appear as obstructive national idiosyncracies, from the perspective of the historian or social scientist these aberrations serve both as valuable clues to their potential use and as barometers of power and pressure within individual societies. Most economists extract these institutions from their social and historical context in an effort to distill common features.[2] Yet the single most characteristic feature of state enterprise is its flexible nature and, almost by definition, its charge to absorb and reflect demands specific to its environment: the national social and historical context.

Rather than placing the emphasis of analysis on the institution in the abstract, we should use the institution as a prism to examine the conjunction of relationships between various social forces that may not often come into direct contact: politicians, workers, businessmen, and bureaucrats. The equation between these forces is much more complex than simplistic notions of political influence or capitalist hegemony, and a study of these institutions should reveal a web of power relationships that together influence society at large. Furthermore, as the balance of power within a given society changes, such social and political changes are reflected in changes at these institutions. While they reflect the status quo, they may also be used to measure shifts, changes, and even revolutions within the status quo. The range of decisions made by the managers of state enterprises reflects considerations unique to the historical circumstances of their society; they can reveal the underlying forces that shape an individual society and may either prevent or facilitate fundamental change in state policies.

The overwhelming power of social and historical forces working on state enterprises are particularly apparent in three major areas of state enterprise policy formulation. First, the initial decision to establish a state enterprise entails a choice of which product or service is to be provided. The choice is usually made in response to a demand from a local group, and discussion takes place in a highly public debate among producers, consumers, and merchants—those with the most to gain and lose from the establishment of the state enterprise.

A second major area of interest is marketing policies, which must be formulated once a state corporation is in operation. These policies are worked out in private, far from public scrutiny, and reveal, in most cases, dynamics between the government and businessmen, or state and capital. Rarely can a government avoid or ignore such accommodations with the business community, and the terms eventually agreed upon explain leverage, power, and state goals.

The third realm of major interest is often the most contentious yet the least examined by economists: labor relations. Although this area is often suspected by economists to be governed primarily by the concerns of politicians, labor relations reflect far more of the complexity of power relations within a given society than either of the other two areas of policy making. It is my contention that labor relations proved to be the most problematic and determinant area of state corporation policies in South Africa, reflecting the balance of power within society. It is not my intention to provide a universal model of state corporation behavior. Rather, I hope to demonstrate that by examining these areas of decision making, the study of state enterprises reveals the social and political dynamics at work in the individual societies in which they operate.

When a decision is made to establish a state corporation, it is usually attended by intense debate—between the government and private businessmen, producers and consumers, taxpayers and bureaucrats—that reveals the deep rivalries as well as the interdependencies within the society. Differences and disagreements are finally papered over with arguments that the enterprise to be established will fulfill a broad social need and will benefit all segments of the nation. And the nature of most state enterprises lends them to such characterizations: most are large-scale, capital-intensive, "upstream," or key industries, difficult for private capital to initiate or continue but crucial for overall macroeconomic performance. Certainly the range of industries normally associated with state enterprise fits this description: steel, electricity, shipbuilding, chemicals, and petrochemicals.[3] Nevertheless, the specific circumstances regarding the establishment of such institutions should reveal far more than an impulse toward economic development.

The establishment of state enterprises in Asia, for example, provides substantial material for an investigation of Asian societies. In his persuasive study of the importance of government regulation and intervention in Taiwan's economic development, Robert Wade argues that the Taiwanese state steel industry was established to feed the country's ongoing industrialization in several areas and specifically to end dependence on imported steel.[4] Similarly, in her influential economic study of South Korea's phenomenal growth, Alice Amsden briefly describes the establishment of South Korea's state steel industry, offering few explanations but pointing out that the government wanted to export some of the steel in order to earn hard currency to pay off debts.[5] Both Asian state steel corporations were markedly successful and deserve study to explain how they could achieve such success at the same time as most industrialized nations watched their steel industries deteriorate. Yet while this industry clearly served a demand, in the competitive international steel market of the 1970s—when both countries took this step—steel hardly seemed the best target for an import substitute, let alone an export industry. And Amsden outlines the apparently overwhelming reasons militating against the industry in Korea: lack of capital, skills, markets, and resources.[6] Although the later success is undeniable, the complex factors that went into making such a risky decision remain unknown.

Even in the late nineteenth and early twentieth centuries, when global industrialization was taking place in a less competitive environment, the creation of such "infrastructural" industries was problematic. The argument was often used that a national steel industry was necessary for industrialization and economic independence at a time when European steel makers dominated the market, and many state steel firms were established around the world. However, these developments, as in South Africa and Brazil, to take only two, have been found not only to reflect general state economic policies but also to be linked with specific national interests—mining and the military, respectively.[7]

Electricity provides another interesting example; abundant and cheap electricity is crucial to any industrial effort. But it may be produced for both residential and industrial consumers, and pricing and distribution may favor one or the other. In his definitive examination of the early history of the electricity supply industry (1880–1930), Thomas Hughes demonstrates that numerous factors—technical, political, and sometimes personal—determined the form and purpose of electricity supply in industrializing economies.[8] While state enterprises obviously fit into broad government economic planning, the choice and timing of industrial intiation cannot be assumed to have little reference to ongoing social and political struggles. Local industrialization may be pursued through many different strategies; the question for researchers is, Why this particular one?

Once established, state enterprises are hardly free from the pressures that attended their inception; whether establishing entirely new industries or rescuing old ones, they enter into markets previously dominated by and servicing others. They may face the competition of foreign firms operating with lower production costs, offering a wider range of products, and controlling well-established marketing networks as well as the "vested" interests of local merchants or even local subsidiaries of the foreign companies. In some cases, as with steel, new producers have even faced world cartels bent on pushing them out of the market altogether. In addition to trying to enter the market and survive—operating as any private firm would—state enterprises are also concerned with either protecting or maximizing profits for constituent groups. They may be interested in helping an important trade partner, protecting local merchants, or lowering costs for local producers—concerns that would be alien to a private firm. A state enterprise is forced to consider the broader implications of its actions for both the local economy and the country's international trade relations. It must try to balance the interests of merchants, producers, local and foreign capital, consumers, and taxpayers.

In this tenuous period, state corporations try to find markets for their goods and enter into relationships to ensure their own survival. Unless they have the luxury of monopoly control over their markets, they must successfully capture those markets and are often forced to compromise some goals to meet others. In Brazil, state enterprises attempted to break the dominance of foreign companies but frequently did so by entering into partnerships with those firms, as well as with local Brazilian firms, increasing their profits by providing them with cheap goods in return for at least partially nationalizing supplies.[9] In South Africa, the state corporations found few ready local allies and instead worked to induce foreign companies to establish South African subsidiaries through the provision of cheap goods, creating local industries but deepening foreign investment.[10] In Taiwan, the government controls all agreements with foreign firms, including those for importing technology, and ensures that "the state holds its own, keeping control over key sectors within Taiwan."[11]

In each case, decisions were made on the basis of local and historical circumstances: Brazil has an entrenched and politically important national capitalist class that dates to the nineteenth century and would not sit back while wealth flowed overseas; the South African economy had been thoroughly saturated with foreign investment since the discoveries of minerals in the late nineteenth century, and it enjoyed relatively limited local capitalist development; Taiwan's statist legacy of Japanese colonial rule was followed by the invasion of the Nationalists who established authoritarian rule on a war footing with the mainland. Each nation followed an economic path that was unique and consistent with its own past.

But even more challenging than facing the demands of local business-men and foreign cartels is the task that places state enterprises most squarely at the center of their own national histories: exerting control over workers. Relations with the work force are most directly tied to specific national circumstances and, as Amsden argues, show "the least consis-tency across countries."[12] There is little consistency because each country has its own history of struggle between dominant and subordinated groups, has its own cultural norms, has its own specific resources; all of these factors and more affect workers and their relationship to employers. Beyond considerations of limited groups of national businessmen, trading partners, or industrial consumers—as in the policy areas mentioned above—labor relations force considerations of broader social relations and historical traditions that must be controlled in order to produce a product at a price that will not threaten the interests of the various groups. And yet state enterprises cannot alienate workers, who are often their voting constituents. They must find methods specific to their own cultures to placate their work force or face either financial setbacks or social unrest.

Adding to the complications inherent in developing successful labor policies, there is additional pressure on newly industrializing countries to rely on low labor costs to propel themselves into full industrial status; South Korea is a case in point. In explaining Korea's dramatic industrial success, Amsden argues that labor considerations are central to that suc-cess. It is Amsden's contention that the creation of a well-trained, rela-tively low-paid work force has enabled newly industrializing countries like Korea to "catch up" and indeed surpass fully industrialized economies: "Learners do not innovate (by definition) and must compete initially on the combined basis of low wages, state subsidies and incremental produc-tivity . . . the strategic focus is necessarily found on the shopfloor, where the achievement of incremental, yet cumulative, improvements in pro-ductivity and product specification are essential to enhance price and quality competitiveness."[13]

In Asian nations, a "strategic focus" on the shop floor has been facili-tated by the fact that there is no historical tradition of labor-union activity. Employers have been able to control workers successfully through the cre-ation of factory-based unions with union officials in the employ of the fac-tory. In South Korea the government has gone even further, relegating labor policy to the Korean Central Intelligence Agency.[14] This particular twist reflects the country's history as a Japanese colony, its involvement in a war against Communist North Korea, and the absence of a union tradi-tion throughout Asia; such a choice would be unthinkable in Britain or even South Africa, where a tradition of strong industrial union representa-tion exists, although labor control may be effected through equally powerful institutions. Yet the success of the Asian model is clear, and it confirms speculation by the political scientist Fernando Henrique Cardoso that state enterprise would be most successful where an authoritarian regime could suppress worker resistance.[15] For even the most successful late industrializing nations, labor control is not just necessary but crucial to that success.

Control over workers must be exerted through methods sensitive to national circumstances, providing useful clues to the relations between dominant and subordinated classes; the Korean model would never work in Brazil or South Africa. In Brazil under the corporatist Vargas regime, the government initially brought workers under control through unionization, part of the regime's ideological populism. Unions, like state enterprises, were all shared by the "people" and controlled by the government. However, once Vargas succeeded in achieving significant government control of the unions, he tried to use them to stifle the workers' voice. Nevertheless, the unions became increasingly vocal and successful in winning reforms throughout the 1950s and early 1960s. In reaction, they were decisively suppressed in 1964 when the military took over the government and stamped out "subversives," notably union leaders.[16]

In South Africa, broader institutions of social control, including disenfranchisement, a legal "colour bar" that structured labor relations on race, and "influx" control, were introduced incrementally to respond to growing problems of labor control. South African state enterprises have had little use for such outright intervention as in the case of Korea because they operate within a broad network of intense labor control. All of these policies clearly reveal important differences between these societies, their social structures, and their histories.

More important, labor problems are never entirely "solved"; they continue to reflect ongoing changes and struggles within different societies. Even under the authoritarian regimes described above, workers find ways to protest their conditions of employment. By the early 1990s, worker discontent in South Africa as well as South Korea erupted in nearly continual unrest, threatening both shop-floor stability as well as the entire low-wage structure of their economies. Indeed, state enterprises often contribute to social unrest by initiating industrialization and thereby bringing into existence a permanent industrial work force that over time develops a clear "consciousness" of its exploitation. As workers become more aware of their position, firms are forced to reformulate those policies that initially brought labor under control.

At state enterprises, however, labor problems become even more complicated, due to the very nature of their operations and their position within the national economy. When production takes place under pressure, as in state enterprises manufacturing industrial inputs usually under monopoly conditions, any interruption or dislocation in the production process can seriously affect both the firm's financial position and the national economy. As Michael Burawoy has argued, factory workers enjoy considerable leverage simply through their position within the production process.[17] Workers with little political power outside the firm and ineffectual union representation or no meaningful voice inside the factory are thus likely to vent their opposition in the form of covert production disruptions. When employers succeed in closing all other avenues of negotiation with their work force—as in the case of South Africa's historical suppression of African workers—they may achieve relative outward calm and avoid strikes and protests; but they risk the high turnovers and poor performance typically associated with "inefficient" production.[18]

An example of the power wielded by workers at state enterprises is the textile industry. On a global basis, textile firms have been one of the least successful industries to come under state control, despite attention to efficiency and costs. State textile firms were established in South Africa in the 1940s and in Japan in the nineteenth century.[19] In both cases, the government imported foreign machinery and foreign technicians to organize the factories and ensure efficiency. Workers at these factories—African males in South Africa and young women in Japan—were paid meager wages meant to supplement the farm income of their families. Despite technological expertise and low wages, labor costs were high because of high turnover, consequent training costs, and a generally unstable work force. In other words, while state enterprise managers ignored political pressures by employing skilled foreigners and forcing local workers to accept low wages, they were still unable to exert complete control over labor costs; the problem was not the overpayment of workers but an inability to control those workers.

How do state enterprises achieve control over their workers? Crucial to the success of the enterprises, labor control has been implemented when policies are adopted that conform to national historical and social reality. State enterprises may often copy private practices that have proven successful in that society; they rarely innovate, tending rather to conform and reflect. Indeed, few enterprises whether private or state owned have successfully transplanted labor models from other societies, as is evidenced by the increasing efforts to use Asian methods in North America. Successful state enterprise labor policies closely reflect the real relationship of workers, political power, and capital and the historical development of that relationship within a given society.

Not surprisingly, South African state enterprises found their greatest success by modeling not only labor policies but also industrial strategies on the country's most lucrative business: the mining industry. Just as in other countries, in South Africa most state enterprises manufacture what are sometimes called upstream, key, or producer goods, as I mentioned earlier. These products, such as steel, chemicals, electricity, and so forth, are produced through processes not unlike the production of gold or diamonds: raw materials (coal, iron ore, phosphate) are obtained through unskilled labor and processed through highly sophisticated technical methods relying on technicians and machinery. In these cases, the work force is split between highly trained technicians, who oversee the mechanical or chemical processes, and an unskilled group, which produces the inputs to the process. These methods promote control over the bulk of workers by reserving the most skilled—and valued—operations to machines rather than to workers.

In South Africa, unskilled workers were also politically disenfranchised, organizationally fragmented, and individually expendable. They have formed the backbone of South African gold and diamond mining for more than a hundred years. The key to their exploitation is their vulnerability in the production process; so long as workers lack skills and are interchangeable, control amounts to dismissal. Workers are "cheap" because their individual skills can be easily obtained. By substituting technology for skills, employers shift costs from labor to machinery, a much more predictable factor. As Alexander Gerschenkron has argued, "The advantages inherent in the use of technologically superior equipment were not counteracted but reinforced by its labor-saving effect."[20] In other words, advanced technology has allowed South African state enterprises to avoid the use of labor that was reputed to be cheap but would in fact have entailed substantial costs.

The choice of such industries elsewhere has not ensured the same level of industrial control, because of differing social and political histories. For example, in countries with strong union representation of a homogeneous work force, such as present-day England and Germany, even unskilled workers could not be so peremptorily replaced. And in the rapidly growing Asian economies—despite the absence of independent unions—industrial strategy is based on the use of highly trained and fully enfranchised workers whose loyalty to the state is traded for low wages. Asian successes depend on the cooperation of these workers, and especially their loyalty, through a mixture of cooperation and intimidation, not outright disregard or brutality. Even in Brazil authoritarian regimes recognized the political importance of the working class and included its unions at the highest levels of government decision making, although eventually coopting and controlling them. Indeed, it is ironic that the postcolonial view of Asian, African, and Latin American countries posited low labor costs as their primary asset in attempted industrialization, whereas in fact control over workers has been difficult and expensive.

In South Africa these industries enabled state enterprises to fit into and reflect the political and historical circumstances surrounding the growth of the African working class. While the growth of the country's economy has been highly dependent on the use of low-paid workers, especially in the high-cost mining industry, South African history has been marked by ongoing struggles to obtain and control such workers. Continued African resistance to subordinated incorporation into the industrial work force shaped the pervasive and oppressive framework of racial stratification. As industrial development progressed, the creation of a permanent African urban work force posed a threat not only on the shop floor, where it had been difficult for these workers to organize resistance, but also to the labor structure of the mining industry—dependent on a reservoir of desperate and impoverished rural Africans—as well as the racially exclusive nature of the state, which workers increasingly challenged.

South Africa's state corporations have grown and developed throughout the twentieth century with due attention paid to the needs of the dominant mining industry, the vocal white working class, and potentially volatile African workers. They have developed industries that conform to production processes that do not threaten the racial division of employment or by extension the racial division of political power; they reflect and expand the traditional political economy that reserves political power to whites and devalues African labor. While adhering to the political demands of the government's apartheid policies, the state corporations cannot be viewed as the tools of that policy—any more or less than they are the tools of capital—but as the embodiment of myriad social and economic relationships that hold both capital and apartheid in place inside South Africa.

In order to consider the future use of state enterprises for socioeconomic change—in South Africa and elsewhere—these institutions must be viewed within the historical context of their growth and operations. Although they are flexible institutions, capable of various methods of operation, they reflect and are constrained by long-term factors of historical, political, economic, and social pressures within their own societies. In the case of South Africa, the state corporations in the early 1990s reflect a society that relies on and at the same time devalues African labor. By changing their own policies, they cannot change the social construction of labor, and without comparable changes in other areas of government control it is doubtful that their own changes will be successful. The historical development of these institutions mirrors the complex history of South Africa; their use as an agent of change will depend upon a real shift in the balance of political and economic power inside South Africa.

CHAPTER TWO

Mine Owners and the State
1886–1918

The rise of the South African gold-mining industry in the decades subsequent to the major mineral discoveries of the 1880s subjected the Transvaal region to a process of economic and political upheaval that extended well into the twentieth century. Afrikaners had only tenuous control over the southern African hinterland before the last quarter of the century, their claims to land and political authority constantly challenged by African societies. Moreover, white settlement in general on the subcontinent was weakly established: the agricultural base of the various colonial communities was uniformly shallow, and few immigrants were attracted from Europe. Gold revolutionized the situation, shifting the hub of economic activities to the center of the subcontinent and enabling whites to establish firm control of the land.

Yet for the Afrikaners of the Transvaal these developments had contradictory effects. White rule was established over black, but English speakers controlled the gold industry that fueled the changes. And these foreigners were less interested in investing their profits within southern Africa than in exploiting the mineral resources to generate funds with which they could speculate elsewhere. In the aftermath of the discovery of gold, therefore, new contests arose in southern Africa, and in the Transvaal in particular, between Afrikaners and English speakers, between those who considered themselves Transvaalers and those they labeled *uitlanders*—outlanders, or foreigners—between, in the terminology of the time, Boer and Briton. Although often taking an ethnic form, and fought usually in political arenas, these contests revolved around control of southern Africa's resources and how they were to be utilized and developed. Indeed, the revolutionary changes set in motion by the discovery of gold often pulsated around such apparently prosaic activities as the generation of electricity and the manufacture of iron and steel.

A Tenuous Rule

The origins of direct state intervention in the South African economy rest in policies adopted in the nineteenth century by the government of the Zuid Afrikaansche Republiek (ZAR) to strengthen itself against African neighbors and British imperialists. Europeans first moved north of the Vaal River in the late 1830s, when Voortrekkers escaping British rule in the Cape had located land suitable for the type of extensive cattle farming that they had practiced in the eastern Cape, land that seemed to them sparsely populated by Africans relative to other parts of the hinterland. Settling in three parts of the present-day Transvaal—which they named Potchefstroom (also known as the South African Republic), Zoutpansberg, and Ohrigstad/Lydenburg—the Voortrekkers established a loosely knit political structure with much power resting in the hands of the leaders of the three separate communities but also incorporating a common *Volksraad*—a representative institution for white males that combined the features of an executive, a legislature, and a court of appeal—and eked out a semi-subsistent living from their livestock holdings and from hunting.[1] Despite earlier claims to imperial sovereignty, the British recognised the political independence of the Voortrekkers in 1852 when, under the terms of the Sand River Convention, they guaranteed Transvaal Afrikaners "the right to manage their own affairs and to govern themselves according to their own laws," so long as the white settlers agreed not to form alliances with any "coloured nations to the north of the Vaal River," or to "trade in ammunition with the native tribes," or to permit or practice slavery in the Transvaal.[2]

Having negotiated British recognition of their autonomy, the Transvaal Afrikaners asserted that God and might gave them the right to rule over all Africans north of the Vaal. In 1860, in response to criticisms by British missionaries, the executive of the Lydenburg Republic argued that "the largest part of the country north of the Vaal river . . . was lawfully purchased by the Dutch emigrants from its earlier owners—the Kaffir tribes who lived there—and a part was acquired by rightfully waged wars, caused by the unwarranted attacks of the natives of that country. Thus we have in our opinion acquired the land by right and in accordance with the tenets of God's word."[3]

Such assertions, however, could not disguise the tenuous nature of settler control over resources when faced with African competition. Afrikaners were engaged in much the same economic activities as their African neighbors and needed to exploit the same resources if they were to survive and prosper. They needed vast areas of land for their cattle, they wanted cheap workers for their farms, and they wanted a dominant share of the ivory trade so that they could acquire the capital necessary to purchase processed foods and manufactured items from the Cape. Thus the 1850s and 1860s witnessed ever-increasing conflict as Afrikaners sought to subjugate their African neighbors. Although initially enjoying superior firepower, the Transvaalers met with little success. With regard to ivory, for example, concentrated by mid-century in the northeastern reaches of the Transvaal, skilled African hunters had acquired so many guns through trade with the Portuguese in Mozambique that by the middle of the 1860s they had succeeded in monopolizing the hunting of elephants and had excluded practically all Afrikaners from the highly profitable trade.[4]

Settler claims to rule all Africans in the Transvaal likewise did not go uncontested. The Kwena and the Ngwaketse defended themselves against Afrikaner attacks in the early 1850s and successfully maintained their autonomy in the western areas of the Transvaal. In the south the Tlhaping kept control of most of their lands, while in the north the Ngwato went undefeated. The Pedi under their king Sekhukhune provided the strongest challenge to Afrikaner land claims, establishing a powerful, well-armed kingdom that ruled over much of the northeastern Transvaal.[5]

In the face of such challenges, the Afrikaners themselves were disunited, arguing over what policies to adopt and becoming embroiled in civil war between 1860 and 1864. Although the war ended with all Transvaal Afrikaners uniting together in the ZAR, the conflict had so weakened them that in 1867 they had to abandon the Zoutpansburg to its original African inhabitants.[6]

Continuing contestation in the late 1860s and 1870s by Africans and Afrikaners for the control of resources undermined the authority of the ZAR state and tore at the fabric of its nascent national economy. To acquire and hold land, the Transvaalers undertook military expeditions against their African neighbors. These expeditions required state financing, but the ZAR lacked a solid tax base and had no reserves of gold or other precious metals. As a result, the ZAR financed its military adventures by issuing currency secured by land instead of specie. This policy produced two detrimental effects. First, because government ownership of much of the land used as security was more a paper claim than physical reality—most was in actively contested parts of the north and east of the Transvaal—the currency quickly became drastically devalued, barter became the preferred mode of carrying out commercial transactions, and the limited system of tax collection became practically unworkable. Second, devaluation of both currency and land set the ZAR off on a further quest for even more land to secure its debts and raise new sources of funds thereby, continuing a cycle of attempts at conquest, greater debts, and increased insecurity. Growing stratification within the Afrikaner community produced even more pressures for conquest, with some individuals becoming relatively wealthy through land speculation while many others grew ever poorer and demanded that the state alleviate their situation.[7] Yet, as Stanley Trapido has summarized the situation reached by the first half of the 1870s, "the administrative machinery of the embryonic Transvaal state was incapable of collecting sufficient revenue to finance both military expenditure and the barest essentials of civil administration, including the collecting of taxes."[8]

In this context of economic and military weakness, the ZAR succumbed to the greater power of African foes and British imperialism. In 1876 President T. F. Burgers led the largest Transvaal army yet assembled in a desperate attempt to destroy forever the power of the Pedi state, newly strengthened by the acquisition of guns that Pedi migrant workers had purchased at the recently developed diamond mines of Kimberley. Burgers' attempt ended in August in a "military debacle" for the ZAR, with Sekhukhune weakened but in full control of Pedi territory and the president deserted by his own army.[9] It was the British, newly interested in the southern African hinterland and its mineral and labor resources because of the discovery of diamonds on the southern margins of the Transvaal, who took advantage of the situation, proclaiming in April 1877 their annexation of the ZAR, an act that the Transvaal Afrikaners acquiesced to without resistance.

Paradoxically, British intervention strengthened the Transvaal state. The British were determined to destroy Pedi power, which they considered a threat to European rule in the interior. Moreover, they wanted to secure greater supplies of labor for the Kimberley diamond mines and believed that this could be achieved by destroying Pedi autonomy and subjecting Africans to land alienation and the payment of taxes. Military campaigns by British forces assisted by African allies in 1878 and 1879 finally resulted in the conquest of the Pedi by the end of 1879 and the destruction of Sekhukhune's power. Thereafter, the British so harshly enforced the collection of taxes from those defeated that in 1879 state revenue from African taxpayers was twenty-four times what it had been in 1876. With their strongest African competitor defeated, and increasingly opposed to again being under British rule, the Transvaal Afrikaners rose up and in 1881 defeated the imperial forces at the battle of Majuba Hill. The British, their interests in migrant labor already secured, withdrew, leaving the ZAR again independent but now with a much more centralized and efficient administration than had been the case before annexation.[10]

The ZAR had won its political independence from the British and no longer faced a powerful African foe, but the economic condition of the state remained perilous. The British had charged their military conquest of the Pedi against the ZAR's treasury, with the result that the republic's public debt rose from £256,678 in 1877 to £425,893 in 1881, an amount that far exceeded total government revenues of only £50,000 in the latter year.[11] Moreover, many Afrikaner "notables" continued to speculate in land, thereby further devaluing the state's currency, which remained secured by contested titles to enormous acreages.[12] By 1885 the financial stability of the ZAR was so poor that the state could not raise any loans from outside institutions, and the Standard Bank, newly established in the republic, feared that government bankruptcy was imminent.[13]

It was this situation of endemic financial weakness that most disturbed Paul Kruger, who became president of the ZAR after the defeat of the British.[14] Kruger had participated in the Great Trek and had fought in many wars against African polities as well as against the British. He feared that economic weakness would undo the victories won on the battlefield and could destroy the republic as surely as any military defeat. He believed that only by developing the economic self-sufficiency of the Transvaal could the strength and integrity of Afrikaner state and society be secured. As he put matters when he assumed the presidency in 1883, a year in which state expenditures exceeded revenues by nearly 30 percent, "the first essential [in preserving the ZAR's sovereignty] is the development of the resources of the country, so that our imports are reduced and our exports increased; or to speak more clearly, so that we export goods and import money and not (as happens too frequently now) import products, to pay for which money flows out of the country."[15]

Kruger believed that a solution to the ZAR's economic problems lay in following a policy of direct state intervention to promote increased local production and reduce dependence on foreign imports. In taking this approach he was following the example set by a number of other nations that felt more and more pressured in a world economy dominated by just three countries—Britain, France, and, to an ever-increasing degree, the United States—which through their industrial and financial muscle largely controlled the terms of international trade. In the 1870s governments in both Germany and Japan had established state-owned industries and granted private businessmen what essentially amounted to state-protected monopolies.[16] Kruger, presiding over a much smaller and financially less viable state, did not have the means to fund the establishment of local industries, but he did grant licenses for private monopolies—termed "concessions"—to ZAR citizens to encourage them to develop import-substitute industries. These concessions included two given in October 1881 and July 1882 to A. H. Nellmapius, a friend of Kruger's, granting him the exclusive right to manufacture "spiritous liquors" and to "erect factories and melting furnaces for the manufacture of all sorts of iron and steel wares and the melting of iron ores." Additional concessions were granted to different individuals for "the manufacture of woollen goods," "the tanning and preparation of leather" and manufacture of leather goods, "the exclusive right to the erection of a machine brick factory," "the exclusive right to establish factories for all sorts of fine and rough earthenware and porcelain," as well as other industries. Under the terms of the concession agreements, the new enterprises were not to be taxed, they were to have a monopoly of production within the ZAR, and for most of them the government would levy special duties to protect them from cheaper imports.[17] Kruger hoped that government protection, in lieu of direct investment, would be sufficient to spur local development and underpin the ZAR's economic and political autonomy.

The ZAR versus the Gold Magnates

The concessions policy had barely got underway when the discovery in 1886 of enormous deposits of gold on the Witwatersrand revolutionized the Transvaal's economy and set in process a series of developments that transformed the social, economic, and political structure of southern Africa. Alluvial gold deposits had been worked in the Transvaal in the 1870s and 1880s, but the amount produced was miniscule, accounting for only 0.03 percent of the world's output by 1885.[18] Soon after the Witwatersrand reef deposits were declared a public digging area in September 1886, however, gold output escalated. In 1887 the Witwatersrand mines produced gold worth £81,022; in 1888, £967,416. Output kept on increasing throughout the 1890s: £1,735,491 in 1890, £7,800,000 in 1894, £11,476,260 in 1897, by which time the Transvaal produced approximately 27 percent of the world's gold.[19]

Huge amounts of speculative capital flowed into the ZAR, practically all of it invested in the gold industry. Robert Kubicek has estimated that between 1886 and the end of 1913 "the Witwatersrand gold mining industry absorbed between £116 and £134 million in equity and loan capital," an amount of European investment three times that put into all Australian or Canadian mining and equal to about 60 percent of total European investment in Russia during the same period.[20] The South African investments were highly profitable, with the Rand gold-mining companies returning £101,815,738 in dividends between 1887 and 1913.[21]

With the dramatic rise of gold mining, the ZAR's revenues and population grew also. Whereas in the fifteen years prior to the Rand gold discoveries ZAR government revenues had averaged £110,000 annually, in 1887 they exceeded £600,000, in 1889 they topped £1,500,000, and in 1898 they amounted to £3,320,958, a thirtyfold increase in little over a decade.[22] Immigration greatly augmented the white population, with nearly three hundred thousand Afrikaners and English speakers living in the ZAR by

1898—up from only forty thousand before the gold discoveries; one hundred thousand of them lived in what had become the newest and largest urban concentration in southern Africa, Johannesburg, the "goud stad" (gold city).[23] Indeed, by the late 1890s, "only the United States attracted more emigrants from the United Kingdom than did South Africa."[24] Gold seemed to have provided almost overnight the factor necessary to spark economic development and buttress the ZAR's political independence.

Yet in many ways the rise of the mining industry threatened the republic's autonomy, because gold dominated the ZAR's economy in such an overwhelming fashion. Gold accounted for practically all exports by value. In 1897, for example, the ZAR exported goods worth £11,965,200, with 96 percent of that amount provided by gold. State revenues, which grew so enormously in the 1880s and 1890s, were largely dependent on the gold industry; more than half of government income was generated directly by taxation on the mines or indirectly by duties on goods used primarily in mining.[25] Nearly all the capital invested in the industry came from outside the ZAR, primarily from England (60 to 80 percent) and Europe, with the result that the bulk of dividends were paid out to foreign investors.

Given the high level of profitability of the industry, this meant that very considerable sums left the ZAR. Between 1887 and 1899, while total government revenues amounted to £28,713,055, the gold-mining companies paid dividends of £19,660,834. In 1898 gold dividends for the first time exceeded government revenues, with the state taking in just under £3,500,000 and nearly £4,750,000 going into the pockets of shareholders.[26] Moreover, aside from the funds obtained through import duties and direct taxation, little of the capital generated by the mining industry found its way into the local economy. To ensure the profitability of their enterprise, the mine owners paid black workers extremely meager wages and kept the pay of white workers as low as possible. They also imported most of the food and other goods sold to their workers in compound stores as well as the bulk of machinery and stores used in the mines, as they found that they could get such supplies more cheaply from foreign sources than they could locally.

The result of such measures was an increasing burden of import payments. In 1897, the year that exports earned just under £12,000,000, imports totaled £13,563,827, at least half of which was for goods utilized directly by the mining industry.[27] In the face of such financial returns, Kruger's earlier concern that the ZAR should not import goods and export money seemed an even more pressing issue after the discovery of gold than before.

The political autonomy of the Transvaal Afrikaners also seemed shakier with the rise of the gold industry. When the industry was first established in the late 1880s and early 1890s, practically all the investment capital had come from the diamond magnates of Kimberley and financiers in Europe, with the result that Afrikaners held not a single significant financial interest in any of the mines. Indeed, the entire industry was owned and controlled by people whom the Afrikaners considered foreigners. And these mine owners and their overseas backers complained constantly at what they considered the onerous taxation policies of the ZAR, complaints made more vociferous by the fact that the same people had already ensured through political influence in the Cape and in England that the diamond industry remained free of any form of direct taxation. Within the mining workplace there was also little room for Afrikaners; experienced English-speaking miners and tradesmen occupied all the skilled jobs, while the mine owners utilized Africans exclusively for the unskilled tasks.

The significance of this development was not just economic but political, because so many newly arrived English speakers found employment in the mining industry that by the beginning of the 1890s they formed a majority of the adult white male population on the Rand and therefore, if they had the vote, could determine who controlled the ZAR. Kruger so feared the threat of this potential voting bloc that, despite constant denunciations by the owners of the gold mines and their supporters in the Cape and in England, he refused to extend the franchise to those whom Afrikaners termed "uitlanders."[28]

Fearing that the British would conquer through investment what they had lost in combat during the 1881 Anglo-Boer War, Kruger returned to the concessions scheme in an attempt to encourage local initiative in industrial development. He believed that "only through the erection of factories could the state become self-supporting."[29] As before, the concessions were to be granted only to citizens of the ZAR, Dutch-speaking descendants of the original Voortrekkers, in order that they should gain a significant advantage over foreign interlopers. Few of the burghers, as ZAR citizens were called, had profited from the mining boom. Those who were farmers—the bulk of Transvaal Afrikaners—engaged in relatively limited market production, were still engaged in a struggle with Africans for control over land and labor resources, and usually found themselves undercut by African competitors and cheap foreign imports of foodstuffs.[30]

The wealthiest of the Transvaal Afrikaners—among whom could be counted Paul Kruger himself, as well as a man who would later become the first prime minister of the Union of South Africa, Louis Botha—were people who speculated in land rather than developed it. Although they made considerable sums of money from such speculation, they did not invest the proceeds in the mining industry.[31] Moreover, much of the land was sold to the owners of mining companies, always interested in acquiring control of as much potentially gold-bearing land as possible. The development of concessions, however, by establishing monopoly industries producing goods necessary to the mines, would offer Afrikaners a way to profit directly from the ongoing radical economic transformation of the Transvaal.

But most burghers lacked the capital necessary to develop the nascent industries, and they either failed to fulfill the terms of their licenses or instead took an immediate profit by selling the new concessions to foreign investors. Concessions for the manufacture of oil from plants and seeds, of soap, of matches, of rope, of paper, and of candles changed ownership several times, and all either lapsed or were canceled.[32] None of them produced any long-term profits for Afrikaner license holders.

The most important concessions—those for the operation of railways, for the establishment of a national bank and mint, for the generation of electricity, and for the manufacture of dynamite and of cement—were foreign owned almost from their inception. Kruger had granted the railway concession to Dutch financiers in 1884 because there were no burghers with the funds necessary to initiate such an undertaking; by 1887 the concession was owned totally by a consortium of Dutch and German banks, which derived relatively substantial profits in large part because the ZAR government guaranteed a 6 percent return on their share capital in the Nederlandsch Zuid Afrikaansche Spoorweg Maatschappij (NZASM).[33] The national bank and mint concession went to a consortium of foreign banks and the Wernher Beit mining house.[34] The German electrical machinery firm of Siemens and Halske obtained a concession in 1894 to build a station on the Rand to provide the mines with electricity, a more economical mode of generating power than the then current steam. Siemens soon handed the concession over to a London-based group, including the Rand mining firm of Goerz and Company, which formed the Rand Central Electric Company (RCE) but remained a major shareholder in the new operation. The RCE was one of the most financially successful of the concessions, paying regular dividends of 6 to 7 percent annually by the end of the century.[35]

The dynamite concession (like that for cement) went to Eduard Lippert who, though a German national and not a burgher, was also a resident of the ZAR and a friend of Kruger's. Perhaps because of such close personal connections, Lippert was able to ignore the concession license's requirement that the dynamite be manufactured locally, and he instead imported all supplies at a huge markup that was charged to the mining industry. He soon transferred a controlling interest in the concession to a French dynamite company and then to a partnership of the French company and the Nobel dynamite company, while acting as the front man for their operations in the ZAR. Selling imported dynamite at markups averaging between 100 and 200 percent, the concession earned profits in excess of £600,000 in 1897 and 1898, the bulk of which went to overseas shareholders.[36]

Such developments failed to benefit Transvaal Afrikaners financially and antagonised both the English-speaking gold magnates and the British government. The magnates denounced the concessions policy as not only corrupt but also a crippling financial burden on a mining industry beset with heavy production costs. The British government echoed these criticisms as well as those concerning Kruger's refusal to extend the vote to uitlanders. With the mine owners calling for imperial intervention to protect the industry's profits, the British in 1899 went to war with Kruger and the ZAR. The South African War of 1899 to 1902 ended in total defeat for the ZAR and Kruger's flight into European exile.[37] Having spent much of his career trying to strengthen the economic and political autonomy of the ZAR, Kruger died in Switzerland in 1904 unable to return to a country that he considered to be controlled by English mining capitalists and British imperialists.

While the concessions policy had failed utterly to achieve Kruger's hopes of economic self-sufficiency, it alerted the mine owners to the great significance of control over local industries for the financial structure of the gold industry. In many ways the industrial development of the Transvaal held the key to the future of mining. New industries could be developed to help lower costs and raise profits, but if they were not to prey on their mining customers as had the foreign-controlled concessionaires, they would have to be controlled or closely monitored by the gold magnates.

Dynamite was a particularly pressing issue. Although the Witwatersrand consumed half the world's production, because of the monopoly granted by Kruger all of it had to be imported at prices far higher than local producers would have charged.[38] Local production of goods would also have cut the heavy costs of long-distance sea transportation. Within southern Africa improved local transportation, particularly by rail, would later reduce costs even further. And the expansion of locally generated electrical power would enable the mine owners to increase production without raising labor costs, an issue of particular significance after the war, when competition for workers was severe and the mines suffered considerable labor shortfalls at the wages they were prepared to offer. In sum, mine owners saw that they could benefit tremendously from the industrialization of the Transvaal, but only so long as they had a considerable say in determining what form that industrialization should take.

Imperial Control, Mining Hegemony, and Electricity

Victorious at the end of the Anglo-Boer War, the gold magnates and the British administration of the Transvaal faced the question of how to continue the region's industrialization under the control of, but not at the expense of, the mining industry. The magnates wanted to see new industries developed that would provide goods at the cheapest possible cost to the mines. Because on the whole they did not expect that these new industries would be profitable—after all, any profits would surely come at the expense of the mines—they preferred not to finance the enterprises themselves but instead looked to other investors and to the state to come up with the money and to run the risks of establishing new businesses. In short, they hoped to appropriate Kruger's concept of government-protected monopolies for their own ends.

At the same time, the British administration under Lord Alfred Milner believed that to promote the "supremacy" of imperial interests (and protect the funds of British investors) in the Transvaal, everything possible should be done to aid the mining industry.[39] The Transvaal economy rested on gold. British investors had more than £100,000,000 in the mines and continued to pour funds into the industry. Between 1900 and 1909 South Africa accounted for 85 percent of all new funds invested in the African continent.[40] Moreover, Milner believed that strengthening the local economy would attract sufficient British immigrants to ensure that English speakers formed a majority of the electorate, rendering futile any continued Afrikaner opposition.[41]

Milner and the mining magnates turned to Kruger's former concessions to achieve their goals. In the immediate aftermath of the South African War, they radically altered the ownership structure of the concessions industries through the Transvaal Concessions Commission. The commission examined each concession and, largely following the recommendations of the mining industry, either canceled the existing licenses, transferred them to new holders, or eliminated the monopoly rights of the existing businesses. The Hatherley Distillery, for example, long an object of attack by the mine owners, who wanted to prevent their black workers from getting any access to alcohol, was done away with entirely.[42] Dynamite, however, was another matter, because of its central importance to the mines. The mining companies wanted to secure their own control over the dynamite production process, and when the Concessions Commission eliminated the monopoly previously held by the Nobel and French companies, the De Beers and Consolidated Goldfields companies built a rival factory in the Cape, which from 1905 on secured sole supply contracts with practically all the major mining groups. The effect of mining control over costs was dramatic, the price of dynamite dropping from £5 a case in 1895 to £2 in 1910.[43]

With regard to railways, the mine owners preferred that the state take on the costs of providing what they considered an essential but perennially unprofitable service. The mine owners were primarily concerned to reduce transportation costs on goods that their industry consumed, especially coal, and felt that the NZASM had taken advantage of its monopoly rights to overcharge for railage. Leading the Chamber of Mines' attack on the NZASM, Percy Fitzpatrick of Wernher Beit, in evidence to the Transvaal Concessions Commission, urged government expropriation on the grounds that "it is inimical to the best interests of the country that so important a monopoly should be in the possession of private individuals and controlled by a Board of Directors at Amsterdam, whose main, if only, object must be the earning of as large dividends as possible."[44] Ignoring the fact that Fitzpatrick's statement could apply just as well to the mining industry, the commission essentially adopted his language in its own report when it argued that "it is injurious to the public interest that the construction and working of trunk lines of railway communication in any country should be a monopoly in the hands of a single private company, and the injury is aggravated by the fact that the monopolist company is foreign, and the seat of its administration in a foreign country."[45] Acting on the commission's recommendations, the British administration in 1902 purchased the NZASM for £13,000,000 and thus brought all rail transport in the Transvaal under state control.

In later years, the administration honored a prior agreement between the mining industry, Kruger's government, and the Portuguese government that in return for the gold industry's being permitted to recruit African workers in Mozambique, the bulk of Transvaal commerce should move through the Mozambican port of Lourenço Marques. The continuation of the agreement (which resulted in 50 percent of Transvaal traffic going through Lourenço Marques, 30 percent through Durban, and 20 percent through Cape Town) was financially advantageous to the mine owners, who retained access to their major supply of recruited labor. But for the British colonial authorities it meant the loss of a considerable amount in customs dues that could have been obtained if the railways had been required to bring all goods through British ports.[46] Moreover, the administration agreed that all rail rates should be lowered to cover costs only. Thus, government control of the railways freed the mine owners from the burden of paying exorbitant profits to the NZASM shareholders, ensured continued access to supplies of cheap labor for the mines, and put the burden of financing a transportation network on the state.

The question of what to do with Kruger's electricity concession was much more complex, particularly as it was of crucial importance to the labor policies of the mines. After the South African War the mine owners faced a severe labor crisis. They wished to continue with their low-wage policy but found it increasingly difficult to attract African workers when many employers in other sectors of the South African economy were also competing for the same labor and pushing up wage rates. Three of the mine owners responded by setting up a central recruiting organization to funnel Mozambican workers directly to the mines, to pressure the administration to extend the implementation and strict enforcement of pass laws, and to import indentured workers from China despite fierce opposition, especially from Afrikaners.[47]

Of greater long-term significance were the efforts made to increase the mechanization of operations in the mines and thereby reduce the dependence on black labor, cut costs, and increase productivity. Indeed, for the mine owners, mechanization had strategic as well as financial advantages. As the engineer of Consolidated Goldfields put matters, by alleviating the industry's almost total dependence on black labor, mechanization "may save labour at a price which makes it, according to the books, not so economical; but if it is a case . . . where labour is scarce [as it was], it may be worthwhile to do it, even beyond that cost."[48] And electrification was the most efficient and cost-effective means to bring about such mechanization. One mining company reported that because of electrification it could process 50 percent more ore; the costs of power, previously derived from steam, had dropped by 37 percent.[49] Largely due to the implementation of electrically powered mechanization the ore output of the gold mining companies, even in a period of labor scarcity, jumped dramatically from a prewar high of 6,651 tons in 1898 to 12,312 tons in 1906.[50] With such returns, electricity was considered vital to expanding production, lowering costs, and increasing the vast profits of the gold-mining industry.

Yet by 1906, the last year of direct British administration of the Transvaal, the growing power demands of the mining industry were clearly outpacing the resources of the two existing electricity-supply companies.[51] In that year, the largest mining company on the Rand, Central Mining (consisting of Wernher Beit, Eckstein, and Rand Mines, which together were known as the "Corner House" group), decided to electrify its operations. Central Mining considered establishing its own private power station, but in reasoning consistent with the industry's investment pattern decided it would be cheaper to let someone else bear the capital costs of erecting the plant.[52] The two power companies already in existence, the RCE and General Electric, operated under concessions granted originally by Paul Kruger in 1894 and 1897, respectively, but neither had a monopoly. The

RCE was much the larger company, supplying twelve mines with electricity and backed financially by the mining house of Goerz and Company as well as the German electrical engineering firm of Siemens and Halske.[53] The General Electric Company was controlled by Consolidated Goldfields, and it primarily supplied mines owned by the parent company.[54] Neither company was large enough to meet Central Mining's demand, which would more than double total Rand electrical usage, nor were their parent companies—mining houses themselves—willing to commit further funds of their own to the establishment of a large-scale electricity industry.

The key to expanding production, providing low-cost power and guaranteeing the financial stability of electricity generation, lay in the creation of a monopoly. The perils of open competition among electricity-supply companies were well illustrated in contemporary London, where sixty-five companies operated, creating a nightmare for regulators and driving up consumer prices through inefficient operations. Electricity was cheapest where it was generated on the largest scale and transmitted by a single company locally. Moreover, once a sole producer achieved domination in production and supply, even if it was not guaranteed a monopoly by the state, it could exert almost total control because the enormous costs and risks involved in starting up an electricity system would make it virtually impossible for any newcomer to enter an established industry.[55]

In search of such domination, the RCE and General Electric competed against one another to expand their operations. The RCE adopted a legal maneuver, requesting the Transvaal administration in January 1906 to extend the company's concession to cover all mining areas along the Rand. If successful in obtaining such a monopoly, the company would then have no difficulty in attracting outside investors with the funds necessary to finance new plant.[56] Within a matter of months, however, the RCE's request was challenged by a new competitor, the African Concessions Syndicate, a British South Africa Company (BSAC) subsidiary holding an unexercised monopoly to generate power at the Victoria Falls. In July the syndicate introduced a private bill to obtain the right to erect power lines and generating stations as well as control over an area of supply covering the entire Rand and extending to Pretoria and Heidelberg.[57]

The General Electric Company, itself linked indirectly to the BSAC in that Consolidated Goldfields was a major shareholder in the BSAC, chose an alternative route to expansion. It negotiated new contracts with additional mining customers and, more important, sought out capital support from German banks eager to finance the acquisition of German machinery necessary for a new power plant. In particular, the banks wanted General Electric to purchase all the equipment required for expanding production from the Allgemeine Elektrizitätsgesellschaft (AEG), the foremost German electrical machinery firm of the time.[58]

The British administration favored the RCE's plans over those of the company's rivals, out of a mix of economic and political concerns. Lionel Curtis, assistant colonial secretary and a close associate of Milner's, decried the African Concessions Syndicate's bill because if passed it would bring about "the creation of what will in practice be one of the most comprehensive monopolies to be found in any country let alone any British colony. I do not hesitate to say that the powers asked for are such that within five years the African Concessions Syndicate, Ltd., would be the only corporation worth mentioning, public or private, in a position to sell electric current in the Transvaal."[59]

General Electric's plans to link up with German bankers and engineering firms received an equally cold response, particularly from British bankers and engineers in the Transvaal, who drew on deep-seated anti-German sentiment among English speakers to bolster their opposition.[60] In November 1906, one month before the granting of responsible government to the Transvaal, the British administration partially granted the RCE's request by extending the company's concession rights, due to expire in 1909, until 1948.[61] The day before the actual transfer of political power, the administration denied a similar request by General Electric.[62] The African Concessions Syndicate's bill met the same fate as General Electric's plans, with British officials arguing that its proposals did not conform to then current regulations.[63]

But within a few months the situation had changed totally, with all three companies—RCE, African Concessions, and General Electric—consolidated into a single new operation, the Victoria Falls Power Company (VFPC), which exercised a virtual monopoly over the generation of electricity on the Rand. In December 1906 the BSAC floated the VFPC, claiming that the new company—essentially the African Concessions Syndicate in a different guise—would supply electricity throughout the chartered company's area of operations from a power station to be built at the Victoria Falls, a scheme that engineers in England described as "amazing," "incredible," and "absurd," largely because of the isolation of the falls and the unreliability of their water supply.

Hidden in the details of the VFPC's plans, however, was a proposal to build a small power station on the Rand, and that seems to have been at the heart of the new enterprise's attractiveness.[64] Consolidated Goldfields then sold the General Electric company to the VFPC in January 1907, primarily in exchange for £100,000 worth of VFPC shares.[65] In February the VFPC purchased the concession rights of the RCE for £175,000 in preference shares and £175,000 in debentures, a price that a director of the Corner

House group regarded as absurdly high, especially considering that the RCE retained possession of all of its capital assets.[66] The largest investor in the VFPC, however, was the AEG and its German bankers, who received £1,500,000 worth of shares in return for supplying all the equipment needed to begin operations.[67] Using only shares and debentures, as yet unsecured by any physical assets, the BSAC and Consolidated Goldfields had by 1907 created a company backed by British mining and German banking capital with the legal right, as embodied in the General Electric and RCE concessions, to a dominant share of electricity supply to the Rand.[68]

The VFPC backers next transformed that dominant share into a monopoly by reaching an agreement in June 1908 with Central Mining, which produced 40 percent of the Rand's gold output. If the VFPC tried to set an electricity price higher than the Central's directors thought reasonable, it risked seeing the Corner House group build a competing power station. Rather than fight among themselves, the mine magnates compromised. Central Mining agreed not to establish its own station or fund any others, while the VFPC formed a wholly owned subsidiary, Rand Mines Power Supply Company, which was to provide electricity to Central Mining's operations only and to pay 25 percent of its profits to Central.[69] Thus the mining companies themselves, without having to invest significant amounts of their own capital, established a monopoly operation for the supply of electricity to the Rand.

The creation of a powerful industrial monopoly, while a boon to the mine owners, drew considerable criticism from municipal and commercial interests, particularly when the VFPC presented a private bill to the Transvaal Legislative Council in 1909 to grant the company expanded rights. The VFPC had decided to build a new, much larger power station near the coal mines at Vereeniging, thirty-five miles to the south of Johannesburg, as the basis for an electricity distribution system covering the entire Rand. The new power station, it was claimed at the time, would "probably be the largest . . . in the world," generating nearly four times as much electricity as all the power companies in London combined, with the bulk of the output going to Rand Mines, part of Central Mining.[70] Before establishing such a station, however, the VFPC needed legal sanction to expand its area of supply as well as to obtain rights-of-way for transmission wires.[71] The bill would have granted the private company the right to run power lines and to supply customers within any municipality without the consent of the local authority.

The major municipalities in the Transvaal immediately objected to the bill, as it impinged on their legal rights as well as threatened the revenue that they obtained from their own lighting stations.[72] The coal-mine owners, other than Lewis and Marks, who ran the mines at Vereeniging, were equally alarmed. The substitution of electrical for coal-fueled steam power on the mines would greatly reduce the Rand's demand for coal, and although the Vereeniging power station would use coal to generate power, its needs would be much less than those of the steam engines in the mines. Of even greater concern to the coal-mine owners was their fear that the VFPC would use its monopoly position in power generation "to create a monopoly of the coal market," because it would become the major customer for coal in the Transvaal. Clearly the Vereeniging station, reliant solely on Lewis and Marks's coal, represented an enormous threat to their economic interests.[73]

Under considerable public pressure the Transvaal administration, self-governing since 1907 under the leadership of Louis Botha, established a commission of inquiry in 1909 to investigate the structure of the electricity industry. The Power Companies Commission was directed to address the concerns of a large number of producers and consumers—including representatives of the gold mines, the coal industry, the Central South African Railways (CSAR, the state-run successor to the NZASM), local engineering firms, municipal authorities, farmers, and employers of labor in general—as to the implications for them and for the Transvaal as a whole of the VFPC's monopoly on electricity supply.[74]

Despite the wide-ranging frame of reference, the commissioners primarily focused on the cost of power to the gold mines.[75] Their narrowness of vision was in large part a reflection of the overwhelming importance of gold to the economy, in the Transvaal as well as the rest of British-ruled South Africa. Gold accounted for two-thirds of South Africa's exports by value and provided the bulk of state revenues, particularly in the Transvaal.[76] Gold was also the largest employer of labor, particularly of white males whose votes could be crucial in determining who governed the Transvaal.[77] Moreover, Botha's government, recognizing the economic dependence of the Transvaal on gold, had recently moved away from the older Afrikaner critiques of mining capital and developed a closer relationship with the mine magnates, particularly in 1907, when the state had helped crush a strike at the mines.[78] The mine owners saw in Botha and his deputy Jan Smuts men sympathetic to the interests of the gold industry. Lionel Phillips wrote to his partner of "the necessity of backing up the men we know to be progressive, like Botha and Smuts, and firing our guns at the people we know to be the traditional enemies of industrialism and industrialists, like Merriman, Sauer, Hertzog and persons of that ilk."[79] This developing alliance resulted in record dividend payments by the gold industry—£10,500,000 in 1909 alone, almost equivalent to the Transvaal's total state revenues that year—and a renewed flood of foreign investment.[80]

Chaired by the general manager of the CSAR, Thomas Price, and with the Transvaal government mining engineer Robert Kotze as one of its members, the Power Companies Commission heard testimony primarily from three interested parties: the VFPC and its associates, the gold industry, and the coal industry. The commissioners rejected the arguments of the coal representatives that the Vereeniging power station should not be built and that the VFPC should be forced to buy its coal from a marketing combine established by the Transvaal Coal Miners' Association. Accepting almost without exception the testimony of the VFPC and the gold companies, they concluded that the gold industry and the Transvaal's economy as a whole would benefit greatly from vastly increased supplies of cheap electricity generated by a private monopoly producer.[81]

But the commissioners also concluded that such monopoly power should not go completely unregulated by the state, for fear that a private producer could (especially if ownership changed hands) take advantage of its position to exploit consumers. Their final report stated: "Since the supply of electric power thus leads to the establishment of a virtual monopoly in a commodity which has become practically a necessity of modern civilisation, it should, while being left as far as possible to private enterprise, at the same time be placed under government control and subjected to regulations which shall secure the equitable supply of power, the public safety, and public interests generally."[82]

The commissioners incorporated both their willingness to aid the mining industry and their concerns about monopoly excesses in the Power Act of 1910. The key provision of this legislation provided for the establishment of a Power Undertakings Board, which would be composed almost entirely of government officials involved with and responsible for the gold industry: the government mining engineer (as chairman), the inspector of machinery, the registrar of mining titles, the commissioner of inland revenue, and a number of others. The board would have sweeping powers over the generation of electricity, with the authority to determine the prices that could be charged and to approve or disapprove the building of new power stations. Indeed, the primary duty of the board was to prevent the "exploitation" and "abuse" of customers, and its approval was necessary for all price changes and for any major expansion of plant that might result in higher consumer prices.

Responding to the concerns of the railways and municipalities, the framers of the act also included provisions giving the government the right to revoke power-generation licenses, to determine whether surplus profits had been taken and how they should be disbursed, and to expropriate compulsorily the entire VFPC operation after forty-two years if then desired. All current municipal rights over territory, supply rights, and distribution arrangements were guaranteed, while the CSAR was assured of a special rate for power if it decided to electrify its operations.[83] The legislation did not, however, make any provision for ensuring jobs for local whites in the electricity industry, or for limiting German investments, or for protection of the collieries from the purchasing policies of a monopoly. In short, the act allowed the VFPC and its Rand Power subsidiary almost unlimited freedom to engage in any business practices that cut their costs and thus the price of electricity for the mines, so long as none of these actions impinged on the revenues of municipal and state agencies.

Botha's government rushed to pass the Power Act just three days before the Transvaal became part of the Union of South Africa. Such speed ensured that, with regard to electricity at least and by implication the whole process of industrialization, the special relationship developed between the state, mining capital, and emerging industrial capital within the new nation's most economically significant region remained a matter for local negotiation only. This was a striking change from the policies initiated twenty years before by Kruger, who had taken an adversarial posture toward the mine owners, hoping to extract some of the gold industry's profits and channel the money into local economic development. Botha largely followed Milner's lead with regard to the economy, favoring the gold industry because its enormous importance to state revenues and the employment of Transvaal whites made it difficult to do anything else.

Botha hoped that, in the long run, state assistance to mining would lead to the growth of the Transvaal economy in general. In the short term, however, the practical result of his administration's policies was the creation of an electricity monopoly that operated to the benefit of the gold magnates, and did so without costing them any of their capital. Indeed, the mine owners felt that the electricity-supply industry was so carefully regulated in their favor by the Power Undertakings Board—an attitude fostered by the fact that the board never challenged a single application made by the VFPC—that they quietly divested themselves of the company's stock, assured that the government would protect them from rising electricity prices and content not to make profits themselves from the generation of electricity.[84]

Within two years of the passage of the Power Bill, the VFPC's Vereeniging station came into operation. Generating 40,000 kilowatts, more than enough to meet the electricity needs of the gold industry, it was one of the largest power plants in the world. Sammy Marks, owner of the Vereeniging collieries and a large landholder in the area, as well as a board member of the VFPC, believed that the new station, together with abundant local supplies of water would, "soon attract other industries" and enable "the creation of a South African Sheffield [the heartland of Britain's industrial sector] on the Rand."[85]

The Mine Owners and the Iron and Steel Industry

A second industry crucial to mining operations was iron and steel manufacture. The mines used steel machinery, hoists, shoes, dies, and drills as well as corrugated iron for buildings. Nevertheless, Kruger's concession for local steel manufacture, granted to Alois Nellmapius in 1882 and thereafter traded among speculators, had not got off the ground and had been canceled in 1901.[86] By 1910 there were no works inside South Africa producing steel from iron ore or even from metal scrap; the mine owners had to import all their requirements from overseas.

Unlike electricity, which by its very nature necessitated local production and transmission, steel could be shipped from long-established overseas producers. Moreover, it was difficult for any local manufacturer to find the huge amount of start-up capital necessary to establish works that could compete in quality and price with international producers. Yet, as with electricity, the mine owners wanted to exert control over the cost of the product to their industry, and they thought the best way to achieve that aim would be to develop local production rather than remain at the mercy of overseas cartels. As in the case of the VFPC, they also wanted the industry to be established with the capital of other investors, not that of the gold industry. It was far more difficult, however, to lure investment into an industry that could not be guaranteed monopoly control—as it was politically impossible to ban all imports of steel goods—or to encourage government involvement in an industry not already operating under a concession. Their early efforts failed, but they also revealed significant interest within the government bureaucracy in the establishment of a local steel industry.

The new South African state was directly interested in establishing an iron and steel industry because of the demand for supplies by the state railways. One of the central elements in Milner's plans for the development of South Africa had been the unification and expansion of the railway network. After the expropriation of the NZASM in 1901 Milner had embarked on a massive expansion program, which continued after his departure and well into the Union period. Between 1900 and 1909 railway mileage in South Africa almost doubled, with 2,977 miles of new track laid. With £73,000,000 invested in the system by 1910, largely in the form of state-guaranteed loans, the railways were second only to gold in the amount of capital at work. Furthermore, they were the largest state revenue producer by far, accounting for 47 percent of the Transvaal's revenues by 1909.

When Louis Botha became the first prime minister of the newly established Union of South Africa in 1910, therefore, the largest state-owned
enterprise was the South African Railways (SAR), a recent combination of
the CSAR with the provincial lines operating in the Cape, Natal, and the
Orange Free State. And it had an enormous appetite for steel.[87]

Even before Union, the general manager of the CSAR, Sir Thomas Price,
had been so eager to obtain steel that he believed the railways should produce its own. A transplanted British colonial official who had risen to the
post of general manager of the Cape Colony's railways before being
appointed to head the CSAR, Price is described in the *Dictionary of South
African Biography* as "the father of the central railway systems of South
Africa."[88] He usually focused on the interests of his department rather
than considered the impact of his policies on other industries. In 1904 he
had sanctioned plans to expand the CSAR workshops in Pretoria to include
an iron foundry for casting necessary parts and had recommended that the
CSAR manufacture iron using its own scrap, "instead of our being in the
discreditable position of sending our scrap out of the country only for it or
its equivalent to be returned again in the manufactured form."[89] When
some private businessmen emerged eager for government support to establish a smelting operation, Price was critical, arguing: "We got a little tired
of people coming along prepared to undertake this work provided the Government found the money or gave a guarantee."[90] In 1909 he decided to
establish the railways' own works for the melting of scrap.

But other officials in Botha's government favored attracting private capital to establish a large-scale steel industry rather than increasing the public debt through more borrowing. The Transvaal's government mining
engineer, Sir Robert Kotze, believed that Price's plans were too limited to
lead to a viable industry. On the basis of his previous experience as an
engineer for the Transvaal Gold Fields Group, Kotze believed that Price's
plans would likely result in the production of steel inferior in quality and
more expensive than the imported product. He recommended instead that
the government investigate the possibility of establishing a large-scale,
integrated steel industry, capable of producing goods for the mines as well
as the railways and under private control.[91] Kotze believed that an iron and
steel industry could be "of greater importance than that of mining," and
he called upon a British engineering expert, F. W. Harbord, for advice on
"the best method of developing the industry."[92]

Kotze was particularly interested in using private capital for such a
venture and hoped that the announcement of government interest in the
project would be sufficient to attract private participation. Harbord
agreed, claiming that "no good purpose would be served in the Government starting a process for the manufacture of steel from scrap."[93] In 1910,

just prior to Union, the Transvaal administration overturned Price's plans for a CSAR smelter, instead giving Kotze permission to use the railways' abundant scrap metal as bait and to offer it to any private business willing to manufacture steel from scrap, on condition that it would simultaneously develop the larger industry.[94]

One of the smaller and poorly performing mining houses, General Mining, eager to establish a local industry under government patronage, quickly interested a foreign firm in the competition for the scrap iron. General Mining, largely owned by German investors, had considerable financial interests in Rand collieries and real estate as well as in gold. It was therefore, among its peers, particularly interested in encouraging any development that would both lower costs to the gold industry and bring about greater industrial development on the Rand.[95] General Mining put up a small amount of capital to induce the British steel manufacturer Edgar Allen to consider Kotze's proposition.[96] Kotze welcomed the participation of Edgar Allen, believing that the British firm would provide the capital and knowledge necessary to establish a successful industry in South Africa.

It soon became apparent, however, that the British steel maker was primarily interested in setting up a minimal local operation to evade the probable introduction of heavy tariffs while continuing to make its real profits by importing British steel.[97] Edgar Allen believed that local industries, like those being established elsewhere throughout the world, would request and indeed require government protection through tariffs, thereby making it difficult for foreign firms to continue to import goods successfully. When Kotze made it clear that a significant amount of the company's profits would have to go into the development of the local firm, not back to British investors, Edgar Allen abruptly withdrew.[98]

The only other firm in serious competition for the government's support was one that lacked any financial support from the mining industry, the notorious entrepreneurial firm of Lewis and Marks. Theirs was a distinctive operation, being one of the few large investment firms inside South Africa involved in local manufacturing. The managing partners, Samuel Marks and Isaac and Barnet Lewis, had originally made their money in diamond mining at Kimberley, and over the years they had gone on to invest in a variety of real estate enterprises under the ZAR concessions scheme, including gold- and coal-producing properties, agricultural land, and even industrial factories.[99]

The mine owners considered Lewis and Marks a threat to their own financial interests, fearing that any local manufacturing industries established would surely look to the mining industry for both markets and profits. Moreover, Marks had already demonstrated in his extensive dealings with Paul Kruger a readiness and an ability to secure political backing for his enterprises. He continued to play a similar role after the South African War, working in particular to assist Louis Botha's political fortunes while stressing the benefits to South Africa of the industrial development of the Vereeniging area, where Lewis and Marks owned 120,000 acres of land. And Marks had forced the mine owners to come to an expensive compromise over the vfpc's Vereeniging power station proposal.[100] By 1910 Lewis and Marks saw the offer of railway scrap as a rare opportunity to establish yet another business enterprise, and they hoped to locate it in the midst of their real estate holdings at Vereeniging, Marks's "New Sheffield." After the withdrawal of the General Mining and Edgar Allen bid for the government scrap, and given Marks's developing relationship with Botha, his firm appeared to be in a good position to win government approval despite the antagonism of the mine owners.

Indeed, the local firm encountered a government eager to come to terms and dispose of the railways' scrap. The general manager of the SAR, William Wilson Hoy, Price's son-in-law as well as his successor, was particularly concerned about the immediate financial situation of his organization, which was faced with enormous costs in merging and augmenting the four provincial systems. Having already seen the amount of rail mileage in South Africa double between 1900 and 1909, the expectation at the SAR was that the lines would have to double again in order to serve fully the bulk of the country. Yet the SAR imported all its steel goods, even though huge quantities of unused scrap lay idle in its Pretoria yards.

The government mining engineer had already investigated a number of steel-making ventures, including an experimental blast furnace in Natal and a proposal by C. F. Delfos—a local merchant—to use a new Swedish steel production process. Kotze had rejected both schemes, the former because his aim "was to start an iron industry in the Transvaal," the latter because the process was relatively untested.[101] Believing that the situation was one of "urgency," Hoy reached agreement to turn the railways scrap over to a Lewis and Marks subsidiary, the South African Iron and Steel Company, Limited (soon renamed the Union Steel Corporation—Usco), which had been formed in 1911 "to establish steel and iron works and rolling mills in the Transvaal and elsewhere within the Union."[102] In return for the railways scrap, for preferential railage rates on the transportation of all scrap and steel products, and for a guarantee of future orders for steel products from the railways so long as its prices and quality of goods remained satisfactory, Usco agreed to expend surplus profits on experimenting with iron ores, though it was exempted from complying with this requirement for the first three years of its operations.[103]

But Usco, lacking significant financial support from either the government or the mine owners, and with Lewis and Marks already well-known for trying to float operations with other people's money, soon underwent a barrage of criticism. The special nature of the agreement concluded with the railways immediately attracted considerable debate, particularly as it had been signed before being published in the *Government Gazette* and thus did not have *"Parliamentary sanction or even knowledge,"* and because it gave one company a "virtual monopoly" in the utilization of government scrap.[104]

A select committee established in 1912 to investigate the issue found no shortage of critics. In evidence to the committee, John X. Merriman, a former prime minister of the Cape, described the Scrap Iron Agreement as "a proposal to sell railway iron scrap . . . [that] *had developed into a monopoly* that was going to end in disaster to this country." Lionel Phillips, a former chairman of the Chamber of Mines and the head of the Corner House Group, argued that although a local industry might have great popular appeal, if it were not to collapse it would have to receive government protection and be allowed to sell at higher prices than did the importers of steel products. He thought that with the agreement as signed, *"the country might be saddled with a most serious responsibility in the future."*[105]

Such criticisms were hardly conducive to Usco attracting further investors. The company had been in operation for little more than a year when the lack of capital began to show; Kotze noted critically in 1913 that "a large amount of capital has yet to be spent to bring these works into a position to influence in any way the Johannesburg market for steel."[106] Usco tried to cut costs by reducing pay rates, particularly by hiring white workers at below commonly accepted union rates. This practice only drew further criticism from the press and within Parliament, where questions were raised as to whether the Scrap Iron Agreement had included—as the questioners implied that it should—any "fair wage" clause.[107] The outbreak of the First World War initially made matters worse for the company, with machine parts difficult to obtain and credit drying up. The parent firm of Lewis and Marks got into "a desperate plight," barely able to raise a loan of £8,000 at the end of 1915 and owing through Usco over £10,000 to the SAR for scrap and railage.[108] Moreover, although Usco's steel production grew considerably, from 272 tons in the first five months of 1913 to an annual output of 7,537 tons by 1917, this was miniscule in comparison with the needs of the South African economy.[109]

At the start of the war an average of 120,000 tons of steel goods had been imported annually, but because of overseas demand supplies were largely cut off, with only 9,000 tons imported in 1917.[110] Usco's production, all of it utilizing railway scrap, hardly made up for the difference.

Nor was there much likelihood of future expansion. In 1916, when according to the Scrap Iron Agreement Usco was to begin at least experimental smelting of local ores, Kotze concluded that "the absence of surplus profit" meant that the corporation could not embark on such a project.[111]

In addition, policies adopted by the company to extricate itself from its financial difficulties worked to the disadvantage of the local iron and steel industry's prime source of support, the railways. Rather than meet all the steel needs of the railways at the set prices agreed upon, Usco took advantage of wartime shortages to sell the bulk of its output to the mines at greatly inflated prices. In 1917, for example, Usco sold more than 80 percent of its production to the mines at a price averaging nearly 43 percent more per ton than the SAR paid.[112] In the same year, in an underhand deal, Usco resold rail sleepers purchased cheaply from the SAR at a great profit to the Tanganyika railways, further angering the general manager of the SAR, especially as the SAR continued to abide by its contractual obligations and sold scrap iron to Usco for one-fifth the price it could have obtained on the wartime market.[113]

Such actions satisfied neither the gold magnates nor the railways. Expensive steel produced by a company that exercised a virtual monopoly over local output, and that was owned and operated by men who had no significant investments in the mines, was not a development that the magnates wished to see continue and expand. When at the beginning of 1917 Lewis and Marks asked the government to provide the financing for the experimental blast furnace that Usco was contractually obligated but financially unable to build, its request was rejected by the Scientific and Technical Committee that advised the secretary for mines and industries on matters of industrial development. The committee had been formed at the behest of the Chamber of Mines and was composed primarily of engineers and consultants to the mines. The committee members' condescending attitude toward Lewis and Marks was well captured in the language of their report, which recommended in June 1917 that no government funds be used to bail out "dear old Sammy and his affable partner."[114]

The report also reflected considerable self-interest, because just two months later a new investment firm set up by Lionel Phillips and a number of other mining magnates, the Industrial Development Company (IDC), agreed to supply Usco with the capital necessary to erect a blast furnace to smelt local ores on an experimental basis. The readiness of Phillips and his fellow magnates to invest a small sum—no more than £10,000—in the local production of iron and steel resulted from several concerns. First, they wanted to keep the state out of steel production, fearing that its needs would not coincide with their own at the time. Just five days before the members of the Scientific and Technical Committee had recommended that no government funds be used to support Usco, the secretary for mines and industries had written to them acknowledging that there were "obvious objections in a general way to the Government assisting a firm of the character of the Steel Corporation," but that "if the Government were to assist, the fact would enable the Government to have a voice in the kind of experiments to be made."[115] The committee members did not find the likelihood of such a voice an attractive proposition. Second, they felt that Usco took advantage of its monopoly position to overcharge the mines and they thought that if the mine owners themselves held some financial stake in the company they could persuade it to adopt different pricing policies. Third, they believed that if industrial development in general could be encouraged, it might well result in less critical attention on the mines' dominant position in the South African economy, attention that had resulted in the gold mines' having to pay a special levy in 1915 and, after 1917, an additional tax on all income and dividends, rather than solely on profits.[116]

Explaining the rationale behind the original establishment of the IDC in December 1916, the general manager of the Standard Bank wrote to his London board as follows: "Mr Wallers [the general manager of Central Mining and a close associate of Phillips's] in reviewing the scheme informed me in confidence that the object of the Mining Houses in interesting themselves in it [industrial development] is not purely philanthropic. They feel that the Mining Industry today overshadows everything else and bulks too largely in the Government eye. They think that it would be an advantage both to themselves and the country if the basis of industry could be broadened."[117] The magnates also thought that this broadening should take place in industries of immediate service to the gold mines. With regard to the smelter funded by the IDC in August 1917, for example, the main concern of Phillips and his fellow investors was to produce local steel of the right quality to manufacture shoes and dies for use in the battery stamps that crushed their gold-bearing ore. Overseas supplies were unavailable, and steel made from scrap soon weakened. The IDC investors hoped that a local experimental smelter would not only come up with a solution to their particular needs but also yield sufficient profits "to refund most if not all the Capital laid out."[118]

The general manager of the SAR, William Hoy, saw things diferently. He believed that Usco was not living up to its contractual obligations. He could see no advantage to the railways in the production of experimental steels for making battery stampers for the gold mines. He wanted large supplies of relatively low-quality steel produced at the cheapest possible cost to meet the needs of the SAR. His proposed solution to these contradictory impulses was to recommend that the state itself should embark on the production of iron and steel. In a memorandum written in August 1917, the very month that the mine magnates were putting some of their own money into Usco and a time when imports had been largely curtailed and local steel prices were still rising, Hoy suggested that the government should "investigate fully the possibility of establishing an iron and steel industry on a commercial basis." He did not favor direct state control as in the case of the railways, since he thought that "business concerns" should not be run "by bodies whose opinions and actions are governed largely by the views of voters actuated more often than not by personal motives or by local or sectional interests rather than by due regard for the policy best calculated to advance the welfare of the country." He did not like the situation with Usco, as he thought that "a private company might be inclined to indulge in profiteering." Rather, he suggested a compromise: a company that would be a private entity and able to earn a profit but in which the government itself would hold the majority of the shares. Such an arrangement he felt would enable the new operation to be run along sound business lines, with expanded production and cheap steel prices for the railways, but without being subjected to the profit demands usually made by foreign investors and local speculators.[119]

Hoy extended his argument to the electricity industry, suggesting in 1918 that state control was necessary if the railways and by extension the country at large were to benefit fully from the expansion of South Africa's power-generating capacity. He wanted to electrify a number of the SAR's lines, particularly those in Natal, where the railways hauled great tonnages of coal, but he could not expect to obtain sufficient amounts of cheap power from the VFPC, which largely limited its business to the Rand mines, or from the only other producers, municipalities, because their plant was inadequate for anything more than meeting local lighting needs. Hoy wrote to Kotze, the government mining engineer, in June 1918, informing him that he had "in mind the advisability of the Government acquiring, controlling or regulating the supply of power and the price at which it should be delivered to consumers." As with his proposal for a state iron and steel corporation, he envisaged an electricity producer able to make a profit, but with a majority of its shares owned by the government.[120] For the moment, nothing came of Hoy's proposals; funds, both government and private, were in short supply at the end of the war. But in the long term, the concept of state-funded and state-controlled corporations directly engaged in the production of what were rapidly becoming basic necessities would have enormous ramifications for both the mining industry and the economic development of South Africa.

Conclusion

By the end of the First World War the gold-mining industry seemed as dominant as ever in the South African economy, if not more so. Minerals accounted for nearly three-quarters of the country's exports, which in turn provided nearly half of South Africa's national income. In the United States, by contrast, total exports accounted for just under 7 percent of the national income, while the average in European countries was closer to 19 percent. In short, South Africa depended on gold exports for its economic well-being.[121]

Moreover, gold's economic dominance had secured a considerable degree of state support, despite the past history of Kruger's antagonism to the mine magnates and the coming to power of a national government led by Afrikaners after the creation of the Union of South Africa in 1910. In 1907, and again in 1913 and 1914, Afrikaner leaders in the Transvaal and in the Union—Louis Botha and Jan Smuts in particular—had assisted English-speaking mine owners in crushing industrial actions led by white workers in the mines. By such actions gold profits and state revenues were maintained.[122]

Yet the economic and political costs of these actions were high. With the mine magnates and the foreign investors who owned the bulk of the gold industry taking their enormous dividends overseas, practically no capital was reinvested in local development. As Lionel Phillips put matters in 1913, his firm had "plenty of money for mining propositions but none for industries."[123] The exception to that generalization, as the vFPC and to a much lesser extent the IDC and Usco attested, was investment in local industries that could undercut foreign monopolies by taking advantage of low labor and transportation costs to produce goods more cheaply than could the overseas manufacturers.

But what was good for the mines—poorly paid labor and low prices for supplies—was not necessarily good for the wider community. White workers, for example, whose votes could go a long way in determining who held political office, discovered that policies which benefited the financial interests of the mine owners did them little good beyond keeping them employed. And even those jobs were under attack as the mine owners sought to reduce the proportion of relatively expensive white labor and replace it with cheaper black labor. State enterprises like the railways, and their bureaucrats, also found increasing cause for concern as gold industry's policies impinged on their financial situation. More and more individuals in government and politics began to conclude during the First World War that state policies would have to be adopted that would offset the worst excesses of the mining industry, though without harming the financial structure of the mines. Gold had enabled white rule to be fully established in South Africa, but it had also set in process a great number of contradictory developments in the economic and political structure of the country.

1. Sammy Marks, one of the founders of the Union Steel Corporation.
Courtesy Iscor Limited.

2. H. J. van der Bijl, chairman of Escom, Iscor, and the IDC.
Courtesy Iscor Limited.

3. C. F. Delfos and his experimental blast furnace in Pretoria. Courtesy Iscor Limited.

4. Mural depicting industrial development in South Africa, Escom House, Johannesburg. Personal collection of Alice Jacobs.

ICATED TO THE IDEAL OF CEMENTING TOGETHER BY COMMON ENDEAVOUR FOR ACHIEVEMENT ALL THE PEOPLES OF SOUTH AFRICA, REGARDLESS OF RACE OR INTO A BROTHERHOOD OF MUTUAL TRUST AND GOODWILL FOR THE WELFARE OF OUR COUNTRY AND THE GLORY OF ALMIGHTY GOD

DEUR VLYTIGHEID TOT MANLIKHEID

5. Mining iron ore at Thabazimbi. Personal collection of Alice Jacobs.

6. White operatives at the Iscor Rolling Mills, Pretoria. Courtesy Iscor Limited.

7. H. J. van Eck, chairman of the IDC. Courtesy Industrial Development Corporation.

8. Black operatives at the Good Hope Textiles' spinning mill.
Courtesy Industrial Development Corporation.

9. Turbine hall, Komati power station, Escom. Courtesy Electricity Supply
Commission.

10. Central control station for the Rand power system, Escom.
Courtesy Electricity Supply Commission.

CHAPTER THREE

The Creation of the State
Corporations

Four decades of mineral-driven growth had wrought enormous changes in South Africa. Political union of the formerly disparate British colonial, Afrikaner, and African states of southern Africa had been established, with white power firmly in place and Africans incorporated as a mostly landless rural and urban proletariat discriminated against in social and economic life and by judicial decree. South Africa had also become the economic powerhouse of Africa. By the beginning of the First World War, European capital amounting to approximately £350,000,000 was invested in the country, a sum considerably greater than that invested in the rest of Africa combined. The annual value of South African exports approached £70,000,000 (of which Transvaal gold accounted for just under £40,000,000), and comprised more than 70 percent of the total exports from Africa. South African gold exports alone were equivalent to twice the value of exports from all British territories in Africa (excluding South Africa) and ten times the value of exports from French, Belgian, and German territories combined.[1]

Such changes had been forged through war, and they depended on the exercise of considerable state force to prevent fragmentation. In the decade after union, South Africa still remained four loosely connected provinces overwhelmingly populated by rural African societies and ruled by a small white citizenry divided along cultural and economic lines. The country lacked an overarching sense of political community, and the economy, centered on gold in the Transvaal but with relatively little development elsewhere, was marked by the "absence of *national* integration."[2] Force held things together. The last war against Africans, who had protested land loss and the imposition of grinding taxes, had only been concluded in 1906, with four thousand Zulus killed, seven thousand imprisoned, and their leader Bambatha beheaded. Since then, state control in rural and urban areas had become ever stricter and more onerous with the implementation of laws determining where people could reside, what jobs they could hold, and where they could move, the whole system of control regulated through the enforcement of the pass laws by the police and the courts.[3]

Afrikaner opposition to British imperialism, which in the nineteenth century had produced two major wars, sparked another in 1914 when men opposed to South Africa's entry into the First World War on the side of Great Britain took up arms against the government. The uprising split Afrikaners—never a single community—with Prime Minister Louis Botha leading an army of forty thousand, most of them Afrikaners and officered by old Boer colleagues from the South African War, against the rebels, who were broken in battle, hunted down, tried, and, in one case, executed for treason. Paradoxically, the first casualty among the rebels, General J. H. de la Rey, a renowned Afrikaner commando leader in the South African War who was killed by police at a roadblock in September 1914, had just eight months earlier led an army of sixty thousand government troops in breaking a general strike by white workers on the Rand protesting efforts by English-speaking employers to cut wages and substitute cheaper black workers for white.[4] The January 1914 labor conflict was the third time in six months that soldiers had been used in an industrial dispute. In June 1913 more than a hundred striking mine workers and bystanders had been killed by British troops, and in September thousands of black miners had been driven back to their jobs "with bayonets and rifle butts."[5] In sum, the forcible exercise of state power was crucial to maintaining the political and economic structure of South Africa.

But force had its limits, especially in the face of developments during and immediately after the First World War that ripped apart South African society. Growing problems in the cost structure of the gold industry led the mine owners to adopt policies that impinged severely on the work conditions and wages of black and white miners. Declining economic conditions in general were particularly harsh in the countryside, where a rising tide of white impoverishment produced both rural discontent and an exodus of unskilled Afrikaners to the cities. With employment opportunities in the gold industry limited, there were few alternative sources of jobs. Those that existed in the country's small but growing manufacturing sector were poorly paid and often taken by black workers rather than white. In this context, discontent grew: among Africans critical of discriminatory legislation and facing lowered wages; among Afrikaners up against the likely prospect of becoming "poor whites" and finding ethnocentric nationalism attractive; among English-speaking white workers radicalized by the worsening conditions in the workplace.[6]

The conjunction of these developments produced what David Yudelman has referred to as a crisis of legitimation for the South African state.

In order to sustain its revenues—to, as Yudelman has put matters, fulfill its role in accumulation—the state adopted policies that favored the gold-mining industry and protected the interests of British capital. But the resulting conflict—in the mines and in the 1914 rebellion—demonstrated that an increasingly large part of the white electorate "simply rejected the validity of the state" and severely tested its ability, with only limited police and army forces at its disposal, to maintain control.[7]

To deal with structural imbalances in the economy and the legitimation crisis, the South African state took a growing interventionist role in the decade after the First World War. Politicians ranging from Botha and Smuts, popularly associated with mining capital and British interests, to J. B. M. Hertzog, ardent Afrikaner nationalist and self-appointed champion of white workers, sought to broaden the base of the South African economy, so as to meet the revenue needs of the state and provide more jobs for white workers. A key development in this interventionist approach was the direct participation for the first time by the state in production. This was done through the establishment of state corporations to produce electricity and to manufacture iron and steel. By the end of the 1920s the Electricity Supply Commission (Escom) and the Iron and Steel Corporation (Iscor) represented a major state role in the economy of South Africa.

Impending Crisis in the Postwar Years

Although the gold-mining industry dominated South Africa's economy as much in the decade after 1910 as it had in the preceding three decades, its cost structure was undergoing new pressures. Between 1912 and 1919 working costs increased while working profits declined, particularly during the waning years of the war and immediately thereafter. Dividends fell, with only £5,500,000 paid out in 1918, a third less than in 1912 and half the record payment of 1909. Yudelman has argued that the major cause of this decline was a combination of world inflation and the fixed price of gold. Whereas in wartime and postwar conditions inflation pushed most prices ever higher, the return on gold, though showing an apparent increase in pound value, actually declined in real terms. Indeed, by 1920, according to Yudelman's calculations, "the price of gold in pounds sterling . . . was the highest ever. . . . But in "real" terms—calculating its purchasing power after allowing for inflation—it was the lowest price in the twentieth century."[8]

Rather than blaming wartime inflation and the fixed price of gold, however, the mine owners singled out high labor costs and government exactions as being responsible for their problems, as these were factors over which they could exert some control. Labor unrest in the gold mines in

1913 and 1914 had been directly related to attempts by the mine owners, Lionel Phillips among their leaders, to increase productivity, particularly in the low-grade mines, by making working conditions in general more onerous, by lowering wages, and by increasing the number of jobs that could be performed by blacks, thereby reducing the number of relatively expensive white workers. By 1916, as a result of the mine owners' efforts, backed up by the state, the wages of black and white workers in the mines had fallen approximately 10 percent from pre-strike figures, while the ratio of blacks to whites had increased by 17 percent.[9]

At the same time, the mine owners contended that these savings were not enough, especially considering the burdensome amounts they claimed they had to pay in taxes, railway transportation costs on supplies, customs duties, and other government charges. They argued that they might have to close a significant number of their less profitable operations, mines that in 1917 "employed 6,000 whites and 48,000 blacks . . . and produced about £7 million of gold per annum." These closures would have had enormous repercussions for the government, as it would have produced great labor unrest as well as cut the gold revenues on which the state depended for the bulk of its income.[10]

In this context of declining labor conditions and growing threats to the profits of the gold industry and the revenues of the state, mine owners and politicians alike proposed that increased industrialization would solve their and South Africa's ills. As we saw in chapter 2, the Chamber of Mines felt that the mining industry bulked "too largely in the Government eye," and it believed that "the basis of industry" should be broadened. In July 1916 the chamber privately informed the government that it was establishing a fund to encourage "sound South African industries . . . at present handicapped by want of capital." The result of these efforts was the establishment of the Industrial Development Company (IDC), primarily backed by Lionel Phillips and his Central Mining Company.[11] However, the financial input of the IDC into South African industrialization was minute. Although the company helped fund Lewis and Marks's experimental blast furnace, it considered only seven out of every one hundred applications for financial assistance worth investing in and had given them a total of only £18,600 by the middle of 1917. Clearly, the gold magnates were not interested in putting up much of their own money to encourage industrialization.[12]

Botha's government also called for more industrialization, and linked the issue to the difficult conditions facing white workers in the economy. In response to a request from the IDC that "the State" take the lead "in developing the resources of the country," the government in May 1917 established an Industries Advisory Board, composed of private businessmen (including the general manager of Central Mining), to advise the Department of Mines and Industries on "industrial matters."[13] In September the board submitted to the government a report outlining the industries most in need of state and private assistance, including iron and steel manufacturing, and suggested that such industries should be required to give preference to white job seekers. "Since economically the white race is inferior in many branches of unskilled and semi-skilled labour to native and coloured people, there is a tendency for factories to reduce the white labour employed to a minimum. Hence when state assistance is given this could be on condition that a certain percentage of whites are employed."[14]

Although the board conducted numerous studies and produced reports that repeatedly wrestled with the form state assistance should take, little was actually done.[15] In a time of economic stringency the government was not ready to commit public funds to the development of private enterprise. Nor was it ready to risk such funds by establishing its own operations. Indeed, one of the few practical results of the politicians' and mine owners' discourse on industrialization was an agreement to fund a small new steel manufacturer, C. F. Delfos, at the expense of Lewis and Marks. Delfos had particular attractions for the mining industry because his operation, unlike that of Lewis and Marks, depended almost entirely on the mine owners for its business and could be counted on to support their interests. The government, accepting the advice of its Industrial Advisory Board (largely influenced by Phillips), abrogated the railways agreement to sell all scrap to Lewis and Marks and instead contracted for the SAR to buy all of its iron and steel goods from Delfos.[16] While good for the mines, this development had little to offer white workers.

Indeed, during the war and after, white workers had little reason to expect better times to come their way through the greater industrialization of South Africa's economy. Numerous scholars have commented on the emergence of secondary industry in South Africa during the war, when the cutting off of overseas supplies and local demand combined to produce a huge growth in manufacturing, and have noted the large employment opportunities that opened up.[17] By 1918 private industries outside mining employed approximately forty-three thousand whites, who comprised one-third of the work force in factories, whereas the mines employed just over twenty-three thousand whites, who accounted for only 11 percent of the men at work in the gold industry.[18]

The most striking feature of this growth, however, was not the quantity of employment opportunities provided (after all, the SAR alone employed practically as many whites as did all nonmining private industry and continued to do so until 1933), but rather the difficult and declining position that whites occupied in manufacturing. Although whites accounted for a third of the work force in 1918, that was down from nearly 40 percent in 1915. Blacks and, to a much lesser but still significant extent, white women took an ever-increasing share of the jobs in manufacturing, and did so for the rest of the 1910s, the 1920s, and after.[19] Moreover, white workers in the manufacturing industries were poorly paid. In 1918, the forty-three thousand white industrial workers received total wages of just over £9,000,000, compared with £10,900,000 for their twenty-three thousand white peers in the gold mines.[20]

Declining economic conditions after the war produced growing civil strife that threatened to fragment the very foundations of white power in South Africa. Real wages in the mining industry kept falling while inflation skyrocketed, pushing up the cost of living by 25 percent in 1920 alone.[21] Harshening conditions also affected the rural areas of the country, where the development of commercial agriculture, particularly in the Transvaal, left many Afrikaners landless and forced to join the second "Trek," this time of "poor whites" to the cities. Some of these people found work in the mining industry (which provided the bulk of jobs available to unskilled whites), where by 1918 Afrikaners made up 75 percent of the white work force; smaller numbers were employed in the growing manufacturing industry (where most jobs were taken by skilled British immigrants). In both sectors, however, they were the least skilled and the most poorly paid of the white workers. By 1920 more than a hundred thousand people were deemed poor whites, most of them chronically unemployed and barely able to subsist, with Afrikaners providing the overwhelming bulk of their numbers. Indeed, poor whites comprised nearly a quarter of the total Afrikaner population, and formed an even larger proportion in the Transvaal.[22]

These Afrikaners, rural and urban dwellers, employed and unemployed alike, were increasingly attracted to the ethnocentric ideas of Hertzog's National Party in the postwar years. National Party propaganda stressed the oppression of Afrikaans speakers by British imperialists and English-speaking Jewish gold magnates, and decried Botha, Smuts, and their South African Party (SAP) as a tool of foreign capitalists. Members of the Afrikaner elite formed separatist organizations in 1918 to benefit the *volk*, such as the economic organizations SANLAM—Suid-Afrikaanse Nasionale Lewensassuransie Maatskappy (South African National Life Assurance Company)—and SANTAM—Suid-Afrikaanse Nasionale Trust Maatskappy (South African National Trust Company)—and the (at first) culturally focused *Broederbond* ("Brotherhood"). Rural supporters of the National Party found ready converts to their cause among farmers who had supported the SAP and been the backbone of Botha's and Smuts's early political careers.[23] At the same time, white urban workers gave increasing support to the Labour Party, which decried the power of the mining industry and denounced the close relationship developed between the mining magnates and the Botha-Smuts government. Throughout the war, both the National Party and the Labour Party called for government ownership of mining and shipping operations, so that the economic discontents of their followers could be alleviated through greater local industrial development and increased export trade.[24] Such developments threatened both the mining industry and the political base of the government.

Poor economic conditions and attempts by the mine owners to make further inroads into the employment of white labor produced a wave of strikes that shook the foundations of the mining industry. In 1916 only 1,420 days of work had been lost through industrial action. In 1919, however, 537,100 days were lost, with 23,800 men out on strike; in 1920 the numbers increased yet again, to 839,400 days lost and 105,700 men striking.[25] The mine owners eventually came to terms with the white workers, though at considerable cost; the white wage bill, which comprised the bulk of the mines' labor costs, rose from a pre-strike annual average of £494 per worker in 1919 to a post-strike average of £627 in 1920.[26] The most threatening strike for the mine owners, however, was the one organized by black workers in February 1920, when more than seventy thousand men, more than half the mines' black labor force, stopped work. To the consternation of the Chamber of Mines, the stoppage did not represent a "riot," as previous labor actions by black workers were usually described, but rather "a regular strike organised on the European model," making it much more troubling.[27] If black workers were to organize effectively, the basis of the cheap labor system that ensured the profitability of the gold industry would be undercut.

The mine owners broke the black workers' strike with armed troops and police, killing eleven and injuring 120. But they recognized that the industry's labor policies would have to change. After the crushing of the strike, the mine owners agreed to increase black wages and to decrease the prices that company stores charged for goods sold to compound dwellers. Ominously for white workers, the mine owners drew attention to the report of the government's commission of inquiry into low-grade mines that had recommended, after the black miners' strike in 1920, that the legal color bar be abolished. They argued that job reservation for whites should be done away with entirely and productivity be increased through greater mechanization.[28] Privately the mine owners, determined to force a showdown with white workers, also established in 1920 a "reserve fund," controlled by the Transvaal Chamber of Mines, to be used when the inevitable dispute broke out.[29]

For the South African state, any major attack on white workers raised serious questions about its ability to govern. A series of government commissions dating back to before Union had drawn attention again and again to the vulnerable nature of white rule in South Africa, particularly in light of the growing problem of poor whites. The Transvaal Indigency Commission in 1908 had argued: "Where the white man directs and the coloured does the work, the relatively incapable white man is bound to be unable to maintain his position as an aristocrat in the economic world and must either merge with the coloured population or become a parasite on the white community."[30] The Select Committee on European Employment and Labor Conditions, deliberating in 1914, concluded: "The European minority, occupying as it does, in relation to the non-European majority, the position of a dominant aristocracy . . . cannot allow a considerable number of its members to sink into apathetic indigency. . . . If they do and they manifest an indifference founded on the comfortable doctrine of letting things find their economical level, sooner or later, notwithstanding all our material and intellectual advantages, our race is bound to perish in South Africa."[31]

By the end of the war, the dire predictions seemed ever more likely to come true. There was a growing influx of poor Afrikaners entering the cities, especially on the Rand, white labor in the mines was under attack, and there were few job opportunities available for unskilled whites in the manufacturing sector. The secretary for mines and industries, Herbert Warington Smyth, warned in 1919 that "unless our rate of industrial growth increases a few years will see a wave of emigration from the shores of South Africa of the best and most enterprising of our young white population."[32] Yet unemployment continued to rise; the number of whites out of work doubled between 1919 and 1921.[33] Adding to the pressures on Botha and Smuts was the growing popularity of the National Party and the Labour Party, whose support was built on Afrikaner and white worker disaffection with the SAP and its alliance with the gold magnates.

In this context of economic and political flux, the government sought to alleviate pressures by pushing for a much-expanded level of state intervention in the economy, particularly in those industries regarded as essential to broad-based industrialization, electricity and iron and steel. The provision of large supplies of cheap electricity and locally produced iron and steel would, the government believed, enable a huge increase in industrial development as well as other sectors of the economy throughout the country.

As I mentioned in chapter 2, William Hoy, the general manager of the railways, had in 1917 and 1918 urged state involvement in electricity generation and the production of iron and steel primarily to meet the needs of his own organization.[34] Hoy's sectional interests were taken up with regard to the economy as a whole by Botha, who had concluded by the end of 1918 that "some central organisation should be established in connection with which the Government might acquire, control or regulate the supply of power and the price at which it should be delivered to consumers. The object of the scheme would be to provide at various centres power, for disposal in bulk, to municipalities; to mines; for agriculture, railway, telegraph and telephone purposes and to large industrial corporations."[35] After Botha's death in August 1919 Smuts, upon his own accession to the prime ministership, followed his mentor's lead and commissioned an overseas consulting firm, Merz and McLellan, to report on the overall supply of electricity in South Africa and its importance for further industrialization. The resulting report stressed that increased electrical power was essential both for the growth of the existing manufacturing industry and to attract "new and permanent industries as rapidly as possible."[36]

Additional support for increased production of electricity and iron and steel came from one of Smuts's protégés, H. J. van der Bijl, who would go on to become the major architect of state-controlled industrialization in South Africa. Van der Bijl was recruited by Smuts in 1917 to become scientific and technical adviser to the government, a post he took up in 1920. The son of a wealthy Transvaal grain merchant, and an old family friend of Smuts's, van der Bijl had obtained a doctorate in physics at Leipzig and taught at German universities before taking up a research position in New York with American Telephone and Telegraph. While there he wrote a book, *The Thermionic Vacuum Tube and Its Applications*, which served as a standard physics text in American universities until the Second World War.

Van der Bijl was appointed scientific adviser not just because of his professional accomplishments and his family connections to Smuts but also because he was the only Afrikaner applicant among a number of exceptionally well-qualified candidates for the job.[37] As the government expert on science and technology, he argued for the centrality of electrification and iron and steel production to economic development. "The electrification of the Union's railways . . . can be made to be one of the most powerful factors in stimulating industrial development . . . by bringing together two of the most important requirements of most industrial undertakings, namely power and transport facilities," while iron and steel was "the foundation of all industries."[38] Still, on the basis of his experiences with ATT in America, van der Bijl thought that both industries would be better managed by the private sector than by the state.[39]

However, the notion of direct state control over production gained increasing support in the face of the industrial unrest that racked South Africa in 1919 and 1920. Hoy felt that government forces could move more quickly to put down disturbances at state rather than at private or municipal power stations. Noting that strikes had already affected the small municipal stations from which the sar drew some of its electricity needs, Hoy argued that "in the event of [further] trouble arising, it would be too late for the government to intervene without perhaps precipitating or increasing the difficulties."[40] The government mining engineer, Robert Kotze, supported Hoy's position, arguing that in addition to "the risk of interruptions from strikes," nongovernmental stations were also subject to "an undue raising of prices due to excessive pandering to labour demands."[41]

Although Smuts's government supported increased state intervention in the economy, it did not want such efforts to impinge on the financial interests of the gold industry. In 1921 Kotze, convinced that the mines were indeed facing a cost crisis, wrote to Smuts that "the time is coming when it will be as necessary in the national interest to support and stimulate mining as any other industry."[42] Smuts himself was readying the state to support the mine owners in their planned assault on white labor, and he had no intention of supporting measures that would in any way add to the costs of the gold industry. For Smuts and Kotze and other members of the administration, as well as for the gold magnates, the attraction of state intervention in the production of electricity in the early 1920s lay in the cost advantages that cheaper power would have for the mines, the fact that it would enable a greater degree of mechanization and less reliance on relatively expensive white labor, and the growth that could be produced in the manufacturing sector, where more jobs could be provided for whites (at the same time as they were pushed out of the mines) and their dissatisfaction with the government and the gold industry could be alleviated.

The Electricity Bill, 1920–1923

While today the establishment of large-scale power systems appears a commonplace occurrence, in 1920 such systems were just beginning to take shape in the industrialized countries of the world. In Britain government had enacted legislation only in 1919 to regulate the plethora of private companies and municipalities. The industrialized cities of Chicago and Berlin were likewise developing regional systems to deal with their power demands.[43] These systems, however, had been established by privately owned companies that were granted public utility status. The Hydroelectric Power Commission of Ontario, which began operations in 1910, was the first solely government-owned power corporation in the world, and remained the only one until the establishment of a similar body in Victoria, Australia, in 1918.[44] Therefore, when the South African government raised the possibility of establishing regional power systems under the direct control of the government, it was hardly surprising that the idea was greeted by rival suppliers and potential customers alike with skepticism, suspicion, and resistance.

The South African Railways and the Victoria Falls Power Company— in the persons of William Hoy, the SAR's general manager, and Bernard Price, chief engineer of the VFPC—took opposing sides on the issue of state participation in the production of electricity. Both men were firmly committed to the interests of their respective organizations. Hoy had worked for the railways all his adult life, had been general manager since 1910, and was the son-in-law of the previous general manager. Price also had presided over the VFPC since 1910 and had ensured its growth into one of the largest electricity suppliers in the world.

Hoy had faced enormous problems during his tenure as he tried to unify and expand South Africa's rail services: financing for increased lines and operations had to be obtained at great expense from overseas because the gold magnates preferred not to invest money in what they thought should be a state service; iron and steel had to be imported at high cost; and local electricity producers had shown no interest in generating low-cost power for the railways. Hoy wanted to see large amounts of cheap electricity produced locally, to benefit the railways in particular and manufacturers and farmers in general, and he wanted the state to have a large role in the production process. Price on the other hand opposed competition from the state. The VFPC had a highly profitable market supplying the mines alone. Moreover, Price was answerable to a London-based board of directors and to primarily English shareholders, who demanded that he make the largest possible profits. If Hoy succeeded in establishing a government-controlled power supplier, Price knew that such an operation would inevitably attempt to tap the Rand's demand for electricity and thereby undercut the VFPC's monopoly. Thus, when legislation was proposed in 1920 to deal with the issue of standardizing the generation and distribution of electrical power in South Africa, both men felt that the very survival of their respective operations depended on the exact framework of the final law enacted.[45]

The first version of the Electricity Bill, drafted largely by Hoy and Kotze and the staffs of the SAR and the Department of Mines and Industries, and presented for public discussion in February 1921, confirmed Price's worst fears. The bill proposed that VFPC be place under the regulatory control of a government body—the Board of Electricity Commissioners—that would set industry-wide prices and determine which companies would supply which markets. The bill also proposed that the board be empowered to advise the minister of mines and industries to establish new power stations under the control of "a Government department or by the SAR for the supply of electricity to Government departments, municipalities and the public generally"—in essence, that the state not only regulate the VFPC but also create competitors for its business.[46] The bill would give the government the authority to prevent the further establishment of private electricity stations in favor of state operations. From Hoy's point of view the bill would ensure government control over the stations supplying the SAR with electricity, as well as fulfill Botha's earlier wish that the government itself establish power "centers" throughout South Africa.

Rather than object to what were for the time revolutionary implications concerning state intervention in industrial production in South Africa, Price focused his criticisms of the bill on the sensitive question of prices, particularly with regard to the mining industry's costs. He attacked "the privileged position" of the Board of Electricity Commissioners compared to private producers. Unlike the latter, which the bill would require to treat all consumers in exactly the same fashion, the government producers would be permitted to vary their charges to meet market conditions, charging some consumers more, some less, so long as the state undertakings did not "in the aggregate" show a profit. What Price feared was that government producers would try to seize the huge Rand market for electricity—the mining industry consumed 91 percent of the electricity generated in South Africa in 1919–20—by offering the gold mines cut-rate prices and charging other customers higher rates.[47]

But even the mine owners saw dangers in government intervention and the establishment of a variable pricing structure for electricity. Unlike Price with his concerns about cheaper state rates for the mining industry, the gold magnates were concerned that the government might well charge them for electricity in order to benefit the railways and to promote growth in other sectors of the economy. The Chamber of Mines did not object in general to the idea of state production of electricity, although it was concerned that such a policy should not impinge in any way on the profits of the gold industry.[48]

Smuts gave prime responsibility for working out a compromise with the bill's critics to his old friend Robert Kotze, the man he had appointed in his capacity as Transvaal minister of mines to be government mining engineer in 1908. Kotze's sympathies for the problems of the mine magnates were long-standing and well-known. He had been a strong champion of the gold industry's interests and had chaired the government commission that in 1919 recommended that the statutory color bar—the only legislative measure that white workers believed stood between them and unemployment—be done away with. In 1921 he told Smuts that the

"national interest" required that the government support the gold industry, and in September of the same year he suggested that the state should
subsidize up to 20 percent of the wage bill of the mines, thereby alleviating
the pressure of costly white wages on the low-grade mines.[49] Clearly he
was not ambivalent in arguing that the government should do everything
in its power to assist the mines.

Indeed, encouraged by the support of Kotze and Smuts, the mine owners embarked on a campaign to break the power of organized white labor
in the last few months of 1921 and the beginning of 1922. In November
1921 the Chamber of Mines announced its intention to abandon the color
bar. It next stated that to reduce the high cost of white labor the mines
were going to employ a higher ratio of black workers. White workers on
the Rand organized to defend their perceived interests, striking first at the
VFPC's Vereeniging power station in early January 1922 and thereafter
throughout the coal and gold mines, bringing work in the gold industry
largely to a halt through all of January, February, and March.

Ominously for the mine owners and the government, the strikers were
extremely well organized, with unions and shop stewards taking a leading
role among both the English-speaking and Afrikaans mine workers. Also,
large numbers of Afrikaner strikers, drawing consciously on the experiences of the South African War and the 1914 rebellion, formed themselves
into semi-military commandos. Together they unfurled the banner that so
caught the contradictions of their position: "Workers of the World Fight
and Unite for a White South Africa." Leaders of the National and Labour
parties strongly supported the strikers. Hertzog believed that "the policy
of the government ha[d] led to a wholesale surrender to Capitalistic influences," while F. H. P. Creswell of the Labour Party thought that the "concentration of Credit Power and Industrial Power" in the gold industry had
become" the great danger to the development of society."[50] Tielman Roos,
the leader of the National Party in the Transvaal, called on all reservists to
disobey any government call-up intended to put down the strike by force.

In the face of such opposition, which threatened not only the economic
concerns of the mine owners but also his own political base, Smuts was
unbending in his resolve to crush the strikers. He called up an army of
twenty thousand men backed by tanks, artillery, and aircraft, and for three
days in March bombarded the strikers into defeat, killing at least seventy-
six of them. Smuts intended that the captured strike leaders be summarily
tried and executed, but at the urging of his colleagues (fearful of the political repercussions) he relented, and although eighteen of the strikers were
sentenced to death only four were hanged. As Smuts's actions demonstrated, state power in South Africa still rested on the exercise of government might. Indeed, he made the point succinctly himself in a letter writ-

ten little more than a week after the crushing of the "Rand Revolt": "Unless society is to go to pieces there must be a solid guarantee of force in the background."[51] Yet while claiming in the letter that it was "madness in their blood" that had caused the workers to challenge the state, he also noted in Parliament that the decisive factor in getting "things going towards revolution" was the movement of poor whites— "people without any calling or education"—into the towns, a problem that still needed great efforts, not least by the state, to resolve.[52]

During the course of the labor struggles and in their aftermath, Robert Kotze redrafted the Electricity Bill. Responding to the criticisms of Bernard Price and the mine owners, he proposed that the near absolute powers previously envisaged for the Board of Electricity Commissioners be split between two bodies. The first, the purely regulatory Electricity Control Board (ECB), would supervise operations of all power suppliers, whether government, municipal, or private, but would not itself engage in production. Kotze fashioned the ECB on the model of the Transvaal's Power Undertakings Board (which had acted as little more than a rubber-stamp operation for the VFPC), and he suggested that it be staffed with officials from the Department of Mines and Industries and other government offices. The second organization proposed in Kotze's revised bill, the Electricity Supply Commission (Escom), would be a power producer and would supply electricity to the SAR as well as other sectors of the economy. While it would meet the immediate needs of the railways, Escom's proposed powers and responsibilities were far less extensive than those initially envisioned by Botha, Hoy, and even the original bill. Escom would not operate as a government department or even as part of the state apparatus but would merely be under government supervision. It would be liable to the same regulation by the ECB as any other power supplier and would not be permitted to charge any group of customers more for electricity in order to subsidize another market.[53]

Despite the watering down of the bill, Hoy was satisfied that it at least provided that the SAR would have access to government-controlled stations, which would enable the SAR to safeguard itself against stoppages due to labor unrest. This was a point of considerable import given that the Rand Revolt had begun at a private electricity station, that nearly 1,500,000 man-days of work were lost in strike action in 1922, and that considerable bitterness remained among white workers after the breaking of the strike.[54]

Kotze's revised bill, however, met with considerable opposition from municipal authorities, the VFPC, and the mining industry, expressed in private correspondence in 1921 and in public testimony in 1922. The key issue in dispute was the role of the state in producing and distributing electricity. The municipal authorities complained that the redrafted legislation still gave the government the authority to determine who should produce electricity in South Africa and to which markets it should be supplied. Under the bill, municipalities were obliged to consult Escom whenever they planned to expand their plant; Escom would then determine whether they or Escom could best meet the additional demand. The municipalities feared that Escom might well use its regulatory authority to seize their local electricity markets in order to finance its own set-up costs and operations.

The municipalities had already been subjected to considerable public criticism for generating inadequate amounts of cheap electricity for their residents and for failing to meet the needs of nascent urban industries. One of the basic purposes of the revised Electricity Bill was to remedy this situation, primarily through the establishment of additional or alternative sources of electrical power generated by Escom. In reaction to Kotze's redrafted legislation, all the major municipalities in South Africa demanded that they retain exclusive rights to sell electricity within their local areas and that Escom be permitted only to provide them with bulk electricity at cost, which they could then resell at a profit.[55]

The VFPC and the mine owners also objected to state production. Bernard Price, in testimony to a select committee investigating the question of power generation in 1922, argued that the establishment of Escom would "effectively close the door to private enterprise" in the electricity industry.[56] The representatives of the Chamber of Mines likewise claimed that state production would compete unfairly with private business, and they argued that the proposed supply commission "should be wiped out altogether in its present form."[57]

Chaired by the minister of mines and including two members from the Rand, the select committee was disposed to sympathize with arguments concerning both the well-being of the Johannesburg municipality (one of the most ardent opponents of Escom) and the well-being of the gold industry.[58] Indeed, the committee members preferred not to create the supply commission, yet they feared that if they did not do something the SAR itself would go ahead and erect power stations and charge the costs to Parliament through the railways' annual budget.[59] In consequence, the committee members waffled, giving back to the municipalities control over the sale and distribution of electricity within their localities and amending the bill to delay the establishment of the commission until "a date to be notified by the Governor-General," rather than "as soon as may be after the commencement of this Act," as originally stipulated.[60] The amended bill was then passed by Parliament as the Electricity Act of 1922, and the Electricity Control Board was established soon after.

But Escom remained a paper entity only. The duplicity inherent in the select committee's language was well understood by the two major contenders in the electricity question—the VFPC and the SAR—in their reactions to the act. Price wrote gleefully to a business associate, "For the time being we have managed to stave off the appointment of a Commission [that is, Escom], which means that the nationalisation of the power supply business in this country has been deferred."[61] In contrast, the SAR's parliamentary adviser, A. C. McColm, who felt that the main purpose of Escom was to have been the provision of electricity for the railways, and who lamented the return of local control to the municipalities, complained bitterly that "money talks and loudly too when you touch the purse strings of private monopolies." The SAR did, however, move to defend its particular interests, ensuring that legislation that gave the railways the right to build its own power stations received parliamentary assent one week before the passage of the Electricity Act.[62]

Price's satisfaction was short-lived. Within a matter of months of the passage of the Electricity Act, Escom was brought into existence and began to exercise its potentially considerable powers. The VFPC inadvertently brought about the establishment of the state producer by proposing in 1923 to build a huge new power station at Witbank. Approximately 150 km northeast of Johannesburg, Witbank was the site of the largest coalfields in the Transvaal. With demand for electricity on the Rand growing, particularly as the gold mines further mechanized operations in the wake of their defeat of organized white labor, Price rushed to get government approval to expand the VFPC's operations, determined to establish a new station as soon as possible in case Escom was established. In an attempt to woo his strongest opponent he offered the SAR special customer privileges at the new station, so long as it contributed £200,000 toward construction costs.[63] Hoy rejected Price's advances, however, foreseeing a VFPC monopoly throughout the Transvaal that would leave the SAR "entirely in their hands." He remained worried by the fact that the VFPC stations on the Rand had been struck by private workers during the labor unrest in 1922. Moreover, he hoped that Escom, once established, would purchase the SAR's own power stations in Natal and Cape Town—thereby partly alleviating the railways' considerable debt—and erect a government plant in the Transvaal to cut further the energy costs of his organization.[64]

Hoy's arguments won the support of his political superiors, who had become concerned that the compromises reached in the Electricity Act had left unresolved the pressing issue of regulating and expanding power generation in South Africa.[65] Furthermore, Price's Witbank proposal raised fears that, if successful, the VFPC would effectively monopolize the supply of power to the Rand for the forseeable future. This was a disturbing prospect for a government intent on encouraging industrialization and a gold-mining industry that did not want to have its working costs controlled by any one supplier. In response to Price's application, Herbert Warington Smyth, the secretary of mines, minuted that "the object of the Electricity Act was to prevent [the] railways having to take power from outside firms," and F. S. Malan, the minister of mines and industries, utilizing the machinery of the Electricity Act, established Escom in March 1923 in order to investigate the VFPC proposal, the very step that Price had hoped to thwart.[66]

As established under the terms of the Electricity Act, Escom was a completely new form of enterprise in South Africa, being neither wholly state-controlled nor part of private industry. Escom's governing board was to consist of individuals appointed by the governor-general, while its funding was to come through private and government loans rather than directly from the government budget. The commission was legally designated a "body corporate," separate from the state and capable in law of suing and being sued, yet with its operations subject to the supervision of the minister of mines and industries. Its primary duty was "to stimulate the provision . . . of a cheap and abundant supply of electricity," and to do so on a nonprofit basis.[67]

The direction of this new type of institution was largely set by the man who became Escom's first chairman, H. J. van der Bijl. Already on record as favoring private enterprise over state intervention (perhaps one of the main reasons that at the age of 34 he was chosen by Mines and Industries to fill such a major position), van der Bijl announced his intention to operate the supply commission as if it were a private company.[68] He felt that Escom should actively compete with private and municipal producers to win access to ever-larger markets for electricity. He argued that the commission should be run on "business lines," and that it should not, like the railways, always look to Parliament to bail it out of financial difficulties. Such policies, he believed, would enable Escom to fulfill what he considered its primary function, the promotion of private enterprise throughout South Africa by a process of industrialization built on a foundation of cheap electricity.[69]

Van der Bijl's vision was less a result of Escom's immediate origins in the labor struggles of the early 1920s than an attempt to resolve the growing fragmentation of white rule in South Africa. The economic dynamism of the mining industry had enabled whites to conquer southern Africa, but the practices adopted to secure enormous profits also produced great stresses. The utilization of low-paid black workers ultimately threatened the privileged position of white workers and drove them toward labor militancy and antimining, anti-"establishment" political parties. The profit-taking measures of the gold industry—trying to pay as little as possible for labor and supplies—and the sending of practically all surpluses to overseas financiers and shareholders left the South African economy short on internally generated investment capital.

By the early twentieth century the rising number of poor whites (essentially a contemporary euphemism for Afrikaners), had started to threaten the political base of mining dominance in South Africa. For Smuts, it was "very ignorant" poor whites, "the flotsam and jetsam of our urban population," led by "advanced Communists" from overseas and supported by Hertzog's "Nationalists," who in 1922 turned a strike into a "revolution."[70] Force crushed the revolution, but the men who provided the bulk of that force, the commandos of rural Afrikaners that Smuts called up in March 1922, came from the same segment of the population that produced poor whites and Hertzog's supporters. If economic conditions outside the mining industry continued to decline in South Africa, then Smuts's commandos too would be likely to end up on the side of revolution.

Escom was established in this context of long-term strains and immediate pressures. Its complex structure and responsibilities exemplified well the contradictions of its origins. It was not to be state-controlled or state-financed, but it was to be state-supervised. It was meant to power industrialization throughout South Africa, particularly by meeting the expanding needs of the railways, but it had to do so without making a profit. It had to be run along business lines and had to compete with private enterprise, but it was not to adopt any practices, like variable market pricing, that would raise the energy costs of the gold industry. Such constraints reflected important contradictions inherent in white political and economic rule inside South Africa and seemed likely to doom van der Bijl's efforts to spur local industrialization and resecure the foundations of white hegemony.

The Iron and Steel Industry

Following the strike of 1922 and the establishment of Escom in 1923, the position of white workers in South Africa continued to deteriorate. In the gold-mining industry the number of white employees dropped by a third between 1921 and the end of 1922, and white wages were reduced by 25 to 50 percent. By contrast, the decade-long decline in black wages was reversed, even if only slightly, and the ratio of black workers to white rose from 8.2 to 1 in 1921 to 11.4 to 1 in 1922. Men without jobs in the mines, and the still-increasing numbers of poor whites moving into the cities, could not hope to find work in the manufacturing sector, where white employment fell between 1921 and 1923 (more so for white men than for white women) and wages also declined. Throughout South Africa, but particularly on the Rand, white unemployment increased, and the specter of the poor-white problem loomed ever larger.[71] Moreover, the political fallout from the government's violent repression of the strike was particularly ominous. Denounced by his Nationalist and Labour foes, now combined together in an electoral pact, as a tool of "big finance" whose footsteps "dripped with blood," Smuts saw political support for his South African Party erode in a series of by-election defeats in 1923.[72] With a general election due in 1924, he faced the likely prospect that his government would be ejected from office.

Determined that the gold industry should not bear the costs of providing jobs for whites, and believing that only general industrialization throughout South Africa would alleviate the growing economic problems of his constituents, Smuts looked in part to the development of a local iron and steel industry to resolve his difficulties. The iron and steel maker Usco established by Lewis and Marks had not amounted to much, producing only 4 percent of the country's steel needs by the end of the war, and its operations were further slowed by the death of its founder, Sammy Marks, in 1920. Smuts's government, with the encouragement of Lionel Phillips and the Chamber of Mines, had in 1920 entered into an agreement with C. F. Delfos for the local manufacture of all of the railways steel needs.[73] But that scheme too had foundered. Phillips and his fellow magnates had quickly withdrawn their initial offer of investment capital once they discovered that Delfos was contractually obliged to offer better terms to the SAR than to the mines.[74]

Conditions got even worse during the early 1920s as intense competition between the few local producers pushed prices down and as increased output from overseas suppliers, which had caused world prices to decline, threatened to flood the South African market.[75] Delfos, already rebuffed by Phillips and other South African capitalists, desperately sought financing overseas to develop his steel plant and make it more competitive, approaching in turn lenders in Britain, Holland, Italy, and America, all of whom turned him down.[76] In July 1925 he entered into negotiations with a group of South African and European financiers, including representatives of the Anglo-American Corporation, Barclays Bank, Rothschilds and Armstrong Whitworth, but he withdrew when they demanded what he considered "rapacious" terms, amounting to two million shares—valued at £1 per share—in his enlarged company in exchange for only £500,000 in new capital.[77] Such experiences reinforced Delfos's earlier conclusion that "the Iron and Steel industry in Europe is really the crux of the whole matter. . . . Our only hope is that . . . we must get our money from South Africa or by the assistance of our own Government."[78]

Smuts saw in local steel production a fundamental means to industrialize South Africa and at the same time meet the urgent need for white jobs, which would not only strengthen the country's economy but also buttress his own political support. Long a believer in the idea that the state itself should not fund secondary industry for fear that such a policy would lead eventually to some of the costs being charged to the gold industry, Smuts tried to find private financing for Delfos. The prime minister invited one of the major German steel makers, the Guttehoffnungshutte (GHH), to investigate the prospects of investing in a South African steel industry.[79] He also introduced the Iron and Steel Industry Encouragement Act—known as the Bounties Act—which provided government monetary rewards for any South African steel producer manufacturing at least 50,000 tons per year.[80] Smuts's 1924 campaign platform also included several proposals aimed at promoting a local steel industry, the most important of which was a plan to establish a large-scale state railway workshop to build locomotives and rolling stock. This workshop, it was claimed, would save the SAR at least £2,000,000 annually on stock and rails as well as provide a huge market for local steel producers, and it would also help meet "the imperative need of providing more skilled employment for the children of the white races."[81]

This was all too little and too late, and in June 1924 disaffected white voters threw out Smuts's government and brought to power an administration headed by J. B. M. Hertzog as prime minister and F. H. P. Creswell as minister of labor and of defense. The Pact government, formed on the basis of the electoral union entered into by the National and Labour parties in the immediate aftermath of the 1922 strike, only won after a bitter campaign that strongly emphasized the need for state protection of white workers, and particularly of unemployed and poor Afrikaners.

Pact politicians accused Smuts of being unable to protect the jobs of whites in the mining industry, of failing to improve the lot of white farmers, and of not having created new industries to employ poor whites. They contrasted the economic problems of white South Africans with the enormous profits of the gold industry (dividends in 1923 and 1924 were almost as high as the record amounts paid in 1909), and they argued that voters had to make a choice between, as Hancock has summarized the rhetoric, "economic stagnation or economic progress; unemployment or civilized labour; South Africa a huge black compound for the big capitalists or South Africa a prosperous white man's country."[82] Indeed, Tielman Roos argued that if Smuts's government continued on its policies for another five years "it [would] be impossible ever to have a large white population. If you [the voters] don't wish to save yourselves, save your children."[83] He and his colleagues called for the introduction of a "civilised labour" policy to create and reserve jobs exclusively for whites. Such rhetoric won the day with white voters who were "utterly tired," in the words of a former president of the Transvaal Manufacturers' Association, "of a Government that promises so much in respect of the support of local industries and performs so little," giving the National and Labour parties an overwhelming majority of seats in the House of Assembly.[84]

Although Pact campaign rhetoric called for an abrupt change in government economic policies, Hertzog's government largely followed the substance of Smuts's policies with regard to the manufacturing industry. Despite the bitter campaign criticisms made of "Hoggenheimer"—the caricature of a foreign Jewish capitalist greedily exploiting South Africa, based on the chairman of the Anglo-American Corporation, Sir Ernest Oppenheimer—Hertzog and his closest supporters recognized mining's central importance to the South African economy, and they saw the impossibility of making serious inroads into the cost structure of the gold industry without causing further difficulties for white society. It was significant that Cresswell became minister of labor and not of mines and industries. Moreover, in arguing against scholars who view 1924 as a major "turning point" in South African history, Yudelman has pointed out that after 1922 South African governments, whatever their political rhetoric, never sought to alleviate white concerns by finding more jobs for whites in the mining industry but looked instead to other sectors of the economy to bear the burden of rural distress and urban unemployment.[85]

Indeed, the policies adopted by Hertzog immediately upon becoming prime minister bolstered the two pillars of the South African economy, farming and mining. He directed most relief programs at the countryside and established new marketing boards to help increase agricultural production and improve the economic conditions of his primarily rural supporters.[86] He chose not to increase taxation on the mines and took no direct steps to increase the ratio and number of whites employed on the mines (both of which grew slightly after 1924 but did not return to pre-1922 levels). Even the 1925 Tariff Act, touted as protecting and promoting secondary industries, exempted goods, such as farm implements and irrigation pipes, used by the agricultural sector from the protective tariffs, thus making it even more difficult for local producers to compete with overseas suppliers. To protect the farmers' access to local markets, the act also instituted protective tariffs against agricultural imports, thereby driving up the costs for the largest existing secondary industry in South Africa, food processing. The Tariff Act additionally exempted goods needed by the mining industry from its provisions, further weakening the situation of South African manufacturers.[87]

The most notable provision of the Tariff Act was the "civilised labour" requirement, a catch phrase that became closely associated with Hertzog and the Pact government through the campaign rhetoric of 1924 and in a series of legislative acts passed in 1925 and 1926. Government protection for industries that hired white workers was not a new policy; Botha and Smuts had expressed considerable support for the idea since 1917, particularly with regard to the steel industry, and in 1922 the government mining engineer had suggested that steel manufacturers be paid a government bounty based on the number of white workers they employed.[88] Hertzog, however, provided a substantial legislative foundation for white preference through passage of the 1925 Wage Act and the 1926 Mines and Works Amendment Act. These acts empowered the government to determine wage rates in nonunionized industries (and thereby set higher rates for whites), and to restrict skilled jobs to white workers in the mining industry.[89]

One of the loudest proponents of civilized labor was Tielman Roos, who saw in the development of a South African steel industry the means to give such a policy practical effect. Known to his supporters as the "Lion of the North," Roos was the powerful leader of the National Party in the Transvaal and the parliamentary representative of a white working-class constituency on the Rand. Born and educated in the Cape, Roos had come to Pretoria to study law immediately following the Anglo-Boer War and became involved in politics. Often considered a "troublesome intriguer," even by his allies, Roos had vigorously attacked Smuts for his handling of the Rand Revolt and had cited the government's failure to help Delfos effectively as further evidence of treachery toward white workers.[90] Roos argued that the establishment of a steel industry in Pretoria would provide jobs for whites, bring about industrial prosperity for the Transvaal, and make South Africa economically independent. Although appointed minister of justice, Roos continued to speak out forcefully for industrial development and to push for greater state support for Delfos.[91]

Delfos needed any help he could get. By the end of 1925, with cheap foreign steel flooding the local market and the capital necessary to establish more technologically advanced, cost-efficient plant unavailable within the country, South African steel producers were almost out of business. Delfos appealed to Roos and other members of the Pact to invest government funds in his operation and establish a "limited liability" company in which the state would hold a controlling interest.[92] Despite Roos's and the Pact's campaign rhetoric, there was no great enthusiasm for the proposal made by Delfos. Money was short, direct state intervention in production was a policy that Nationalist politicians had attacked in the past, and the possibility of tariff-protected, higher-priced local steel raised alarm in the gold industry.[93] Delfos was left to teeter on the brink of bankruptcy.[94]

Although white distress failed to get a government response, the formation of a cartel by European steel makers in 1926 propelled Hertzog into action. The German steel manufacturers had recovered from the war and again dominated the international market. In 1926 they began reaching agreements with other European producers to set market shares. A rail cartel was formed in March and the International Steel Cartel in September, as formal mechanisms through which quotas could be negotiated.[95] This development was particularly ominous for South Africa, as the British manufacturers that supplied the bulk of steel goods used by the railways and the mines also joined the cartel. The director of stores and shipping for South Africa was greatly concerned, reporting to his government from London in March 1926 that the British manufacturers had "dispos[ed] of the trade of the British Empire [in negotiations with the cartel]. . . . Thus, it will be seen that the non-producing Dominions such as South Africa, have become the chief victims of this Cartel. South Africa's position is most unfortunate of all, because we had launched heavy and important schemes of new construction based on the low price of rails."[96] Without competition, the price of steel would rise enormously, and South Africa would be at the mercy of the cartel.

High prices for foreign steel posed a dire threat to the cost structure of the railways (which employed fifty-two thousand white males in 1926) and the mines (which employed twenty thousand men).[97] The mines alone consumed approximately 40 percent of all iron and steel sold in the country, and this in turn accounted for more than 20 percent of the mine owners' expenditures on stores.[98] In the aftermath of the 1922 strike, the gold industry had reduced its working costs considerably and certainly did not want to see that development reversed.[99] The SAR was also threatened by the foreign cartel, especially as Hoy had recently begun a major rail expansion program that had been delayed since 1913. With more than £2,000,000 spent annually since 1921 on steel imports, and the railways running in the red, Hoy had no wish to see prices rise.[100]

Yet the issue of local production had long engendered differing views. Since 1909 the government officers responsible to the railways and to the mining industry had been debating the extent of government involvement desirable in a national steel industry. Thomas Price and later W. W. Hoy had both consistently argued for a high degree of government ownership and control over a South African steel industry, whereas the government mining engineer, Robert Kotze, had maintained that the industry should be under private control, even if it amounted to a private monopoly.[101] On the eve of the formation of the European cartel, the secretary of mines and industries, Herbert Warington Smyth, had continued to oppose government involvement "in view of the precedent it would create . . . and the fact that [private producers] are really pushing on with the industry."[102] The central issue was the hope of SAR officials that government control would ensure low steel prices for their operations and the fear of mines and industries officials that a government monopoly would mean higher prices and costs for the mine owners.[103]

Bureaucratic stalemate was broken when the Department of Mines and Industries came under the temporary control of a politician well known for his antipathy toward the mining industry, F. H. P. Creswell. At the beginning of 1926, just prior to the formation of the European cartel, the minister of mines and industries, F. W. Beyers, left the country, and in his absence Hertzog appointed Creswell to fill the position. Already known for his belief that white workers only should have been employed on the mines, Creswell also argued that mine owners were more interested in sweating every last penny of labor out of their workers than in running the mines on cost-efficient lines. He contended that the use of white skilled workers was a more productive way of mining gold, and he predicted that the replacement of unskilled, low-cost black workers by skilled, high-cost white workers would actually increase industry profits.[104]

Delfos had likewise argued that the steel industry could best be run by a combination of skilled whites and machines, with few if any black workers.[105] Still, when Creswell proposed in February 1928 that the cabinet endorse a plan to create a state-owned steel industry, he did not use labor as his chief argument but focused on the issue of international trade: "With the present day tendency of the control of the iron and steel world to be concentrated in the hands of a few large combines, it is not likely that we shall be able to develop our own resources and become self-dependent in this respect unless we commence on a large scale with the instalment of works under the direct control of the Government."[106] In view of the impending European cartel and supported by the SAR, Creswell won cabinet approval for the establishment of a state-owned steel industry.

In addition to meeting the needs of South Africa's biggest steel consumers, Creswell's proposal addressed political expectations that had largely gone unmet during the first two years of Pact rule. Hertzog's government had experienced numerous setbacks to its goals of "civilised labour" and South African independence. Passage of the "civilised labour" laws had not resulted in greater white employment or higher wages. White male employment in secondary industry had actually declined, as had wages, although the number of white women and children at work had increased.[107] The attraction of a state steel producer was that it would meet both of the Pact government's political imperatives—to provide jobs for whites and to bring about economic growth—and could be inaugurated at a time when the mining industry at last favored local production. Moreover, Hertzog was engaged in a campaign to stress the nationhood and independence of South Africa—making Afrikaans an official language alongside English, introducing a new national flag in place of the British Union Jack, and negotiating with Britain for greater autonomy. A government-owned steel producer would be another important symbol of the new nation-state.

Framing the Iron and Steel Industry Bill, 1926–1928

While the mines and railways welcomed the establishment of a domestic supply of steel, they voiced serious reservations over the creation of what would in practice amount to a government monopoly of steel production and supply in South Africa. Even more than in the case of Escom, both groups worried over the role of a government supplier that in this case would have no local competitors (Usco and Delfos were practically out of business) and would not be subject to the same type of regulatory limits imposed on utilities. The state enterprise envisioned by the Pact government—the Iron and Steel Corporation (Iscor)—would be the only producer of steel from iron ore inside the country (the existing producers were limited to making pig iron from scrap metal), and it would therefore, if provided with tariff protection as seemed likely, dominate the local engineering and other manufacturing firms and exercise a near monopoly over the supply of steel to the mines and railways.

Unlike the drafting of the Electricity Bill under Smuts's administration, the Pact government framed the Iron and Steel Bill with little consultation among civil servants and practically no discussion with private businessmen. Indeed, many of the senior officials involved in the earlier legislation had been passed over for promotion, had quit, or had retired.[108] Instead, Creswell turned for advice to the reconstituted Board of Trade of Industries, which was charged by the Pact government with encouraging new enterprises in South Africa. The board "accepted the principle that protection of industries should primarily mean the protection of South African [white] labour," and it submitted a report to the select committee prepared by a young chemical engineer, Frederik Meyer.[109] Meyer had obtained his doctorate in Germany, and in 1925 he had been contracted to advise the Pact government on industrial matters. He fully supported government control of steel, arguing that steel "will be of considerable benefit to the country and its industrial and agricultural development . . . if the government of the Union takes part in this enterprise to such an extent as to have the controlling influence on the sales policy of the iron and steel works. . . . In this way the dangers to the development of the country inherent in a monopoly of such a key industry can be eliminated."[110]

Yet complete government control over steel prices was exactly what both the railways and the mine owners feared. They wanted cheaper steel than was available from Europe, but they also wanted to determine the prices charged by local producers rather than vice versa. Nevertheless, Creswell took Meyer's advice and in 1926 framed legislation to create a state corporation under the direct control of the cabinet. The corporation would be financed by the sale of shares to the public. However, the government would always retain control over the corporation, regardless of the percentage of public investment. Creswell also stipulated that the corporation's labor policies would be exempt from the provisions of South African law and be detetermined by the cabinet, especially with regard to "the conditions of employment (including provisions as to minimum wages and hours of labour) governing employees of the Corporation, or any class of such employees."[111] The implication of his last provision was that the cabinet would be even more favorable in its treatment of white labor than were the laws in force at the time.

Creswell's draft legislation met with considerable criticism. Kotze's replacement as government mining engineer, Hans Pirow, brother of the Nationalist politician Oswald Pirow (later minister of justice), had worked for many years as a mining engineer on the goldfields and was much more sympathetic to the concerns of the industry than was Creswell. Immediately upon taking up his new position in January 1927, Pirow reiterated Kotze's opposition to government control.[112] Creswell ignored his senior adviser and published the draft bill in the *Government Gazette* in February 1927. William Hoy voiced strong objections to the bill and announced his refusal to accede to a section that bound the SAR to purchase as much iron and steel from Iscor as the proposed state corporation could produce.[113] To mollify his critics Creswell relented somewhat on the extent of state control, agreeing to the establishment of a board of directors composed of representatives of government (with majority control) as well as private interests. He also dropped the special provisions covering labor policies. With these important changes made, the bill went to Parliament where, because of the controversy surrounding the issue, it was referred to a select committee for further investigation.

The hearings organized by the select committee were weighted heavily in Creswell's favor and exhibited none of the strife evident at the Electricity Bill's hearings. Not one representative of the mines or the railways was called to testify, nor was the government mining engineer permitted to voice his objections even though representatives on the committee of Smuts's SAP demanded that Pirow be called.[114] The Pact-appointed majority listened only to testimony from the Board of Trade and Industries, the Department of Finance, the Federated Chambers of Industries, two steel manufacturers (Usco and Delfos), a geologist, and the former scientific adviser to Smuts and current chairman of Escom, H. J. van der Bijl. Although van der Bijl was called in order to testify to the success of the first state electricity corporation, in his evidence he diplomatically criticized the Iron and Steel Bill for the high level of direct government control over the industry, which he considered "not compatible with good business."[115] More forcefully expressed opposition to the bill came from Sir Ernest Oppenheimer, an SAP-appointed member of the committee and chairman of the Anglo-American Corporation. Oppenheimer repeatedly criticized the bill on the grounds that "the lives of the mines should not be curtailed in any way by the production of very expensive steel," and he attempted to elicit evidence from witnesses in favor of eliminating the government's proposed control of Iscor's board of directors.[116]

In the face of these criticisms Creswell made a number of concessions. His representative to the committee, Frederik Meyer, who was the government's primary technical adviser on the bill, testified that the SAR would be free to negotiate prices and the quality of steel purchased from the state corporation, and that the mine owners would gain some protection through the establishment of a system of geographic pricing, which would result in consumers on the Rand being charged the lowest prices in the South African market.[117] These concessions were sufficient to mellow the bill's strongest critics. Although neither the mines nor the railways were able to get direct control over the proposed state corporation—Creswell and his Pact allies were intransigent on that issue—they did derive some temporary satisfaction from the fact that they would not be subject to totally unregulated steel pricing by a monopoly local producer.

Debate in Parliament on the redrafted bill was acrimonious. Smuts denounced the proposed governing structure of Iscor and accused the government of advocating "State control [and] State socialism."[118] Oppenheimer argued in similar fashion that the National party "had been infected with the bacillus of socialism" and warned that if Iscor proved unsuccessful there would be "much greater [pressure put on the government to introduce protective tariffs] than if it were owned by private enterprise."[119] Indeed, so strong was the opposition's resolve to prevent passage of the bill that a parliamentary crisis ensued. Although the bill passed easily through the House of Assembly, where the Pact had a majority of members, it was blocked in the Senate, where the SAP still held sway. Utilizing a parliamentary stratagem that he had already had recourse to when forcing through earlier legislation, Hertzog called a joint sitting of the two houses of Parliament and used his overall majority to get the Iron and Steel Bill passed into law.[120]

The Iron and Steel Industry Act of 1928 met the political needs of the

Pact government and provided long-term security without posing an immediate threat to steel consumers. The act allowed the government to establish a steel industry and thereby to promote the country's industrial independence. Most important, all parties accepted that the industry would also provide preferential employment for the white population. One member of Parliament pointed out that the consulting reports on Iscor had recommended that there be "four whites employed to every three natives" in the industry.[121] Indeed, the issue of labor at Iscor was not debated during discussion of the bill, as no South African politician was willing to alienate white voters. Certainly the mine owners were not going to raise the sensitive issue of the employment of whites, considering their own record in that area. Rather, they welcomed such an outlet for frustrated unemployed whites, who would otherwise focus on employment in the mining industry and give political support to the National and Labour parties.

The mine owners were concerned about the possibility of having to buy what might prove to be expensive locally produced steel, but for the time being their fears were alleviated by the exclusion of iron and steel products from the regulations of the Tariff Act, and by the fact that no attempt was made to amend that legislation after the passage of the Iron and Steel Act in order to assist Iscor. Any such attempt at amendment was sure to be a difficult political battle, as it would have ramifications for numerous sectors of the economy besides the gold mines. Moreover, to signal government continuity with previous policies and as a measure of reconciliation with Smuts and the SAP, Hertzog appointed van der Bijl as Iscor's first chairman.

Conclusion

The creation of these two state corporations—Escom and Iscor—marked a compromise between state and capital in South Africa rather than a victory or defeat for one or the other; the economic and political issues were too complex for any simple resolution. The growth of mining had provided the initial basis for the expansion of the country's economy, and it remained the foundation on which continued development and prosperity rested. Yet at the same time the gold industry leached the South African economy of capital and left it weak. Mining was also the foundation on which white rule had been erected and sustained in South Africa, but many of the policies adopted by the industry created divisions within white society and failed to benefit economically the majority of the white population.

The conjunction of economic distress and political discontent laid the

bedrock for an alliance between ethnic nationalism and white labor organization, which before 1924 threatened the dominant partnership of state
and big capital and after 1924 became the government itself. Governments, however, faced enormous constraints in responding to the concerns of their constituencies. Smuts created Escom to assuage disgruntled
whites facing rural poverty and urban unemployment, yet he erected an
institution that would have to fight for its markets against strong established producers. Hertzog's and Creswell's strident advocacy of "civilised
labour" produced Iscor for much the same reasons as Escom had been
established—to promote industrialization and provide jobs for whites
outside the mining industry. But Hertzog and Creswell too had to compromise with the mining giant, for the profitability of gold continued to
determine government revenues, as well as ensure that Iscor did not
impinge on the cost structure of the railways, still the employer of twice
as many whites as the mining industry. The fundamental nature of these
economic and political compromises left the two state corporations in a
difficult situation at the time of their establishment, with neither open
markets nor low production costs guaranteed. Still, in facing an uncertain
future they were both to be led by a remarkable individual in the person
of H. J. van der Bijl, whom Smuts was later to call South Africa's "greatest industrialist."[122]

CHAPTER FOUR

Strategies for Survival

Since their establishment by the South African Parliament, the state corporations have been identified with the strongly nationalist and even anticapitalist rhetoric that surrounded their political birth. In particular, they have been characterized as the antagonists of foreign business. Although the rhetoric and the terminology used vary by time and author, the message is much the same: the state corporations represented the interests of local—sometimes termed national—capital, while the rest of South Africa's economy functioned in the interests of foreign—or imperial—capital. The South African government has been the most vociferous in making this claim, portraying the state corporations in glowing patriotic terms: "The success which Iscor ultimately proved to be was the death knell of economic colonialism in South Africa."[1]

Although less ready to use such heady language, scholars from a wide political spectrum have likewise argued that the early development of the state corporations represented a battle between national and foreign, or industrial and mining, or, sometimes, Afrikaner and English forces for control of the economy—a struggle in which ultimate victory went to the national/industrial/Afrikaner forces. Thus, Belinda Bozzoli has contended that the establishment of Iscor reflected "the most telling conflict between imperial and national capital, with victory going to the latter"; Robert Davies and others have argued that the state corporations represented the "cornerstone of . . . national capitalist development"; and Heribert Adam and Hermann Giliomee have concluded that the corporations were "attempts to diminish English and foreign control of the economy."[2] In short, official and scholarly sources have argued that the state corporations fostered an isolated, nationalistic segment of the economy, which functioned in a manner at odds with the rest of the country's business enterprises.[3]

The parameters of the debate about the early development and role of the state corporations were in large part set by the political rhetoric that accompanied their founding. When Smuts proposed the establishment of Escom in 1922, following the boom and bust of the immediate postwar years and in the wake of the Rand Revolt, he argued that it was part of the government's policy "to broaden the basis of our [South Africa's] economic existence. We want more independence in that connection, and that can only be done by quietly furthering an industrial policy."[4] Iscor, founded in 1928 by the Pact government, which had won control of Parliament on a platform stressing the need to protect South African industries and to create full employment for whites, was proclaimed the embodiment of both goals. As F. H. P. Creswell put matters in presenting the Iron and Steel Bill to Parliament, "The country [will] reap the full benefit not only in getting our own steel in this country, but also in getting it at a cost to the consumer which would immensely stimulate the creation and establishment of other industries in the country . . . the complete and entire justification of the Government's action will be to establish a really adequate steel works which will supply the consumer of steel in the secondary industries with steel products which will tend to stimulate the general industrial development of the country."[5] In other words, Iscor would provide the necessary heavy industrial base for the development of light industry and manufacturing in South Africa, which would in turn increase white employment prospects generally, while its own operations would offer a new and state-protected source of jobs for whites.

Yet in contrast to the political rhetoric of the time, examination of the state corporations during their formative years—the 1920s and 1930s—suggests that they were not antagonistic to foreign capital or hesitant about using black labor rather than "civilised" labor, and that in fact their very survival and success depended on the extensive utilization of both foreign money and black workers. Indeed, they displayed considerable independence from official policies of the day and found governments unwilling to press policies on them that would undermine their financial performance. The governments of Smuts and Hertzog, whatever their political differences, faced similar problems in promoting industrialization and perpetuating white control in a country dominated by a single extractive industry—gold mining—that had already made clear its opposition to industrial investments and the subsidizing of national industries. Neither Smuts nor Hertzog thought it economically or politically feasible to nationalize existing enterprises or to institute total and continuing subsidization of new businesses, and they had to negotiate with the foreign interests that dominated the South African economy—not only for, in some cases, their business but also, in other cases, for investment capital and market shares.

Electricity generation and steel manufacture both required enormous investments in expensive plant, and although successive governments agreed in both cases to fund initial developments, the state looked to private capital to finance expansion.[6] At the same time, the existing markets for electricity and steel in the 1920s were controlled by, in the case of electricity, a number of municipalities and a monopolistic private company owned by overseas shareholders and, in the case of steel, by weak local producers and a powerful foreign cartel. To obtain capital and acquire market shares, each government in turn, whatever its political rhetoric, had to negotiate compromises with the existing private operations, agreeing not to pursue competitive production and guaranteeing them considerable profits. Such compromises imposed a heavy burden on the new state corporations, and they were met in the method generally adopted by the mining industry: when faced with higher fixed expenses, reduce labor costs. Because of the agreements concerning production and market shares, Escom and Iscor alike paid scant lip service to the "civilised labour" policy and relied instead upon cheap black workers.[7] By the end of the 1930s the state corporations, while not absorbed by private enterprise, were not antagonistic to it. This was more than just a temporary tactical compromise; indeed, a form of partnership had been created between state and private capital.

Struggle for the Electricity Market

Smuts had established a state corporation to generate electric power for two reasons: to provide large amounts of relatively cheap electricity so that South Africa could industrialize and lessen its near-total dependence on the far from stable gold industry; and to enable the state to control the production process and thereby both prevent labor unrest and provide new employment opportunities for white South Africans. Yet there were two major impediments to achieving these goals. First, municipal and private companies (the latter closely tied to the gold industry), under legislation dating from 1910 and 1922, already controlled the major markets for electricity in South Africa: the urban areas and the Rand. If Escom was to succeed, it would have to do so either at the expense of or in league with the existing suppliers. Second, labor unrest could cause grandiose plans for industrialization to unravel. A 1919 strike by power-plant workers in Johannesburg and Pretoria, followed by the 1922 Rand uprising, left a deep impression on government officials, who were concerned about the "rank socialists and bolschevists [sic]" involved and feared future labor disturbances.[8] The South African Railways in particular, which government officials thought would be the key institution in promoting economic development, was so concerned about the specter of strikes that it wanted power generation in the hands of the state.[9] It was van der Bijl's task to bring these apparently contradictory aims and forces into some form of alignment and so establish Escom on a viable footing.

Expanding the Electricity Market

The economics of electricity supply required that Escom increase its number of customers if it was to sell to the railways cheaper power than the SAR could generate for itself. In most capital-intensive industries, maximum use must be made of plant in order to reduce unit costs; in electricity generation this principle is complicated by the fact that the product cannot be stored and transmission must be immediate. Moreover, Escom had to have the productive capacity to meet peak demands—such as during railway rush hours—even though for much of the rest of the time the plant would be standing idle. In short, to spread costs and lower the price per unit, Escom had to find customers ready to consume power when the generating plant would otherwise be underutilized by its main customer, the railways.

Domestic and industrial markets offered a solution to Escom's problems, but both were already under license to other power suppliers. Indeed, this was the major political compromise made by the government mining engineer, Robert Kotze, in the final draft of the Electricity Bill when he incorporated measures to prevent the proposed state corporation from impinging upon the markets and cost structure of the municipalities, the VFPC, and the mines. Municipalities held the legal right, under the Electricity Act of 1922, to be the only providers of power to their local inhabitants, a right they guarded jealously, as it promised increased local government revenues.[10] Industrial power consumption was likewise effectively "monopolised," in the words of the Department of Mines and Industries.[11] The VFPC not only held a twenty-five-year license to supply the entire Rand but since 1910 had also had exclusive contracts with all of the major mining houses—including the Corner House group, the Goldfields group, General Mining, Neumann, JCI, Consolidated Mines, and Goerz. These contracts guaranteed that the gold companies would take their power needs from the VFPC so long as it disbursed a share of its "surplus profits" back to them as consumers.[12] With the Rand and all other urban areas out of bounds, Escom was practically excluded from the major markets for electrical power in South Africa.

Still, the Electricity Act did contain a key provision that could be used to favor increased state control of power generation and thereby strengthen the financial structure of Escom. Although the act guaranteed the existing power companies the markets they already held, it stated that whenever new or enlarged power stations were needed to meet expanding consumer demand, new license applications had to be made to the main regulatory body, the Electricity Control Board. The ECB would then conduct an investigation of the proposal on its own or request that Escom do so. If Escom determined that it could produce the electricity more cheaply than the existing supplier—and the commission was legally bound to sell its electricity at cost—then Escom would receive the license to build the plant. The act did require, however, that Escom then enter into negotiations with the existing suppliers to sell power to them at cost; they could then resell it at a profit to their industrial and urban customers.

Almost immediately after enactment of the Electricity Act in 1923, conflict over the supply of electricity to the Rand not only brought Escom into existence but also gave van der Bijl the opportunity to extend the commission's control over a large share of South Africa's power generation capacity. While the Electricity Bill had been under debate in Parliament in 1922 and 1923, the VFPC and the municipalities had refrained from expanding their own operations. Once the bill was passed, the existing producers flooded the ECB with applications for new licenses, hoping to extend their market control before the formation of Escom.[13] The most significant of these applications was the VFPC's proposal to build a huge new power generating station at Witbank, the site of the largest coal reserves in the country.[14] The company claimed that working costs on the mines had been greatly reduced since the 1922 strike and that as a result "the demand for power again increased by leaps and bounds." Its sales, which had fallen from approximately 800,000,000 kilowatt hours in 1921 to 700,000,000 kwh in 1922, were again rising and exceeded 900,000,000 kwh in 1923.[15]

In addition to this increased demand, the company saw a chance to lower its costs considerably by building anew at Witbank. Transportation costs on coal brought from Witbank to the VFPC stations eighty miles away on the Rand were the company's largest expense, with fully half of expenditures being paid to the railways.[16] Transmitting electricity from Witbank to the Rand would be far cheaper than carrying coal. Moreover, the timing of the proposal seemed propitious to the VFPC. The SAR had announced plans to electrify lines on the Rand and in the eastern Transvaal, and Witbank was the only logical place to build a power plant to meet its needs.[17] If the VFPC secured control over both the Rand market and supplies for the SAR, it could not be seriously challenged by any new producer, whether government supported or not. Indeed, it was because of the enormous ramifications of the VFPC proposal that the ECB established Escom in March 1923 specifically to investigate the Witbank question.

The VFPC's proposal with its ramifications of private monopoly elicited unanimous condemnation from the state officials most directly involved with the mines, the railways, and the formulation of industrial policy. The secretary of mines and industries, Herbert Warington Smyth, argued that "we should not be rushed into giving rights to a private electrical undertaking which might come very near [to a] monopoly of supply to the railway sections." William Hoy of the SAR was even more alarmed: "If [the] VFPC is granted the licence, they will have a monopoly and we will be entirely in their hands." Van der Bijl, in his new position as chairman of Escom, saw enormous dangers for his own organization. "If the VFPC gets a footing at Witbank it means that the door is closed to the Commission and that the Victoria Falls Company has a complete monopoly so far as the industrial areas of the Transvaal are concerned."[18] If Witbank went ahead under VFPC control, Escom would in all likelihood be shut out for decades from the Rand electricity market.

Van der Bijl's major difficulty in opposing the VFPC application was that Escom had no customers of its own to supply from a station at Witbank. The SAR had developed long-term plans for electrification in the Transvaal but did not contemplate their immediate implementation. The province's major city, Johannesburg, provided its own electricity and was not interested in making any agreements with Escom. The largest consumers in the country, the mines, were already tied contractually to the VFPC. And the company held the exclusive license to supply the Rand. Moreover, Bernard Price of the VFPC made a strong case for his company's proposal by stressing that the terms of the VFPC's existing license required it to supply consumers' needs, and that any delay on Witbank jeopardized the company's legal position and laid it open to court action by disgruntled customers. He even proposed to provide the railways with electricity if allowed to build the power station.[19] Van der Bijl countered that he would agree to the VFPC's putting up the station immediately "in view [of the] urgency represented," but that the final decision on the ownership of the plant should await a lengthy investigation by Escom. If the commission determined that it could produce cheaper electricity, it would expropriate the plant and reimburse the VFPC. Moreover, to prevent the company from building a competing station in the event of expropriation, he wanted the VFPC to agree to buy Witbank electricity in bulk.[20] Dissatisfied with these terms, Price proceeded with the VFPC's application to the ECB to build and control Witbank.

Van der Bijl, however, was a skillful political infighter, and he sought to bring considerable pressure on Price by arousing the suspicions of the VFPC's most important customers, the mine owners. Escom challenged the VFPC application on the grounds that the company would not be passing any of the savings gained from the more cost-efficient production of power at Witbank to its customers. Indeed, the criterion for obtaining the license was to provide power at the cheapest possible cost. Because the prices in the mines' supply contracts with the VFPC were firm, consumers could not, van der Bijl argued, "reap the benefit from the lower costs at the Witbank station" unless the contracts were revised or a different supplier, such as Escom, sold the electricity at cost to the mine owners. Van der Bijl also requested that all relevant financial data be made public in order to determine the fairness of VFPC prices.[21]

The VFPC wanted to avoid making such a disclosure at all costs. It consistently posted very large profits on its invested capital. Moreover, it was contractually required to pay 25 percent of its "surplus profits" to the mining companies. To avoid public criticism of its high profit margins, and to keep the definition of "surplus profits" as narrow as possible, the VFPC had engaged in a considerable amount of imaginative bookkeeping, which it did not want subjected to public examination.[22] Van der Bijl's request for public disclosure was enough to cause the Chamber of Mines to demand a renegotiation of the industry's power-supply contracts. Escom weighed in on the chamber's side but agreed to drop its requests for more information if the VFPC would negotiate a new contract with the mines and take power from the commission at Witbank.

Under pressure from the mines and van der Bijl, Price compromised on VFPC control of the proposed Witbank station. The VFPC would build and operate the station, but ownership would be vested in Escom, which would provide the construction costs. Escom would be entitled to sell electricity to the SAR, collieries, and other industries in the Witbank area, and to the Johannesburg municipality if and when that market opened up; the VFPC in turn agreed to purchase at cost from Escom as much additional power as the Witbank station could produce for resale to customers on the Rand.[23] The mines also won three important concessions in their new contract: the fixed price they paid for electricity was lowered, they were given an additional 17.5 percent discount on total charges, and their pro-rata share in the VFPC's surplus profits (now to be more carefully figured) was increased from 25 percent to 50 percent.[24] In sum, the VFPC was freed from meeting the capital costs of erecting the Witbank plant but got to sell much of the electricity generated at a profit, while the mines succeeded in negotiating reduced energy costs. Escom paid for and gained ultimate control of the new power station, becoming in the process the largest "wholesaler" of electricity in South Africa.

Although the secretary of mines and industries hailed the agreement between Escom and the VFPC as "the best practicable scheme for this important station," the commission still failed to gain direct access to the Rand market because of two principles written into the new contract negotiated by the VFPC with the mines. First, during the twenty-year life span of the new contract, the mine owners agreed not to purchase electricity from any supplier other than the VFPC. This meant that should the mines' requirements increase, they would be unable to contract with a second supplier, a stipulation that had immense importance ten years later when mining on the Reef expanded enormously. Second, Price persuaded the Chamber of Mines and the ECB (primarily consisting of civil servants from the Department of Mines), which had to approve the contract, to agree to a clause that waived the periodic government review of prices required under the Electricity Act. This waiver effectively protected the VFPC from any future government pressure to lower prices.[25] So long as its prices remained firm, the company could expect to reap increasing profits as production costs at Witbank dropped. Although agreeing to Escom's ownership of the new power plant, Price had secured the VFPC's monopoly over electricity supply to the gold mines for another twenty (eventually to become twenty-five) years.

Van der Bijl was anxious to justify Escom's massive financial involvement in the Witbank power station—which was of immediate benefit only to the mines—by providing electricity to domestic and industrial consumers. A large part of the political justification of the Electricity Act had been to encourage industrial development outside the mining industry. In this regard, Johannesburg's power supply had been the subject of government concern since 1915, when officials determined that the city was unable to provide services for all of its consumers. By 1921 the situation had become critical, with new applicants for power being put on a five-year waiting list. Fearing that "industrial development within the Johannesburg Municipal area . . . [was] being most seriously impeded," the Board of Industry and Science urged the secretary of mines to apply pressure on the city to take power from the VFPC.[26] The company already supplied power to the mines, industrial concerns, and all other municipalities surrounding Johannesburg. But the Johannesburg municipality refused to reach any agreement with the VFPC, fearing a loss in the revenues it collected for electricity supply. At the same time, however, the government was drafting the Electricity Bill and believed that the "intervention of an independent third party such as electricity commissioners" would solve the problem.[27] Van der Bijl stepped into this situation in 1923 and began trying, in a process which lasted for more than two years, to convince Johannesburg to take power from an outside supplier.

Paradoxically, Escom's position at Witbank made an agreement with Johannesburg very difficult. Van der Bijl had agreed to sell power from Witbank to the VFPC at cost, which the VFPC redistributed to its consumers at a profit. In making an offer to Johannesburg, van der Bijl risked undermin-

ing the vfpc's position on the Rand if Escom charged the municipality the
same rates for wholesale electricity as it did the private company. The
commission had agreed privately to charge the vfpc 0.115d. per kwh, while
the company in turn charged its consumers 0.4418d. per kwh, a profit of
nearly 300 percent on state-generated electricity.[28] Mines and municipalities under contract to the vfpc would clearly protest if neighboring Johannesburg bought its supplies at such a reduced rate. After some discussion
with the company and representatives of the mining groups, van der Bijl
offered to sell electricity to the Johannesburg municipality at 0.4d. per
kwh, just below the vfpc's official price to its customers.[29] This arrangement ensured that Escom did not compete with its own biggest customer,
the vfpc, while also protecting the vfpc's market share.

But the Johannesburg municipality turned down the offer and renewed
efforts to build its own station. Citing the reports of its engineers—which
Escom officials disputed—the city claimed it could produce electricity at
a cost below the commission's selling price. An application to the Transvaal administrator for permission to expand the city's power station was
denied nonetheless, on the grounds that the municipality simply did not
have the capital funds available.[30] In addition to the Town Council's financial motivations for expanding its power station, there were also political
issues involved: Labour Party members on the Town Council were committed to rehiring the so-called power station agitators—fired during the
1922 Rand Revolt—in an expanded Electricity Department.[31] The Labour
Party members of the council attempted to exert political pressure on the
newly elected Pact government and demanded that the minister of mines
and industries introduce legislation to amend the Electricity Act so as to
exempt municipal stations from state regulation or control.[32] Although
their attempt was unsuccessful, Johannesburg's obstructions staved off the
commission; by 1925 neither the municipality nor the commission had yet
obtained authority to supply the city with additional power.

Van der Bijl finally broke off negotiations with Johannesburg in October 1925. The Witbank agreement had been signed, assuring the commission that the vfpc would take as much power from the station as Escom
could supply. And van der Bijl could count on government support, as the
minister of mines and industries had turned down Johannesburg's requests
to expand the municipal power plant on the grounds that Escom was a
more efficient producer. Van der Bijl, however, decided not to pursue the
Johannesburg municipal market when he discovered that local officials
had used government approval given for the temporary installation of a
generator in the Johannesburg plant as an excuse to begin construction on
a completely new and permanent station. Concluding that "the source
from which Johannesburg obtains its electrical energy does not affect the

Commission's position," he refused to have anything more to do with the municipality, thereby leaving South Africa's largest city perenially short of electricity until the middle of the 1930s.[33]

Van der Bijl's negotiations on the Rand partly secured the commission's two primary objectives: to prevent the VFPC from completely monopolizing the Rand, and to get access to a broad range of markets for the Witbank power station. The agreement reached between van der Bijl and Price resulted in the commission's becoming the primary supplier of electricity to the gold mines, even if it did have to distribute its output through the VFPC. It also ensured that the SAR, when it chose to electrify its Transvaal lines, would not have to take supplies from the VFPC.

Concurrent with the Johannesburg negotiations, van der Bijl tried to reach an agreement with the Cape Town municipality to get access to an urban market that he considered much more important to Escom's immediate financial success than that on the Rand. Under the terms of the Electricity Act, the SAR requested Escom in 1923 to build a plant that would meet the rush-hour power needs of the Cape Suburban Line. The plant would, however, lie idle during the rest of the day unless further customers were found. The logical customer to make use of this generating capacity was the Cape Town municipality, but it preferred to operate its own plant and late in 1923 applied to the ECB for a license permitting the expansion of municipal production. Escom referred Cape Town's application to the British engineering firm of Merz and McLellan, who were consultants both to the commission and to the municipality. Charles Merz, the principal electrical engineering adviser to the British government and a strong proponent of the development of national grids, recommended to the ECB that it grant the license but also persuaded the municipality to enter into an "interchange" agreement with Escom.[34] Under the terms of this agreement, whenever the municipality needed additional power in the future it would draw upon an Escom power station for supplies, obtaining electricity at cost and then reselling it at a higher price to its own customers.[35]

An additional opportunity for Escom to expand its market arose in Durban, where the SAR intended to electrify its lines. The SAR planned to build power stations at Congella and Colenso to supply electricity to the railways' harbor facilities at Durban, to the Natal Main Line between Durban and Pietermaritzburg, and to the continuation of the line further inland to Glencoe.[36] The SAR decided in 1922 to proceed with the electrification of the larger section first and to delay work on the Durban–Pietermaritzburg section—and the Congella Station—for the immediate future. However, in November 1922 the Durban Municipality applied to the ECB for a license to enlarge its own plant. At the time, the commission had not yet been formed, and the ECB decided to delay the matter, suggesting that representatives of the municipality meet with Escom officials once they had been appointed. The ECB made it clear that it was prepared to issue only one license in Durban, either to the municipality or to Escom.[37]

Van der Bijl was in a difficult situation. Escom, having no formal structure of its own at the time, was not in a position to consider the construction or operation of a station in Durban. Yet van der Bijl could hardly force the municipality to go without necessary power. Therefore, the city obtained several concessions from van der Bijl in light of what one Escom official termed the commission's "delicate" position.[38] First, van der Bijl agreed that Escom would purchase any additional plant necessary to meet Durban's immediate needs and install this equipment in the municipality's Alice Street station until such time as Congella began operations. Second, the municipality was guaranteed a low price for its electricity for the next three years.[39] Third, the government amended the Electricity Act to prevent the takeover of any Escom station—which might place the Durban municipality at the mercy of a new supplier—unless such action was deemed by the minister of mines and industries to be in the best interests of consumers.[40] In exchange for these terms, Durban agreed in April 1925 not only to purchase electricity from the commission but also to "link" its station with Congella, thereby forming one supply system, under Escom control, for the Durban area. As in Cape Town, Escom would become the primary producer of electricity, while the municipality would retain control over the retail market and thereby build up local revenues.

Through these negotiations with the VFPC and the Cape Town and Durban municipalities, van der Bijl consolidated Escom's control over the production of electricity in South Africa while allowing existing suppliers to retain control of distribution and marketing. In all three cases van der Bijl used Escom's advisory powers to persuade the ECB to grant it licenses for power generation when the markets it coveted, but could not reach, needed additional supplies. Van der Bijl's early efforts set a pattern of accommodation through which the commission was able to balance its own financial interests with those of the established power suppliers.

The SAR's Challenge for Control

But this arrangement did not find favor with SAR officials, for whose benefit the stations were primarily meant to be built. Between 1928 and 1932 Escom faced its most serious challenge from its own progenitor, the railways. In part, the conflict arose from SAR concern at the special terms offered by Escom to the municipalities and the VFPC. Although the agreements entered into by Escom ultimately benefited the SAR—by reducing the cost of electricity to the railways through producing power for a wide range of customers—the SAR's administration objected to the fact that (in the short term at least) the price charged the railways for power was higher than that paid by either the municipalities or the VFPC. The SAR further resented Escom's "quasi-governmental" status, which exempted the commission from the sort of parliamentary review to which the railways were constantly subjected, a form of government overview that had already led to the public exposure of the SAR's practice of juggling its books. While representing in part bureaucratic wrangling and in-fighting, the SAR complaints also sparked an official review of Escom and revealed divisions within the government over the commission's mandate.

Although William Hoy had been a prime author of the Electricity Act, his successor, J. R. More, who became general manager of the SAR in 1928 after having been in charge of electrification on the Durban line, soon determined that the establishment of Escom had not led to immediate cost advantages for the railways. Indeed, on examining the figures covering Escom's first year of commercial operation, More discovered that the electricity prices charged to the SAR were far higher per kwh than those paid by the VFPC or even the municipalities. Whereas the SAR was paying 0.81d. per kwh for power from Natal's Colenso station, municipalities in Natal taking power from the same station paid 0.73d. and the VFPC paid only 0.1d. per kwh.[41] Such differences were the result of van der Bijl's negotiations: low prices were necessary to induce the municipalities and the VFPC to take supplies; without these additional customers the stations would have been far more expensive to run and SAR prices much higher. The logic of this pricing policy by a state producer that had been established to supply cheap power to the railways escaped More, who complained that "the Electricity Act is of no benefit to the working of the Railways" and began a long fight to break up the commission, overturn the Electricity Act, and take control of the Escom stations.[42]

Some of the major costs in power generation were of the railways' own making—railage on coal for the Colenso power station was more than three times the cost price of the coal, and the SAR had been largely responsible for the great cost overruns in the construction in 1929 of the plant. But More ignored these factors and mounted an attack on Escom's management, demanding stricter government overview.[43] He blamed high electricity charges on Escom's administrative and financial policies, which, under the provisions of the Electricity Act, were kept secret. Although the railway administration went through a yearly ordeal of presenting and justifying its budget before Parliament, Escom was bound only to an audit by a private company, which simply reported to Parliament whether the business was being run on sound lines.[44]

The general manager's suspicions about Escom's secretive policies gained validity with the disclosure of a number of financial irregularities in Escom's pricing policies. Van der Bijl had included in the 1929 electricity prices charged to the railways funds to repay the government loan that had been used to set up the commission, even though the Electricity Act had specified that such repayment charges should not be assessed until 1930 at the earliest. Van der Bijl had decided to build up a reserve fund to repay the loan as a way of assuring private investors—whose funds were necessary to finance any expansion in Escom's operations—that the commission was indeed run on sound business lines.[45] In response to More's charges and van der Bijl's disclosure, the Treasury restructured Escom's finances. The government funds advanced to Escom—a total of £8,000,000—were divided into two loan accounts. One of £5,000,000 did not have to be paid back until 1941 and would be allocated to the construction of power stations to meet railway electricity demand, and one of £3,000,000, which would have to be paid back from 1930 on charged primarily against the revenues of the Witbank power station. Repayment of the latter loan would thus fall principally on Witbank's customers, meaning primarily the vFPC and through it the gold mines.[46] More expressed considerable satisfaction that these developments "effectually dispose[d] of the allegation that the Railway complaints of high charges were unfounded."[47]

The controversy engendered by More prompted officials in the Department of Mines and Industries to investigate Escom. In July 1930 the new secretary of the department, L. P. van Zyl Ham, decided that the commission's records should be openly reviewed for the "proper protection of the public."[48] Van der Bijl had already testified publicly in 1927 that he did not share all information with the department as stipulated under law. "As a matter of fact, I have not complied fully with the provisions of our Act in that respect . . . and we have had practically a free hand to run the Commission on business principles." After More's accusations, van Zyl Ham sensed possible embarrassment for his department.[49] With his initial attempts to obtain financial records from Escom rebuffed by van der Bijl, van Zyl Ham drafted an amendment to the Electricity Act: "The Minister may at any time cause an inspection to be made of the books and records of the Commission and may at any time call for . . . detailed information on any matter or subject relating to the business or affairs of the Commission."[50]

The amendment was never introduced in Parliament, however, and van der Bijl continued to interpret the act and the existing regulations of the Department of Mines and Industries as giving him the authority to run Escom without outside interference. He responded to van Zyl Ham's requests for financial records with annual reports and monthly production statistics that were already available in the public domain and that, in the

secretary's eyes at least, gave a wholly inadequate picture of the commission's internal administration.[51] Not ready to force a showdown with van
der Bijl, the Department of Mines by the end of 1930 largely accepted the
fact that Escom was beyond its reach; as one official in the department
concluded, "We cannot press the Commission for information which they
are not bound by law to furnish, especially as the Commission appears to
resent such enquiries as being inquisitorial."[52]

But the general manager of the SAR, not satisfied with a partial bureaucratic victory, continued pressing his attack on Escom. Having proved that
Escom illegally overcharged the railways, he argued in 1931 that the SAR
should itself take responsibility for power generation in South Africa, at
least in Cape Town and Natal. Under Section 6 of the Electricity Act, any
consumer of more than two-thirds of the power supply of any one station
could petition for control of the station after five years. As the railways
took more than two-thirds of the electricity at both the Colenso and Salt
River stations and the five-year periods were about to expire, More suggested in March 1931 that the SAR acquire both plants and followed up
with a formal application to the ECB in 1932.[53]

The SAR's plans caused alarm among municipal producers as well as at
Escom. In Cape Town the municipality was negotiating a "pooling" agreement with van der Bijl and had no interest in the railways' moving in and
excluding the city from what promised to be a very profitable source of
revenue. The municipality threatened that if the SAR suceeded in its application, Cape Town would pull out of the pooling arrangement and go it
alone, which would leave the Salt River power plant (run by Escom for the
SAR) essentially an expensive white elephant, since without urban customers the cost of electricity generation to the SAR would skyrocket.[54] The
SAR's application to take over the Colenso power station in Natal met with
similar opposition. The Durban municipality feared that electricity pricing would favor the railways at the expense of all other consumers, while
Escom concluded that the loss of its own power-generating capacity would
effectively cripple the commission and force it out of business. Not ready
in the midst of the Great Depression to oversee the dismantling of a state
corporation created to promote industrialization and provide jobs for
whites, the ministers of railways and harbors and of mines and industries
agreed in 1932 to deny the request of the SAR.[55]

Consolidating the Electricity Market

By 1933 Escom was well established as an electricity producer. It
owned five power stations, which sold a total of 890,735,162 kwh in
1932—up from 551,018,733 kwh in 1927 when the commission's stations

had begun operations.[56] Moreover, the demand for power in South Africa's urban areas was growing. In Cape Town demand had outstripped the generating capacity of the existing plant by 1932 and resulted in Escom's being licensed by the ECB to expand local production and take over responsibility for the production of power for all local consumers, including the railways, the Cape Town municipality, and other customers.[57] The Johannesburg municipality had also accepted that it could not hope to generate sufficient power itself to meet urban needs and decided to engage an outside supplier, although it chose to do business with the VFPC rather than Escom, where the bitter taste of its previous dealings remained strong.

A major limit on Escom's financial strength and the commission's growth was that almost 80 percent of electricity sales were for redistribution by other power bodies—the municipalities and the VFPC. If Escom was to fulfill its mandate and become the largest producer of cheap electricity in South Africa, it needed direct access to markets where, by negotiating contracts with a broad range of consumers, it could spread the costs of power production in a much more efficient manner. Such access would also enable van der Bijl to operate Escom more effectively along business lines, rather than see the commission used as a wholesale producer that generated enormous profits for private companies like the VFPC.

Van der Bijl got the chance to break into new markets when mining development exploded along the Rand in 1933 as South Africa went off the gold standard and the price of the precious metal rose rapidly. The jump in the price of gold—by 45 percent in 1932 alone, resulting in gold revenues growing from £49,200,000 in that year to £72,300,000 in 1934 and increasing thereafter—brought outlying areas thought to be unprofitable into production.[58] Under the terms of the Electricity Act, Escom could apply for a license to supply the new region and thus gain its own mining customers, but all new development work was being carried out by firms already contractually bound to the VFPC. Even if Escom got a license the contracts between the VFPC and the mining companies took legal precedence. Nevertheless, van der Bijl determined to obtain the new license and indicated his intention to oppose any new applications that the VFPC might make to expand its own production capacity. In a bold move in 1933, he informed the VFPC and the government that Escom would permit no further expansion of the company and would exercise its right of expropriation, granted under the Electricity Act, forcibly acquiring the VFPC's assets once the company's license to supply the Rand expired in 1948.[59]

Given that Escom's right to expropriate the VFPC was legally unassailable, Bernard Price decided to reduce his company's costs and try and make as much profit as possible in the fifteen years of operations remaining. He reached an agreement with van der Bijl granting Escom rights both to the ownership of a huge new power station, named Klip, to be built on the Rand and to the license to supply the new mining areas. As with the Witbank agreement, Escom would sell the electricity generated at the Klip station to the VFPC for resale to the VFPC's mining customers (still bound by contracts as binding as Escom's right to expropriation, but now having renegotiated their share of the VFPC's surplus profits up from the 50 percent ruling at Witbank to 70 percent at Klip).[60] The VFPC earned enormous profits from this deal in its remaining years of operation, but for Escom that was a small price (and one that it did not have to pay) for getting access to the much-enlarged market for electricity on the Rand.[61]

Both the Department of Mines and Industries and the Chamber of Mines feared that van der Bijl had reached the agreement at the expense of the mines. After all, he had agreed to a continuation of the mines' contract and had not obtained any reduction in the price charged by the VFPC. The government mining engineer, Hans Pirow, argued that the arrangement would mean lower profits to the mines and in turn an annual loss to the government of £73,500 in uncollected taxation, and he advised his minister to oppose the granting of the license to Escom.[62] The Chamber of Mines also objected, demanding a reduction in prices commensurate with the reduction in costs brought about by larger-scale power generation.[63] Pirow and the Electricity Control Board (ever concerned with helping the gold industry) allied with the mine owners and refused to grant Escom the license until the base price of electricity had been reduced. Furthermore, the ECB demanded the right to review these prices "periodically" to ensure that any increased profits were shared with consumers on an equitable basis. As the ECB, under the terms of the Electricity Act, was on firm ground, van der Bijl and Price were forced to accede to these demands.[64]

Still, from 1933 onward Escom's position as the major power generator on the Rand went unchallenged because of its successful rebuff to the SAR and the working partnership that it had forced on the VFPC through the threat of expropriation. Electricity demand increased, and Escom expanded its plant to meet the Rand's needs. In 1936 the SAR electrified its lines in the Transvaal and agreed to take power from Escom's Witbank station at a price that left both organizations satisfied.[65] By 1938 the increasing requirements of the gold mines prompted Escom to plan another power station to augment the supply from Klip and Witbank. The commission applied for a license, received it immediately, and again put into force an arrangement similar to those at Klip and Witbank, whereby the VFPC bought electricity at cost and sold it at a profit.[66] With its political and economic strength obvious, the commission succeeded in raising loans exceeding £4,000,000 on the public market to finance this expansion.[67] The predominance of Escom as South Africa's major generator of electricity was clearly demonstrated by its 1939 production returns: during that year Escom produced 3,500,000,000 kwh—almost four times its production level in 1932, and nearly half of all electricity generated inside the country.[68] Indeed, South Africa's total electrical output was six times greater in 1939 than it had been in 1922 before the passage of the Electricity Act and the establishment of Escom.[69] While the bulk (50 percent) of this electricity still went to the mines, an increasing proportion (14 percent in 1939 compared to approximately 8 percent in 1922) was used by other industries (most of them on the Rand) and by domestic consumers (10 percent in 1939, up from 6 percent in 1922).[70] To an ever-increasing extent Escom was meeting one of the main aims of its founders—that it provide the energy necessary to industrialize the South African economy outside the mines.

Manipulation of the Steel Market

Although van der Bijl had established a relatively secure financial base for Escom by 1934, he was only just beginning production at Iscor and still faced many of the same difficulties that he had encountered in beginning state electricity production. As with Escom, Iscor's primary function was to furnish the railways with its products at a cheap price. Like Escom, Iscor found the SAR a tough customer, whose idea of a reasonable price was far below the Corporation's conception. To ensure Iscor's survival, van der Bijl had to find other customers for the corporation's steel. But in attempting to enter the South African steel market Iscor faced two major problems. First, the South African market was overwhelmingly dominated by foreign producers who, working together in a cartel, could raise and lower prices at will (especially by "dumping" goods) and thereby destroy Iscor's competitive ability. The corporation could not rely on state protection through the setting of import duties and tariffs, because the gold industry had convinced the government that such constraints on free trade would only lead to higher prices for all consumers in South Africa.[71] Second, the cost of producing steel in South Africa was higher than in the well-established plants overseas, often by as much as 10 to 20 percent. While much of this difference in cost was a result of the greater economies of scale adopted in European steel mills, a considerable amount was also due to the large-scale utilization of white labor in Iscor's plant.

To satisfy the political rhetoric that accompanied Iscor's founding, van der Bijl had announced that it was his "intention to man the works with white labour with possibly a few exceptions. We believe that this policy would yield better results in a modern highly mechanized works such as are being built at Pretoria and *our estimates of production costs are based on white labour entirely.*"[72] White workers were not only more expensive than black but also organized in legally recognized trade unions, which demanded both higher wages and the adherence of the corporation to a policy that preferred white labor. The fundamental contradiction van der Bijl faced was to strengthen the financial foundations of a local steel producer in a market dominated by a foreign cartel when political demands required that the corporation fulfill its original mandate to provide jobs for whites, both within Iscor itself and by supporting industrialization in the rest of the South African economy. It was this contradiction that van der Bijl had to resolve if he was to make Iscor a successful operation.

Laying Iscor's Foundations

Iscor had been established on the basis of an extremely detailed investigation into South African steel needs made in 1924 by the German steel firm, the Gutehoffnungshutte (GHH). The GHH's report envisioned a completely integrated steel plant capable of producing steel from iron ore and transforming it into numerous products ranging from rails, rods, and structural sections that could be manufactured in a rolling mill—part of any steel plant—to other important products like sheets, wire, pipes, and nuts and bolts, which would require more specialized production processes. The report made provision for the manufacture of all of these items, proposing the building of five different mills. It assumed that one-third of the production—primarily of such basic items as rails and structural steel—would go to the SAR, with much of the rest being specialty items that would be sold more generally on the South African market.[73] As with Escom, the SAR was anticipated to be the main customer of the Iron and Steel Corporation.

But van der Bijl, appointed chairman of Iscor in 1928 in addition to his duties at Escom, soon determined that at least half of the GHH blueprint for success was unrealistic. In consultation with various engineering experts, he discovered that the cost of the plant envisioned under the GHH's 1924 report had risen by at least 25 percent by the time construction of the plant was actually intended at the end of the 1920s, yet there was no likelihood of Iscor's getting state funds additional to those the government had already determined on the basis of the original report.[74] As a result, the extensive proposals of the GHH had to be scrapped. Although the size of the proposed enterprise had to be reduced, van der Bijl still wanted to maintain the overall steel output of the plant. The government had conceived the corporation partially as a measure to replace imports, and van der Bijl wanted to secure at least a one-third share, amounting to 150,000 long tons, of the South African market.[75] The only solution was to reduce the amount of finished goods produced, thereby eliminating the cost of some expensive rolling mills, and to increase the amount of raw and semi-finished steel. While leaving room for the future expansion of Iscor's plant, van der Bijl turned in the short term to the production of large quantities of raw steel only and abandoned plans to produce finished products.[76]

The corporation's major problem would be to find customers. South African steel consumers consistently purchased their requirements from overseas producers, primarily steel makers in Britain and Germany. Even the major (and by the early 1930s the only) South African producer—the Union Steel Corporation (Usco), whose headquarters and shareholders were in London—had been unable to find a local market for more than 20,000 tons per year of raw steel ingots. Iscor had to sell almost eight times that amount if it was to cover the costs of its establishment and provide an adequate return on operations. Van der Bijl's solution was to encourage private firms to establish "subsidiary industries" that would become the main consumers of the corporation's steel. Making a virtue out of necessity, he argued that a "fundamental principle" of Iscor's operations would be

> to confine our efforts, as far as practicable, to the production of primary steel products, such as rails, sleepers, building sections, sheet bars, light plate, billets, ordinary merchant requirements, and reinforcement and wire rod, believing that where opportunity offers for the development of subsidiary industries private enterprises will not fail to seize it. We are of the opinion that the best results will be obtained by working amicably together with subsidiary and cognate industries and by encouraging the establishment of further subsidiary industries. It will certainly redound more to the benefit of the Steel Corporation if our efforts are directed towards assisting capital which has been invested in such industries to earn more and so to encourage further development.[77]

Van der Bijl was hardly setting a precedent, as C. F. Delfos had already tried to get foreign producers to participate in local plants and Usco had in fact succeeded in doing so. The British firm of Stewarts and Lloyds was planning to erect a pipe works at Vereeniging adjoining the Usco works and using Usco steel. Baldwins, a British steel sheet manufacturer, had also been contacted by Usco but failed to reach an agreement before the introduction of the Iron and Steel Bill.[78] Van der Bijl lost no time in following Usco's example and, during 1929, reached preliminary agreements with Baldwins and with Usco—and by extension with Stewarts and Lloyds—to provide these companies with Iscor steel. Usco was prepared to take at least 20,000 tons per year of raw steel, and Baldwins was considering 30,000 to 40,000 tons per year, which they would then process into finished goods.[79] These agreements went a long way toward assuring Iscor of a market.

The agreements with Usco and Baldwins not only provided Iscor with two important customers but also formed the basis of the corporation's marketing operations. As in the case of Escom, van der Bijl acquired access to the custom of the mines through private intermediaries. Both Usco and Stewarts and Lloyds had been doing business in South Africa for years, building up contacts and a large group of customers. Usco's principal customers were the mines, to which it sold light rails. It also indirectly sold them raw steel, which was further processed into machine parts by foundries on the Rand. This clientele was especially important to Iscor. J. H. Dobson, a member of Iscor's board at the time of the negotiations with Usco (of which he eventually became chairman), explained the situation in March 1931 as follows:

> [Iscor] felt that it would be a wise policy to have friendly relationships with a possible potential competitor like [Usco] . . . because they have created numerous friendly trade relationships and general goodwill throughout the country . . . [and] it would have been a very unsound principal for a State Promoted Institution like the South African Iron and Steel Corporation to adopt an antagonistic policy towards private enterprise, because the sales of the products from the Pretoria Works (outside Government requirements) will be dependent to a very large extent upon the goodwill of those engaged in private enterprise, who are the chief consumers of steel products throughout South Africa.[80]

The situation was basically the same with Baldwins and a second major sheet importer, Lysaghts, which sold the sheets used for ventilation pipes in the underground mines. Van der Bijl told the minister of mines and industries, A. J. P. Fourie, that "this arrangement would secure to Iscor a very large proportion of its South African market which is now held mainly by Baldwins and Lysaghts."[81] He also testified to the Board of Trade and Industries that "these people know the commercial side of the business and if we got in with them we would get that service for nothing."[82]

Final agreements with both Usco and Baldwins made provision for the establishment of marketing organizations. Iscor joined with Baldwins and Lysaghts to form Iscor Baldwins Lysaghts (IBL), a company that sold Iscor's total output of sheets throughout the country at the same prices as the British imports.[83] Likewise, Iscor and Usco formed the Steel Sales Company, which sold the remainder of Iscor products along with Usco's and later included the products of all other Iscor subsidiaries, excluding only those sold by IBL. Through these agreements Iscor immediately entered the largest private markets for steel goods in the country; in return, the private companies retained control over the retail markets from which they derived the bulk of profits produced in the marketing of steel.

But it was the government markets that eventually gave the corporation its greatest difficulties. In 1929 van der Bijl believed that Iscor could count on sales to the SAR of at least 70,000 tons per year of heavy rails.[84] Moreover, the Iron and Steel Act had stipulated that the SAR should purchase its steel requirements from Iscor, though the act left the terms of the proposed transaction so vague as to guarantee nothing to the corporation. Most important, the method for the determination of the price of such goods delivered to the railways was very prejudicial to Iscor. Under the terms of the act, Iscor had to match the SAR's lowest price, plus any dumping duties levied by the government.[85] Van der Bijl soon discovered that the SAR had several advantages in determining its prices. The SAR carried its own supplies, and therefore the prices of European competitors did not include railage costs. Further, ocean freight costs did not provide Iscor with a competitive edge, as the SAR had negotiated extremely low rates with its suppliers, lower even than the government contract rate. Iscor had to compete with prices already pared to the bone.

Although van der Bijl insisted that Iscor could compete against British home prices, the ninety-six pound rails used by the SAR presented a special case. These rails were supplied by British firms but were not priced according to "home" consumption values, because they were used, and purchased, exclusively in South Africa. The price was set without regard to any market other than South Africa, meaning that the British firms could undercut Iscor prices. In 1934, the average British price for these heavy rails was £5/14/11 per short ton, while Iscor charged £9/5/-.[86] The competition was a serious problem, as these rails represented 65 percent of all SAR purchases and were Iscor's largest single item of manufacture.[87] Van der Bijl needed to sell the rails, but the SAR was only prepared to buy them at prohibitively low prices.

Van der Bijl pressed for dumping duties on imported steel, the sole protection afforded the corporation under the Iron and Steel Act. Taking his case to the government body responsible for recommending tariffs and protection, the Board of Trade and Industries (BTI), van der Bijl proved that overseas suppliers, particularly those in Belgium and France, were dumping certain steel goods on the South African market. Yet when dumping duties were accordingly levied by the BTI against Germany, Belgium, Luxembourg, and France in December 1934, van der Bijl's attempt to extend the sanctions against the SAR failed. Even though van der Bijl proved that the SAR got its steel from Britain at dumping prices, Hertzog's government refused to order the SAR either to pay penalties or to shift its business to

Iscor. By 1935 the railways still employed 50 percent more white males than did the gold mines and almost as many as did the entire manufacturing industry. No government was going to take any action, particularly in the aftermath of the Great Depression, that would impinge on the finances of, and the employment opportunities offered by, such a significant organization. The SAR refused to purchase more than an insignificant amount of steel from Iscor, while Hertzog's cabinet voted against imposing any form of protectionist tariffs that might have a detrimental effect on the business of British-based steel manufacturers.[88]

Subsidiaries, Private Enterprise, and Government

Rebuffed by potentially his most important customer, van der Bijl decided to shift Iscor's production almost exclusively to the private sector. The SAR rails were to have been manufactured in the same heavy mill that produced blooms, billets, and bars—the intermediate steel goods used in the production of a variety of finished goods. Van der Bijl proposed that the corporation produce the "semis," as the intermediate sections were called, and market them to private firms. Finding the new customers was a somewhat complicated matter, but van der Bijl had an answer for that too: the corporation would join with several private firms to establish new companies to purchase the steel. Furthermore, he proposed that Iscor itself put up most of the money needed to build the new factories yet also develop partnerships with foreign firms. Iscor would underwrite the new companies and secure representation on their boards, while the foreign firms would supply the remainder of the capital as well as significant expertise.

The focus of the subsidiary buildup was in Vereeniging, Sammy Marks's "New Sheffield," where Iscor held a controlling interest in the Usco steel plant in partnership with the African and European Investment Company.[89] Van der Bijl had invested in Usco because it had seemed likely in 1930 that the Lewis and Marks subsidiary was on the verge of bankruptcy.[90] Van der Bijl's first addition to the Vereeniging plant was a wire works, which had originally been planned as part of an Iscor factory.[91] In 1934, Iscor's first year of production as an independent steel maker, Usco further expanded under van der Bijl's direction by acquiring the South African Bolt and Nut Factory. Usco moved its new acquisition from Johannesburg to Vereeniging and, in collaboration with the British firm of Quest, Keen and Nettlefolds, which held a 50 percent interest in SA Bolts and Nuts, built a large new plant.[92] The following year Usco entered into a similar arrangement with a Canadian firm, McKinnon Chain Company, to establish a steel-chain factory at Vereeniging.[93] These additions in Vereeniging—and further developments, including the manufacture of drill and tool steel and agricultural implements, as well as the establishment of the African Cables factory—produced a considerable jump in Usco's output and sales.[94] By 1937 annual production at Usco reached nearly 70,000 long tons, compared with 20,000 in 1930, and sales through the Steel Sales Company amounted to £1,216,393.[95]

But van der Bijl did not limit his efforts to expanding Usco. In 1935 Iscor joined Hubert Davies, a South African engineering firm, to establish the Pretoria Steel Construction Company (Presco), which would manufacture fabricated steel products for the exclusive use of Iscor.[96] In 1937 van der Bijl embarked upon another iron and steel venture, the African Metals Corporation (Amcor), this time in collaboration with all of the firms most closely interested in the South African industry—Usco, Stewarts and Lloyds, Baldwins, Dorman Long, the African and European Investment Company—and for the first time one of the mining houses, Sir Ernest Oppenheimer's Anglo-American Corporation.[97] With Iscor and Usco together holding more than 50 percent of the stock, van der Bijl was appointed chairman and managing director of the firm. Amcor was originally founded for two purposes: to develop iron ore on Iscor properties and to produce ferro-alloys for use in steel manufacture.[98] Van der Bijl soon developed larger plans for Amcor and hoped to open a factory at Vereeniging, but his scheme never came to fruition, because of the outbreak of the Second World War.[99]

Iscor's financial interests stretched far beyond the iron and steel industry per se, as van der Bijl moved to expand the corporation's control over all phases of production. One of its first allied enterprises involved developing a supply of coal, necessary to produce coke for the blast furnaces.[100] The corporation had inherited some coal near Witbank from the old Delfos company and, fearing that it would be left "entirely at the mercy of coal owners," proceeded to investigate the possibilities of coking these deposits.[101] Finding the coal satisfactory, van der Bijl leased Iscor properties to the Johannesburg Consolidated Investment Company (JCI), which undertook to supply Iscor with the coal mined from the property.[102] The two companies—Iscor and JCI—then proceeded to establish a third company, the Phoenix Colliery, for the purpose of carrying on the mining.[103] Owning the major assets of the Phoenix Colliery, Iscor in effect controlled the company and the corporation's supply of coal without appearing to be expanding into a vertical monopoly.

But monopoly was precisely what the corporation achieved in its control over the market for tar. A by-product of the steel production process, tar was produced at a rate proportionate to steel output. Van der Bijl had always hoped that the sales of by-products would help offset production costs for steel, but in the corporation's first year of production nearly

£22,000 worth of tar remained unsold.[104] Van der Bijl's goal was to market the tar for road construction, but he found that the only road construction company in the Transvaal, the Fowler Tar Spraying Company, preferred asphalt to tar. His solution to the problem was simply to buy Fowler. Rather than own the company lock, stock, and barrel, however, van der Bijl encouraged several private companies—Anglo-Transvaal Consolidated Investment Company, Barlow and Company, and Satmar—to take up shares, while the corporation maintained overall control.[105] Once again van der Bijl secured the participation of private capital in jointly owned monopolies.

Through the buildup of subsidiary companies, van der Bijl further expanded Iscor's markets and ties with private capital. Following the initiation of its own production and accelerating after the failure of the negotiations with the SAR, the development of subsidiaries gave Iscor new customers and an outlet for its products. As a result, sales jumped from 88,092 long tons of steel in 1935 to 335,264 long tons in 1939.[106] At the same time, private firms—including many of the mining houses, such as Anglo-American, JCI, and Anglo-Transvaal—were guaranteed profits from their investments.

Protecting the Market

Yet even as Iscor expanded its markets, these remained vulnerable to overseas competition. Shifting production from rails to other products helped to spread the corporation's risks, but it also placed Iscor in direct competition with a number of European finished goods. Moreover, European steel producers had again formed a cartel and saw in South Africa a profitable market for dumping some of their excess production.

In November 1934 a confidential Dutch report on the Continental cartel—Germany, France, Luxembourg, and Belgium—that described efforts to combine with the British steel industry came into van der Bijl's possession. The report specifically referred to the South African market and proposed cartel efforts to undercut local producers.[107] In August 1935 the British industry joined the cartel, which then set about determining export quotas for the international trade.[108] Soon after, Belgium again began undercutting South African producers on steel sections by between 32/- and 48/- per ton, and on sheets by at least 14/- per ton. The main trade, however, was in light rails, sold to the mines at prices that were 34/- to 39/- less per ton than Usco's.[109] Van der Bijl was already aware that dumping duties were not effective in combating this kind of competition. The duties were based on the difference between the "home" price of such goods in Europe and the supposedly lower prices charged by the European producers in South Africa. Yet many of the goods, like Britain's ninety-six-pound rails, were not sold in the producer's country, and the Europeans were able to set artificial home prices deliberately lower than Iscor's production costs. In these cases—many of them involving steel from Belgium and Luxembourg—it was impossible for Iscor to obtain any protection.

Van der Bijl sought without success to enlist government protection of local steel production. He proposed that the government establish an average level of prices for steel goods, below which no products could enter the country without penalty. The suggestion was initially rebuffed by the Board of Trade and Industry, which called it "a radical departure from the principles which the Union has thus far applied in its trade relations with other countries," and which suggested that the SAR should increase the carriage rates it charged in imported steel so that the price of foreign steel would equal the price of Iscor's.[110] However, Oswald Pirow, the minister of railways and harbors, replied that legal advice prevented the SAR from adopting variable pricing based on the country of origin of the goods in question. Pirow also refused to implement a flat increase on the railage for all imported steel.

The Department of Commerce and Industries for its part rejected any protective customs duties that might have raised local steel prices or hindered foreign trade. Hertzog's government had entered into a "barter" arrangement with the new Nazi government in December 1934, under which Germany traded its products—principally iron and steel goods— for South African products (principally wool).[111] The agreement was very important to the government, which was seeking to revive rural sheep farming hit by the Depression-related slump in the prices and sales of wool. Officials in the Department of Commerce and Industries were already concerned that previously enacted dumping duties had unfairly penalized German trade and advised the minister, A. P. S. Fourie, against instituting any more duties in Germany's case.[112] Moreover, because Iscor's own production could not possibly meet the whole of South African demand, tariff protection of any kind raised fears among consumers, especially the gold mines, that the implementation of such a policy would result in higher prices for steel within South Africa.

With no hope of getting government protection of local steel production, van der Bijl opened direct discussions in December 1935 with the European producers to end dumping. The cartel was eager to make an arrangement that would obviate the need for costly competition and permit steel prices to rise. In February 1936 van der Bijl and the cartel reached an agreement that reserved 350,000 tons—approximately one-third of the South African market—to local producers. The rest of the market would be shared by overseas producers who would, in consultation with Iscor, set prices below which steel would not be imported. Any party that tried to break the terms of the agreement would be subjected either to special tariffs or to a sales tax (enacted in June 1936). The agreement was mutually acceptable because each producer was guaranteed a share of the market at prices that would ensure a profit for all. Furthermore, as van der Bijl pointed out to the minister of mines and industries, the agreement essentially erected a screen that insulated the government from the taint of price fixing, although that is what the deal between local and foreign producers essentially constituted for South African consumers.[113]

The cartel arrangement mirrored the earlier local agreements between Iscor and its domestic competitors. Van der Bijl joined with private producers to control the market and determine prices. The demand for steel in South Africa had nearly doubled since the expansion of gold mining in 1933—from 450,000 tons per year to 880,000 tons in 1936—leaving ample sales for everyone set at price levels that would return a healthy profit. Local producers, primarily Iscor, supplied one-third of the steel, while the overseas producers accounted for the balance required. The only loser in this arrangement was the consumer; in the absence of competition, prices would naturally rise. For example, whereas the average price in 1934 of imported structural sections was £6/11/8 per ton, by 1938 the agreed price was £9/18/4.[114] Contrary to the aims of the 1928 Iron and Steel Act, the establishment of Iscor had not led to a lowering of the local price of steel.

The main steel consumers subjected to this development were the owners of the gold mines. In June 1936 the Gold Producers' Committee of the Chamber of Mines commissioned a thorough investigation into Iscor's operations by the dean of the Faculty of Commerce at the University of Witwatersrand, C. S. Richards. A well-known advocate of free trade and marketing, Richards strongly criticized the cartel arrangement in his report, completed in July 1939: "The price and production Agreement with the Cartel should not be necessary, nor should it ever have been sanctioned by the Government. It has operated to the detriment of the whole country, has placed Iscor (and the whole steel industry) in the position of a privileged Government monopolist . . . and has enabled it to charge the mines, its principal customers, monopolistic prices."[115] When it received Richards's report in December 1939, the Gold Producers' Committee immediately drafted a letter to van der Bijl, detailing Richards's criticisms and concluding by saying, "The Gold Mining Industry is being called on to pay too high a price, and it is the price factor which is of paramount importance to this Industry." Although the draft was sent to the Department of Commerce and Industries, it was never formally delivered to van der Bijl: instead, scrawled across the letter in long hand was the notation "Not issued owing to war conditions."[116] As the country entered the Sec-

ond World War, the gold industry had to depend entirely on Iscor for its
supply of steel goods.

Lowering the Costs of Labor

By 1936 van der Bijl had succeeded in securing the steel market through
the creation of subsidiaries and the stabilization of price competition. But
once the corporation began full-scale production, he realized that market
control was not enough to ensure success and that costs would be his
major problem. To continue subsidiary development, van der Bijl needed
capital, which could only be produced if costs were cut.[117] In 1936 his business and works managers conceded that their costs were still prohibitively
high, as much as £1 per ton higher than European producers', because of
heavy capital costs.[118] With Iscor still saddled with these costs in 1938—as
it would be for years—the commercial manager, A. C. McColm, explained,
"Even if we could produce as cheaply [as overseas producers], our overheads
are greater as the capital required for large inland industries is over 50%
greater than the capital required for a similar factory in Europe, due to sea
and land transport of the plant, customs duties and the higher construction
and erection costs obtaining in South Africa."[119] Capital costs were fixed,
and there was no way van der Bijl could lower them. The only means to
lowering costs further was to attack labor charges, and that would mean
either reducing the labor force through further mechanization, adding to
already high capital costs, or lowering wages. In the face of much opposition and controversy, van der Bijl chose to cut wages.

Despite government rhetoric about providing "sheltered employment"
for poor whites, these workers had little more protection at Iscor than they
had in the country's gold mines. In 1934 the government mining engineer,
Hans Pirow, had decreed that the corporation, because of the considerable
extent to which it was engaged in mining and processing iron ore, fell
under the terms of the Mines and Works Act and not the Factories Act
(which afforded slightly greater protection for white employees).[120] In
addition, Iscor had not joined the Engineering Industrial Council, through
which employers and employees could negotiate wage agreements, nor
could the corporation's white employees have their grievances heard by the
government's Wage Board, because they were organized into labor unions
that were required, by law, to use the Industrial Council to settle disputes—a "catch-22" situation for the workers. The only protections
afforded white Iscor employees were their right to strike and the Pact government's policy of "civilised labour." Because the "civilised labour" policy was principally enforced through the granting of tariff protection to
those industries employing whites—tariff protection that Iscor had

notably been refused—even this avenue of protection was of little use to the corporation's white employees.

Moreover, despite the increasing poor-white problem during the Depression, government pressure on the corporation to hire white labor became increasingly fainthearted. At the beginning of the construction of Iscor's steel plant in 1930, F. H. P. Creswell in his capacity as minister of labor persuaded van der Bijl to hire whites for site leveling by offering to subsidize their wages.[121] In May 1931, Creswell arranged for a subsidy of approximately £22,000 for whites to lay the foundations of the plant.[122] Otherwise, Iscor's Board of Directors opted for cheaper black labor, preferring to let the government pay the difference for white workers if it so desired.[123] During 1933, when both the political and economic situations changed dramatically, the government became increasingly less ready to take such action: the Labourites and hard-line Nationalists were out of the government, and Hertzog had formed an alliance with his old enemy Smuts, while the economy began to expand after South Africa abandoned the gold standard and more job opportunities arose for poor whites. Under these conditions, hiring white labor at the corporation on a permanent basis seemed a minor priority.[124]

Van der Bijl remained concerned about the possible political fallout from doing without whites. As he told his Board of Directors in July 1933, the "ratio [between] white and native labour is [a] matter of [the] utmost importance economically and politically."[125] The board subsequently reached a rather ambiguous decision to allow the general works manager to determine the ratio of black and white workers on the basis of "efficiency and economy" rather than remain committed to van der Bijl's earlier promise that white labor alone would be used at Iscor.[126]

When production began at Iscor's Vereeniging plant in 1934, whites comprised only 55 percent of Iscor's work force. Compared to the employment figures at Usco and Stewarts and Lloyds, where whites represented only 28 percent and 23 percent, respectively, of the work force, Iscor's figures were impressive.[127] Closer scrutiny of the distribution of labor gave rise to certain complaints, however. Whites alone worked at two of Iscor's mines, but blacks far outnumbered whites at the third, the Thabazimbi iron-ore mine. While black labor in the mines was nothing new or unexpected, it was in the factory itself that the labor policy was surprising. Van der Bijl had stated that blacks would not be used at the works but only at the mines, yet there were almost as many blacks as whites in the factory when it opened.[128] In January 1934 the Board of Directors, citing cost factors, had reversed its original policy and had decided to employ blacks in the steel plant, though it did state that these men would be replaced with whites "as soon as convenient."[129]

Yet the supposed "unsuitability" of blacks for factory employment was one of the cornerstones of the "civilised labour" philosophy, and it did not take long for the public to catch on to Iscor's heresy. A deputation of private citizens from Pretoria called on the minister of mines and industries and complained about "a very large number of Natives" at Iscor, prompting in turn an investigation by the minister. He discovered that the true labor totals—1,715 whites and 1,356 blacks—were quite different from the projections he had been given in November 1933 (850 whites and 350 blacks). Encouraging van der Bijl to reduce black employment—but not threatening any diminution in government support—the minister explained that, right or wrong, the public perceived Iscor as a government undertaking, funded by the taxpayers for the employment of "die seuns van die volk."[130]

What the minister did not know, and van der Bijl chose not to explain, was that not all of Iscor's white employees were "sons of the people." The Iscor Board of Directors had decided in 1932 to import skilled steel workers from Europe "for the starting up and operation of the plant."[131] Some were hired from the European contractors working on the plant, but most were recruited overseas by van der Bijl himself or by Iscor agents.[132] The managers of major departments within the factory were recruited primarily from Britain and Germany, while the bulk of the imported men were brought from Britain to work on the sheet mill.[133] The number of imported men reached about two hundred by the beginning of 1936, out of a total of nearly twenty-five hundred white employees.[134]

What was significant about these men was not their numbers but their terms of employment. To induce them to come to South Africa, they had been offered an "importation allowance," which had initially amounted to a 25 percent supplement to their wages.[135] After the majority of the imported employees had arrived, they expressed dissatisfaction with their wages and demanded a 75 percent increase.[136] Through the South African Boilermakers, Ironworkers, and Shipbuilders' Union, they declared a labor dispute and requested that a conciliation board be formed under the terms of the 1924 Industrial Conciliation Act.[137] The corporation decided to settle the matter informally, perhaps to avoid public attention, and agreed to a raise in the importation allowance to 40 percent of the foreign workers' wages.[138] By comparison, South African whites, had they performed the same jobs, would have received no such additional payment, and their wages would have amounted to only 71 percent of those of the European workers.

The white South African employees, most of them Afrikaners, demanded equal treatment. Even though they were rank-and-file members of the Boilermakers' Union, they had received absolutely nothing as a result of the union's negotiations with Iscor. When they requested greater representation on the union's Executive Board—dominated by British immigrants—their request was denied. As a result, more than a thousand members left the union in May 1936 and formed their own, the South African Iron, Steel, and Kindred Trades Association. In statements to the press, they complained in particular that the interests of Afrikaans speakers were being ignored. In contrast to the old union, 80 percent of the executive of the new union was Afrikaans speaking.[139] More important, the new union represented the semiskilled and unskilled poor-white workers at Iscor, who resented the immigrants' higher wages yet feared replacement by cheaper black labor. Immediately after its formation, the union contacted Iscor management in order to discuss three points of contention: increased wages, changes in the bonus system, and, most significant for these workers, reversing the corporation's practice of replacing white workers with black.[140]

The union's timing was unfortunate, however. By May 1936 van der Bijl had already committed the corporation to several large-scale subsidiary ventures. He had invested £163,000 in Usco, Presco, Fowler, and the Steel Sales Company.[141] In addition to these initial sums, van der Bijl expected to continue incurring costs for these ventures. At the same time, Iscor's financial results were due to be published and would show that the corporation had suffered a loss of £12,309 for the fiscal year ending 30 June 1936.[142] Unable to consider issuing dividends, van der Bijl desperately needed to lower Iscor's costs if he was to attract foreign investors, and he could hardly consider raising wages or continuing to employ white labor when he could easily hire much cheaper black labor. Indeed, in 1936 Iscor management began reclassifying "white" jobs as "general labourer" jobs for blacks, with extremely low wages.

Moreover, the new union's efforts to protect white jobs were easily defeated. One legal option open to the union—to petition to join the Industrial Council for the Metal Engineering Industry, comprised of employers and employees empowered to settle industrywide disputes— was soon foreclosed when only two months after the formation of the union, the council disbanded itself.[143] Therefore, the union sought the establishment of a conciliation board to deal with the policies existing at the corporation and threatened to strike if one was not formed. The government agreed to the establishment of a board, so long as the men did not strike and the issue of black labor did not come up for discussion.[144]

Yet the matter of black labor emerged again and again in testimony before the board. The union members argued that preference should be given to the hiring of white workers in all sectors of the steel industry, while the general works manager of Iscor, Frederick Meyer (the same man who had originally helped draft the Iron and Steel Bill), consistently refused even to consider reversing the policy of replacing whites with blacks.[145] So divisive was the issue of black labor that one committee of the conciliation board concluded:

> It became apparent very early in the proceedings that whatever the outcome of the negotiations may be on other matters, there was one important question on which the Board would be shipwrecked. This was the declared policy of the respondent [Iscor], in every department to reduce posts hitherto held by Europeans to General Labourers' jobs, for which the remuneration would be such that no European could possibly accept same. The applicants [Iron and Steel Union] refused to agree to the introduction of this policy on principle, especially after it appeared that respondents had in fact in at least three instances and during the negotiations already brought this policy into practice.[146]

Nevertheless, the union agreed to consider the regrading of certain jobs, which it believed involved 171 men, only to find out later that the proposals involved 171 job titles—a total of more than 400 men.[147] Accusations were made by the union that Iscor was going to save four times as much as it was prepared to give in response to certain wage demands. Meyer, head of the Iscor delegation to the Conciliation Board, refused to reconsider, and negotiations finally broke down completely in September 1937.[148] Arbitrators were appointed with the agreement of both sides and issued a report in December that mirrored the terms of an industrial agreement negotiated by a reconstituted Industrial Council during the proceedings. The new agreement, and the report, gave Iscor everything it wanted.[149]

The union continued its appeals to the government, but to no avail. It filed legal charges against the minister of labor, J. H. Hofmeyr, Iscor, and the Industrial Council for having published an industrial agreement during the Conciliation Board hearings that left any board decisions moot, but it failed to have the decision of the arbitrators or the agreement changed in any way.[150] Throughout 1938 the union continued to complain about Iscor's black-labor policies, charging in the leading Afrikaans newspaper, *Die Transvaler*, that Iscor had already replaced three hundred whites with blacks and that the government was creating a *swartman-swerkplek* (black man's workplace), just like the Usco factory at Vereeniging.[151] Indeed, Iscor's compound for black migrant workers at Pretoria, across the road from the plant, was so busy that the corporation erected a trading store inside the compound to relieve the city of the "nuisance caused by hawkers in the vicinity."[152] The opposition Purified National Party, formed in 1934 by Afrikaners who had felt betrayed by Hertzog's alliance with Smuts, seized upon the issue in late 1938, at the time of the centennial commemoration of the battle of Blood River, and organized protest meetings in Pretoria when thirty more white employees were fired.[153] The outbreak of the Second World War however, brought the issue to a close, as all workers were quickly subjected to government control.

In sum, neither political pressure nor union agitation helped Iscor's white employees. When it became apparent that white labor would become ever more expensive as a result of the actions of organized labor, van der Bijl became intransigent on the issue, believing that Iscor's profits would evaporate if he was forced to use white workers rather than black. Although Hertzog's government was publicly committed to the use of white labor, neither Hofmeyr, the minister of labor, nor Fourie, the minister of commerce and industries, took any steps to change Iscor's policies. Indeed, Hofmeyr's signing of an industrial agreement in 1937 effectively cut much of white labor out of the iron and steel industry and indicated tacit support for Iscor's policies. From 1937 until the beginning of the war, Meyer continued to replace white workers with black, although the ratio of white to black still remained relatively high—1:2 at the corporation compared with 1:7.5 on the gold mines.

The financial results of van der Bijl's actions—the subsidiary policies, protective agreements, and new labor policies—were considerable. Although the corporation had sustained losses in its first two years, in 1936 it showed a profit of £435,665 and in 1937 £669,279. These profits were hardly unexpected, given the high level of market protection, price stabilization, and subsidiary development attained. In 1936 alone, when the European cartel agreement took effect, the value of sales rose by 108 percent. By 1938 both the amount of steel sold by Iscor and its prices were relatively stable, with increases of only 8 percent and 19 percent, respectively, over the previous year. Yet profits in 1938 rose to £1,236,122—an increase of 84 percent over the previous year's figures. This dramatic rise was largely attributable to lowered production costs, which in turn were the result of the implementation of the labor arbitration award. In short, market agreements with private-sector producers and the adoption of harsh labor policies secured the corporation's strong financial standing.[154]

Conclusion: Escom and Iscor

By the end of the 1930s Escom and Iscor were both in production, supplying the energy and steel needs of South Africa's rapidly growing economy. Hertzog's abandonment of the gold standard at the end of 1932 had spurred massive change, with the price of gold doubling in the 1930s, gold industry revenues increasing by two and a half times, and government receipts from the mines tripling.[155] Economic growth was particularly evident in the manufacturing sector, with the value of its output doubling between 1932 and 1939. Indeed, whereas manufacturing had ranked fourth behind agriculture, mining, and commerce in its contribution to the national income in the mid-1920s, by the end of the 1930s it was in second place and continuing to grow in a process that would have it permanently outstripping the frontrunner gold by 1943.[156] Much of this growth was powered by Escom, which was largely responsible for electrical generation increasing by five and a half times between 1922 (when Escom was first established) and the end of the 1930s (from 1,192.4 million kwh to 6,574.3 million kwh).[157] Although the mines were still the biggest consumer of electricity in South Africa, their proportionate share declined (from 75 percent of all power generated in the mid-1920s to 49 percent by the late 1930s) as demand in other sectors of the economy grew at a much faster rate. Between the mid-1920s and the late 1930s electricity usage expanded fivefold in the manufacturing industry, sixfold in the supply of power to domestic users, and fourfold in the railways, in descending order the three largest users after the mines.[158]

Iscor's output was no less impressive. From an initial production of 103,666 tons of steel in 1934, the corporation's output rose in just four years to an annual figure of 1,031,495 tons. With the Iscor plant at Pretoria producing primarily heavy steel products, and its Usco subsidiary at Vereeniging concentrating on engineering and foundry products (a division of responsibilities that became less apparent over time), the corporation developed an enormous range of products: "tube mill bars, palisading hexagons, triangular bars . . . pig irons, sheets and plates . . . road tars . . . drill steel, steel castings and forgings, steel wire, bolts, nuts and rivets and copper products."[159] The bulk of these products (88 percent) went to the gold mines and the manufacturing industries, while 9 percent was purchased by the railways and 3 percent by other government departments.[160] Such a large output and wide range of products was particularly important to the growth of South Africa's metal industry. Between 1932 and 1939 the number of metalworking establishments, most of them sited in or near Vereeniging, grew by 38 percent (from 322 factories and workshops to 445), while their output mushroomed 340 percent in value (from £2,737,000 to £9,285,000).[161]

Industrial growth meant more jobs. The labor needs of the mining industry expanded dramatically in the 1930s, with 84 percent more whites and 48 percent more blacks employed in the gold mines in 1939 than in 1932. The railways also posted large gains during the same period, with white employment growing by 30 percent and black by 64 percent. The increases were proportionately greatest, however, in manufacturing, with the number of white workers expanding by 77 percent and of black workers by 106 percent. During the 1930s total employment in the three industries grew from 469,415 in 1932 to 763,856 in 1939, with the largest number of whites at the end of the decade having jobs in manufacturing (102,490, compared with 68,566 on the railways and 43,183 in the mines) and the largest number of blacks working in the gold industry (321,400, compared with 173,362 in manufacturing and 54,855 on the railways).[162]

But while employment increased overall, the ratio of white to black at work changed little, despite the political talk about "civilised labour" and the state corporations' initial commitment to alleviating the problems of white workers. For whites the greatest change took place in the mining industry, where the increased mechanization of operations (which put a premium on hiring more "skilled" than "unskilled" workers) resulted in the ratio of black to white falling from 9.3 to 1 in 1932 to 7.5 to 1 in 1939.[163] By contrast, the ratio of black to white workers at the railways, the strongest adherent of the "civilised labour" policy, grew from 0.7 to 1 to 0.8 to 1. In manufacturing, supposedly the salvation for unemployed whites, blacks were more likely to find jobs than whites were; although the numbers of whites at work rose, the ratio of black males to white increased, standing at 1.9 to 1 in 1932 and at 2.2 to 1 in 1939. Moreover, an increasing number of "white" jobs in manufacturing were being taken by women, who were paid lower wages than were men.[164]

The state corporations themselves reflected industrywide practices in their hiring patterns. At Escom and other publicly owned power stations 38 percent of the workers were white, hardly any different from the figure of 35 percent in privately owned firms.[165] At Iscor by the end of the 1930s, 47 percent of the work force was white (a better showing than the 40 percent operative in the metal industries in general), but that was still a considerable drop from the 55 percent employed in 1934, the first year of steel production, and very different from van der Bijl's 1932 claim that he planned to use "white labour entirely" in the production process.[166]

The state corporations' original mandate to provide cheap and abundant supplies of energy and steel was also compromised by the economics of production. With no South African government in the 1920s or 1930s ready to bear the enormous economic and political costs of nationalization and direct state subsidization, the state corporations had to enter already established markets and operate either in competition or in league with existing producers. Both Escom and Iscor, under van der Bijl's leadership, chose to develop marketing partnerships, as competition would have been far too costly.

In the case of electricity, the capital costs of beginning production were so high that new entrants into an electricity market could be crushed by established suppliers, unless the newcomers were ready to accept heavy initial losses (which no government was ready to carry, especially during the Depression). In the case of steel, the problems of production and marketing were particularly complicated. Foreign producers could, and were ready to, dump steel on the South African market at prices much lower than the cost of local production, yet consumers opposed tariff protection for Iscor, since that would certainly have led to higher prices. The resulting compromise, necessary if Iscor was to be run on business lines and not be directly subsidized by the state, was the agreement negotiated between the corporation and the European cartel in 1936 that set market shares and prices at levels that would guarantee profits to all producers, whether foreign or local. The development of partnerships between public and private producers, and the negotiation of collaborative market agreements, while making it possible for the state corporations to be run on business lines, resulted in electricity and steel prices that the main consumers for these products in South Africa—the railways and the gold mines—considered excessively high.

Indeed, two major studies commissioned in the late 1930s—one by the Chamber of Mines, the other as part of Lord Hailey's African Research Survey—strongly criticized the impact of government policies on the mining industry. The report by Professor C. S. Richards, dean of the Faculty of Commerce at the University of the Witwatersrand, argued that although Iscor had been mandated to produce steel at a cost "'as low as the lowest in Europe' . . . [and with] *no protection*," the "difference between promise and performance" was in fact "enormous."[167] Richards denounced the agreement reached between Iscor and the European cartel as a mechanism that eliminated competition, produced a monopoly, and resulted in the overcharging of local consumers. He pointed out that the relatively large-scale use of white workers, even if as a smaller proportion of the work force than originally intended, resulted in "high labour costs," amounting to 42 percent of the total costs of manufacturing.[168] Drawing attention to what he considered the major problems facing not just the steel industry but the whole South African economy—"the problem of state intervention and its relation to industry; the development of economic nationalism with its restrictions on free international trade; the problem of monopoly and its expression [in] discriminatory and non-competitive prices"—he concluded that "the State should sell out its interest [in Iscor] to private capital," and that "some recompense" should be given to the "gold mining industry."[169]

S. H. Frankel, professor of economics and economic history at the same university as Richards, drew particular attention to the problems of the South African gold industry in his 1938 survey of the colonial economies of Africa, *Capital Investment in Africa: Its Course and Effects.* Frankel produced figures demonstrating that not only was gold the primary producer of national income in South Africa, but since 1932 its contribution to state revenues had increased from less than 10 percent to nearly 33 percent.[170] He argued that the high rate of taxation on the South African gold industry—which he calculated at 42 percent of all taxable profits, compared with rates of 18 percent in Australia, 23 percent in Rhodesia, and 14 to 18 percent in the United States—prevented reinvestment in the further development of mining and "other unassisted primary industries." Instead, it resulted in the uneconomic protection of local manufacturing and agricultural enterprises that were "unable to stand on their own in the markets of the world."[171] Manufacturing, Frankel argued, was an especially weak sector of the South African economy. Its most striking features were a "low average productivity per worker"—the value of production per head of employees was about half that of factory workers in Australia, Canada, and New Zealand—and an "artificial wage structure" that resulted in white workers getting the bulk of wages and salaries paid. Frankel calculated that this process had gone furthest in the government undertakings he had examined (not specified in his text), where whites comprised 66.3 percent of the work force and got 91 percent of the total wages and salaries paid.[172] Escom's and Iscor's white labor complements were a smaller proportion of their respective work forces, closer to 40 percent than 60, but still considerably larger than the 12 percent that whites accounted for among gold-mine workers. Like Richards, Frankel believed that monopolies, protective market agreements, and the adoption of the "civilised labour" policy posed enormous threats to the long-term profitability of the mining industry as well as undermined the strength of the South African economy.

Van der Bijl did not disagree with the arguments made by Richards and Frankel favoring greater productivity and the restriction of state constraints on the operations of private business, as he himself remained a strong proponent of private enterprise. Indeed, in the face of growing criticism of Iscor's monopoly position, he proposed in 1939 that the majority of the corporation's shares held by the government be put up for public bid. He hoped that such a move would eliminate the objections of the "industrial community" to "Iscor doing anything beyond the making of raw iron and steel products." He further suggested that a new company, the African Metals Corporation, be formed, state-supported but not state-owned and working in partnership with existing private steel firms, that would aim at manufacturing twice as much steel as Iscor then produced.[173] These plans, however, had to be shelved with the outbreak of war.

As the experiences of Escom and Iscor in the late 1920s and the 1930s demonstrated, entering into market agreements with overseas-owned producers and giving some preference at least to the hiring of more white workers, rather than adopting an overwhelmingly black-labor policy, were necessary economic and political costs for doing business in South Africa. The commission and the corporation could not have done otherwise without crippling their operations. By the end of the 1930s these economic and political costs were becoming more than the gold industry was willing to bear, but the outbreak of the Second World War in 1939 made matters moot: energy needs soared at the same time as South Africa was cut off from outside supplies of steel. In the context of war production, the state corporations restructured their operations, while the gold industry reassessed its attitude to state intervention in the economy.

CHAPTER FIVE

War and the Transformation of Industry

The problems that plagued South Africa's industrial development in the 1920s and 1930s came to a head during the crisis years of World War II. Prices to consumers, especially to the mining industry, soared during the war, while more and more African workers were drawn into the country's cities and factories. With South Africa entirely reliant on domestic production due to a cutoff of imports, local industries boosted production by hiring growing numbers of "semiskilled" African workers and boosted profits by taking advantage of their monopoly position. During the war years, profits in the foundry and general engineering industries—directly affecting the mining industry—jumped by 400 percent.[1] Mass production made such profits possible, especially in view of the increasing numbers of low-paid African workers being used in industry: between 1935 and 1945, the number of Africans in manufacturing industries rose by 119 percent, comprising more than 54 percent of the work force by the end of the war.[2] Most important, these Africans were not being drawn into exclusively unskilled work and instead constituted 5.8 percent and 34.2 percent of the skilled and semiskilled jobs, respectively, in manufacturing.[3] Rising costs, shifting job categories, and a marked urban migration of blacks out of increasingly impoverished rural areas all threatened the precarious nature of white political and economic power.

The Smuts government, coming to power on the heels of Hertzog's resignation over South Africa's entry into the war in 1939, masked these problems under emergency regulations and spent most of the war years trying to formulate long-term solutions. The use of black, Coloured, and female workers—tellingly termed "dilutees"—in factories during the war was officially attributed to a scarcity of white males, while high costs were blamed on imports. However, high costs were certain to continue after the war if the dilutees were replaced with white workers, and postwar trade competition would put such expensive industries out of business. Smuts and his advisers feared, in the words of H. J. van der Bijl, that "the spectre of our economic system breaking down appears to loom up in such disturbing proportions that no steps which we know will combat it can be too big or too bold."[4] Thus, van der Bijl, H. J. van Eck, and others were charged by Smuts to solve the country's economic dilemma by the end of the war, creating jobs for whites and at the same time lowering costs to the mining industry.

The predominant opinion in government circles favored increasing the scope of the country's industrial activities as the answer to South Africa's problems. The Rural Industries Commission issued its report in 1940, proposing numerous industrial ventures that could utilize the country's natural resources, provide employment for whites, and, as a result of being located in the countryside, revitalize the rural economy as well as stem the urban flow of migrants.[5] At the same time, Smuts established the Industrial and Agricultural Requirements Commission (IARC) to investigate the productive capacity of both rural and urban South Africa, with a view to promoting new industries.[6] And Parliament, at the request of the prime minister, was also discussing legislation to establish a third state corporation, the Industrial Development Corporation (IDC), to promote the development of local industries.[7] By 1942, the government turned most of its attention to the anticipated postwar economic situation. Smuts established the Directorate General of Supplies (DGS), with van der Bijl at its head, to extend government control throughout the economy, and the Social and Economic Planning Commission (SEC), with van Eck at its head, to chart the future direction of economic development.[8] Increased industrial development was identified as the panacea to local problems and was unanimously urged by all commissions.

But in addition to endorsing increased industrial activity, most government planners were concerned about the entire nature of industrial production inside South Africa and, in particular, the use of labor. Mass production in the wartime factories created new "semiskilled" positions, which fell outside the racially defined legal classifications of "skilled" and "unskilled" labor previously obtaining inside South Africa. If racial stratification were continued, these new jobs would have to be classified as either exclusively for blacks or for whites, with serious ramifications for production costs in either case. Most government commissions were eager to reform the prewar labor structure, which they attacked as expensive and inefficient. The IARC privately laid out the principal criticisms against South Africa's traditional labor structure in detail:

> Skilled wages, as compared with other countries, were very high in South Africa. The overall cost of wages, however, was less in South

Africa than overseas as unskilled labour was so cheap. . . . Being cheap [Non-Europeans] were used in greater numbers than they should for work which could be done more competantly by the mechanisation of industry [and their use] kept industries on a non-precision manufacture basis, stopped mechanisation, and lowered production per labour unit. Thus, although on a short-term assessment, unskilled non-European labour was cheap, on a long-term basis it was expensive.[9]

Commission members went so far as to advocate the abolition of the "colour bar" and the use of African workers in semiskilled and even skilled positions. They believed that without refashioning South Africa's racially divided work force, further industrialization would merely extend unproductive and noncompetitive methods of operation.

Such revolutionary proposals, however, seriously threatened Smuts's political survival. As an official of the Directorate General of Supplies put matters, "The immediate future prosperity of the country, and possibly even the survival of the Government in power, will depend upon the successful handling of this difficult transition stage [to find employment for returned soldiers and those now employed on war production]."[10] Continued use of the dilutees in the postwar period was not politically acceptable. Smuts fully recognized the importance of the postwar employment situation and even pledged to pay unemployed white workers and soldiers a living wage until they could find work. But he balked at establishing statutory regulations that might either rule out the use of black labor in factory production and ensure high prices to local consumers or, alternatively, exclude whites from the definition of semiskilled labor, incurring the wrath of labor unions, the National Party, and the bulk of the white electorate. Fearing attack from voters and businessmen alike, Smuts refused to address the legal definition of semiskilled work and, as a result, left the future composition of the industrial work force an ambiguous component of economic growth.

Without a clear government policy concerning the direction of South African industrialization, van der Bijl and the other government planners were forced to devise their own strategies for shaping the country's economy. During the war they began to identify the two most serious challenges to their operations: first, the increasing propensity of their private partners to increase profits at the expense of state enterprises; and, second, the difficulties in exerting control over workers, black and white, under changing industrial conditions. While the first problem could be dealt with through financial means, the problems of labor costs and control proved much more formidable. As van Eck complained, "In defining practical lines of manufacture, the inability to predict wage rates, and, more partic-

ularly, output per worker and the direct cost of his labour per article manufactured, presents the biggest obstacle in the calculation of the economic
feasibility of the project."[11] African urban workers began to demand an
improvement in their wages and working conditions and proved increasingly adamant in calling for change. And white workers exercised all of
their legal rights through their trade unions to protect their elite status
within the work force. During the war, it would be necessary to formulate
new methods to lower costs and ensure control over changing modes of
industrial production.

The state corporations were central to South Africa's wartime redefin-
ition of the country's industrial methods and labor utilization. Most of the
increased production both for military and for civilian purposes was performed either by the state corporations or, through them, by their private
partners. During the war years van der Bijl and his managers were forced
to address changing labor requirements and problems with or without government guidance. If they could not bring labor under control, the country's war effort would fail. And their resulting policies were formulated to
carry the state corporations well into the postwar period. The policies
fashioned by van der Bijl, van Eck, and the managers of the state corporations in the war period would prove so successful that they would fore-
shadow the future direction of South African industrialization—growth
that would threaten neither the mining industry nor the white electorate
and would continue to disadvantage the growing numbers of black factory
workers.

War and the Costs of Private Production

As soon as South Africa declared war on Germany in September 1939,
the state corporations assumed a central role in meeting the country's
wartime needs.[12] South Africa had neither airplanes nor ships for its armed
forces and lacked adequate arms for its troops.[13] Moreover, the country
was suddenly deprived of most of the imported manufactured goods on
which it depended. Forced back upon local resources, Prime Minister
Smuts formed a Directorate General of War Supplies to meet the country's
military and industrial needs and put the man in charge of the state corporations, H. J. van der Bijl, at its head.[14] As South Africa's "economic
czar," van der Bijl had overall responsibility for ensuring that the country
obtained all of the military and economic goods necessary for its survival. Van der Bijl and his lieutenants—H. J. van Eck, Frederick Meyer,
and A. M. Jacobs—lost no time in organizing the manufacture and purchase of essential equipment, placing the state corporations at the center
of the country's war production. The demands on the corporations were

now considerable, especially as in June 1940 Smuts had agreed to supply the Allies with £1,000,000 worth of munitions each month, manufactured from Iscor's steel, and to acquire in exchange the ships and planes necessary for the defense of South Africa.[15]

With the outbreak of war, most of the steel imports that had caused van der Bijl so much concern in the 1930s came to a halt. Nearly half of the country's steel imports had come from Germany and the countries under its control, now wartime enemies. Supplies available from South Africa's allies contracted as well, British steel imports dropping from close to 250,000 tons in 1936 to less than 30,000 tons in 1941. Although the United States filled the gap at the beginning of the war, shipping more than 200,000 tons in 1940, by 1942 its contribution had fallen by half that amount.[16] Hoping to make up for the loss in imports, in 1941 van der Bijl hastily tried to arrange for the expansion of Iscor's annual production to 600,000 tons, approximately double its prewar capacity.[17] But it proved extremely difficult to obtain plant from overseas. Furthermore, the corporation had to shut down in turn each of its two blast furnaces for relining, operating in 1941 for three months with only one blast furnace. Because of such constraints, steel production that year amounted to only 316,000 tons.[18] Thus, despite the country's urgent demand for steel, the supply available was severely restricted due to Iscor's limited productive capacity.

Van der Bijl had to rely on production by local private companies to meet the country's immediate need for steel. Although he disliked the division of the steel market (with Iscor producing low-profit bulk goods and the private firms high-profit finished goods), it had been a basic cost of establishing state production without requiring enormous government subsidies or highly controversial protection policies.[19] In the context of wartime needs, van der Bijl had to depend even more heavily on the private firms, as they had the sophisticated machinery and the skilled workmen necessary for speedy production of finished armaments from raw steel. The only alternative to working with these firms would have been government expropriation, and that was not a politically attractive or viable option in the context of wartime needs. Indeed, the demand for war goods was so sudden that the country could not wait for the establishment of separate government plants. As the head of Technical Production at the Directorate of War Supplies, T. P. Stratten, explained in 1941, "the urgency of supply was such that to plan the programme ahead on the basis of first building special purpose plants for each of the items required . . . was quite unthinkable . . . the Technical Production Section 'farmed out' work on components to a large number of different shops."[20]

In all, Iscor entered into contracts with approximately forty private engineering firms for the production of military goods. Most of Iscor's armored plates went to Dorman Long (Iscor's major customer for plates before the war as well), which then engineered and reassembled them into military vehicles, bridges, and aircraft hangars.[21] Likewise, van der Bijl's Directorate of War Supplies established the country's major shell factory at Stewarts and Lloyds, Iscor's pipe and tube manufacturing partner, and spent more there on new plant than at any other nongovernmental "annex."[22] Usco produced bombs in its foundry as well as manufacturing bolts, nuts, and copper wire for defense requirements.[23] In addition, the government financed the expansion of SAR workshops, the new Central Ordnance Factory in Johannesburg, and several mine workshops, all of them enterprises that already had on hand skilled mechanics and specialized tools. By the end of 1942 van der Bijl had installed nearly £6,000,000 worth of state-purchased equipment at private factories producing war materiel.[24]

But the increased use of private firms to produce steel restricted Iscor's own operations more and more to the production of raw steel rather than manufactured steel goods. Although Iscor had been designed as a fully integrated steel mill to produce increasingly complex goods using its own products, the growing arrangements with the private firms caused Iscor to cut the process short, routing its raw billets to its partners rather than using them itself for further processing. As a result, by 1943 Iscor's output of steel billets had risen 35 percent over 1939's output, while the corporation cut back its own limited production of semifinished goods, such as merchant bars, as well as its finished rails (dropping from 66,312 tons in 1939 to 23,753 tons in 1943). To a much greater extent than before the war, Iscor had become a wholesale supplier of raw products to private enterprise.[25]

The result of such a development was declining financial returns for Iscor and growing profits for the private firms. The corporation's profits fell by nearly half between 1939 and 1942, despite price increases in 1941 and 1942.[26] With huge wartime demand and operating plant paid for and provided by Iscor, the corporation's private partners posted much better returns. They continued to supply the gold mines with such products as tubes, pumps, and castings but were able to expand production in general, due to their defense contracts. Those firms with defense contracts, such as Usco and Stewarts and Lloyds, took advantage of expanded production to hire increasing numbers of Africans in semiskilled work. All in all, output at both Usco and Stewarts and Lloyds more than doubled during the war, and profits rose considerably. Usco's profits grew by a third during the war, while Stewarts and Lloyds regularly paid 20 percent dividends on its ordinary shares.[27]

By contrast, those steel manufacturers that were not affiliated with

Iscor and did not have major defense contracts—Dunswarts, George Stott, and Scaw—all suffered falling rates of profit. They were cut off from access to Iscor's cheap steel, had no commensurate growth in production, and continued to rely almost solely on the gold mines for their sales.[28] It was clearly to the financial advantage of steel producers to do business with Iscor and the government, even though the strategic benefits to the country had to be offset by the weakening financial condition of the state corporation.

Escom found itself even more vulnerable to exploitation by private partners during the war. Expansion in manufacturing activity along the Rand also meant increasing demands for electricity throughout the war. And since most manufacturing took place in areas serviced by Escom, responsibility for increasing power generation fell to the state corporation. Escom, however, like Iscor, was constrained by van der Bijl's prewar agreements with private firms. In fact, the commission was even more limited by its arrangements with private companies than was Iscor, because Escom was under contract to sell all of its output on the Rand to one private company, the Victoria Falls Power Company. Indeed, practically all the electricity sold by the vfpc on the Rand was produced by Escom-owned power stations. When the vfpc had first started producing electricity in cooperation with Escom, the company's own four stations generated 50 percent of the electricity that the company sold. By 1939, however, its own production comprised only 13 percent of total sales, while by 1942 its proportion had dropped further, to 10 percent.[29] Moreover, the largest power plants, though owned by Escom, were operated under contract by the vfpc, with the result that the vfpc was able to use Escom's equipment rather than its own to generate power, cut its own overhead costs considerably, and make growing profits.

With Escom-owned plants providing the electricity, the vfpc took advantage of increasing wartime demand to raise the prices it charged its customers. The Rand gold industry was the company's largest customer, accounting for more than 80 percent of vfpc sales.[30] Prior to the war the vfpc (acting under government pressure) provided the mines with a complicated series of rebates that effectively reduced the actual price of electricity (as compared with prices charged other consumers) by about a third. During the war, however, the vfpc unilaterally did away with the rebates, arguing that special war taxes—which rose from a prewar figure of £161,000 annually to £1,747,000 during the war years—were cutting too severely into profits.[31] As Renfrew Christie has demonstrated, however, the company suffered no financial burden from the increased taxes and actually racked up increasing profits, which it kept hidden through imaginative bookkeeping procedures.[32] Indeed, with its operating costs remaining fairly stable throughout the war, the VFPC secured its profits largely by charging the mines three times the price it paid Escom for wholesale electricity. As Escom paid the operating costs of the power stations, the only additional charge borne by the VFPC was transmitting Escom's power into its own grid and distributing it across the Rand, a very small part of the costs of generating and supplying electricity.[33] During the war the VFPC's markup produced a gross profit on mining sales alone of £25,000,000.

Moreover, the VFPC was also expanding into industrial and municipal markets, where it could charge even higher prices for the electricity it purchased so cheaply from Escom. Among these new customers were the munitions factories established along the Rand by Iscor's engineering partners. The VFPC supplied electricity to Germiston, where two of the largest plants were located—Dorman Long and East Rand Engineering—as well as to the municipalities of Boksburg, Brakpan, Krugersdorp, Vereeniging, and, beginning in 1939, Johannesburg, where the remainder of the war plants were located. The VFPC did not provide electricity at a reduced price to these municipalities but charged them the "standard" price—which at 0.34d. per unit was approximately six times what it cost the VFPC to purchase the power directly from Escom.[34]

By the end of the war, the arrangement between Escom and the VFPC had netted the VFPC handsome profits, though bookkeeping measures still hid the full extent of the amount involved. In 1945 the VFPC's published accounts showed a profit of £582,050, and the company publicly declared a dividend of 47.5 percent on ordinary share capital. Within two years, however, as the result of government investigations, an additional £6,900,000 was suddenly discovered in the company's reserves.[35] By contrast, Escom at the end of the war posted a loss for the first time in its history.[36] Because of the marketing restrictions built into its prewar contractual agreement with the VFPC, the commission could not even supply directly the newly established munitions factories with cost-price electricity. Clearly, the agreements that had once enabled Escom to get access to consumer markets worked to the benefit of the VFPC and the detriment of the commission, the mines, and of South Africa's strategic needs.

Poor economic returns to the state corporations and problems of market access caused van der Bijl to reassess the value to Iscor and Escom of their contractual ties to private firms. While firms like Dorman Long and the VFPC had helped van der Bijl meet South Africa's strategic needs, the cost of doing business with them was becoming unacceptably high. Before the war van der Bijl had considered the development of close ties between state and private bodies, despite the short-term financial costs to the state corporations, necessary to the long-term development of the corporations. He was a strong believer in the need for the state corporations to work in concert with private enterprises, even to the extent of privatizing the state corporations themselves. And indeed both Iscor and Escom supplied goods and services to the private sector and would continue to do so long after the war; they could not afford to weaken the private companies or to antagonize private businessmen so long as these remained major customers for steel and electricity. Nevertheless, the nature of the agreements was stifling the expansion of the state corporations and draining them of their profits, markets, and even control over their own production. Furthermore, the private firms exploited their positions by raising prices to consumers, particularly to the gold industry in the case of the VFPC. The growth in wartime demand had exposed the serious limits of these agreements, raising problems for postwar cooperation.

During the war years van der Bijl began to move to establish a new basis for the operations of the state corporations by establishing monopoly control over the markets for electricity and steel. He took the most direct action in solving Escom's marketing problems by deciding to buy out the VFPC. Under the terms of both the 1910 Power Act and the 1922 Electricity Act, the government had the right to expropriate any private power company once its government-granted license had expired. Ever since the negotiations over the Klip station in 1933, van der Bijl had considered expropriation a desirable option. At that time he had confided to Hans Pirow, the government mining engineer, that "I intimated to the Power Company that the Commission intends opposing the granting of any further licenses to the Power Company and that the Commission would itself seek to obtain such Licences."[37] Since 1923 he had feared that the VFPC would try to establish a monopoly over the Transvaal's industrial areas in addition to the gold mines, thereby shutting the commission out of the entire Rand.[38] Such fears had been borne out during the war when the VFPC, relying to an ever-greater extent on Escom's power generation, had successfully captured a de facto monopoly of electrical supply over the mining areas and the new industrial market. Anticipating burgeoning demand for electricity after the war, van der Bijl was determined to prevent the VFPC from taking these new markets away from the commission as well.

In 1943, five years before expropriation could be legally carried out, van der Bijl began his campaign to take over the VFPC.[39] Writing to Smuts, he argued that the company's profits were antithetical to the spirit of the Electricity Act and urged that the company be forcibly acquired by Escom:

The underlying principle of the Electricity Act is that electricity shall be sold without profit for the benefit of the public and of industry in particular. In the developments that have taken place since then I have always borne in mind that the Falls Company's system must eventually be brought to comply with this condition. . . . Since the Power Company has been making very large profits, I take it that it would be the wish of the Government that the Falls Company be expropriated at the expiration of their Franchise.[40]

Furthermore, van der Bijl claimed that expropriation would result in "the saving to the Gold Mines alone . . . of the order of £2,000,000 per year."[41]

Yet strong opposition to van der Bijl's plans prevented their being put into force during the war. The VFPC denounced state expropriation as threatening the rights of private enterprise. The members of the Electricity Control Board, most of them tied to private companies and the mining industry, also remained unswayed by van der Bijl's arguments. The chairman of the ECB, Dr. S. A. van Lingen, who had long felt that Escom should be more fully under the control of his own organization, took up the old arguments of the SAR that the VFPC could supply electricity more cheaply than could the state corporation, and he persuaded the rest of his board that denying van der Bijl's request for government expropriation would result in lower power prices for the gold mines rather than higher.[42] Facing opposition from the ECB and from the VFPC, and with the gold industry as yet unconvinced that Escom's appropriation of the VFPC would lead to lower prices, van der Bijl dropped the matter during the latter years of the war.[43] But he remained determined on the basis of his wartime experiences that, once the political environment was suitable, he should compulsorily expropriate the VFPC and establish Escom as the monopoly producer and supplier of power to South Africa.

With regard to Iscor, it was impossible for van der Bijl to envisage gaining control over foreign producers in the same way as he could hope to use government powers to acquire the VFPC. The foreign manufacturers were clearly beyond the reach of the South African government, and they were far larger operations than the VFPC or any similar local operation. But with the outbreak of the war they had also withdrawn from the South African market, leaving considerable room for van der Bijl to plan major changes in South African steel manufacturing. Van der Bijl felt that Iscor should establish a vertically integrated operation, mining iron ore and coal, producing raw steel, and manufacturing the steel billets into finished products in mills and manufacturing works for which Iscor-controlled subsidiaries had provided the machinery. These plans, he believed, could be carried out with the assistance, and to the financial benefit, of foreign manufacturers.

Even before the outbreak of the war he had discussed his plans for establishing a South African heavy-engineering industry with representatives of the British firm of Ashmore, Benson and Pease in 1939. During the war, the difficulty of obtaining foreign machinery enhanced the attraction of his plans, and in 1944 he sent representatives to Europe and the United States to discuss his ideas. Van der Bijl was convinced that new agreements with foreign firms, unlike the existing relationships with such firms as Stewarts and Lloyds, Baldwins, and Dorman Long, would give Iscor far more control over the local market, because the foreign companies, rather than establishing their own operation in South Africa (as was the case with Dorman Long and others), would provide only the financial and technical expertise needed to enable Iscor to build up the steel industry. Under newly negotiated contracts, the overseas operations would sell Iscor the necessary plant and blueprints but would not enter the market themselves. Van der Bijl concluded the first of these new contracts in 1944 with an American company, the Mesta Corporation, which agreed to assist him in establishing a local firm (to be named the Vanderbijl Engineering Corporation—Vecor) to manufacture machinery in South Africa.⁴⁴ Van der Bijl then persuaded some of his old partners like Stewarts and Lloyds to invest in the new company by suggesting that if they did not do so Iscor would cut off their supplies of steel.⁴⁵

Van der Bijl had only begun to embark on his plans for transforming the nature of state intervention in the electricity and steel industries by the final days of the war, but his intentions were clear. He planned to eliminate as far as possible the partnerships with private capital that had been so necessary in the early years of the state corporations, so that Iscor and Escom would not be hindered in their operations by uneconomic marketing arrangements. He did not oppose private enterprise—indeed, he was already on record as favoring the privatization of the state corporations—but he did want to ensure that the state enterprises be payable operations, fully capable of controlling both the production and marketing of goods essential to the military and industrial strength of South Africa. But renegotiating partnerships, expropriating the VFPC, and establishing Escom and Iscor as the primary producers of electricity and steel were still very expensive projects, for which little direct state funding was available at the end of the war. If van der Bijl was to win the necessary support of politicians and businessmen (especially those in the gold industry), he would have to ensure that the state corporations themselves demonstrated that they were highly efficient and financially well-managed operations.

Controlling the Work Force

The main challenge to production costs at the state corporations came from labor. Prior to the war, van der Bijl had experienced serious problems in labor costs at Iscor, particularly because of the efforts made by white workers to renegotiate their conditions of employment. During the war, changes in production processes brought new challenges to the cost structure of the state corporations. As manufacturing production expanded rapidly throughout the country—the value of output jumping 53 percent between 1939 and 1944—it became apparent that old labor policies, based on strict race and skill differentiation, would not sustain such dramatic growth.[46]

Factories needed workers with certain skills and could not wait for white artisans to be found to do the work. Instead, during the war years, a growing number of factory jobs were filled by workers with limited training in particular tasks who were designated as "operatives"; they could operate but not assemble or repair the machinery on the factory floor. Whether white or black, these workers were crucial to the successful operation of the wartime factories. The appearance of the operatives confused the old racial divisions in the work force formerly defined by level of skill. The lines drawn between white artisans and black laborers were not reflected within the categories of operative tasks, yet white workers continued to enjoy far greater rights than blacks. Such developments caused considerable changes in the work-place policies of the state corporations, as van der Bijl and his lieutenants grappled with the issues of labor costs and control.

Iscor and the Demands of Continuous Production

The new problems of labor control under industrial expansion were best exemplified at Iscor. Because of the nature of steel production, Iscor's managers faced a range of labor problems. From the mining of iron ore through its conversion into raw steel, rolling into workable sizes, and final shaping into consumer products as well as fashioning and maintaining complicated machinery, Iscor's prewar operations required both skilled and unskilled workers, black and white, local and foreign. Due to van der Bijl's arrangements with the private steel firms during the war, which largely restricted Iscor's operations to the mining of iron ore and the rolling of raw steel into billets, the corporation was able to cut back on its use of skilled white labor and relied instead on a combination of black laborers and semiskilled white operatives.

At the same time, however, the managers of the mines and the rolling mills found that they had to develop a range of different labor policies in order to control increasing worker discontent and maintain high output levels. Pressed to keep production up while facing shortages of labor and supplies, as well as demands for wage increases from black and white workers, Iscor's management chose not to try to intimidate its work force—likely to be an unsuccessful strategy anyway—but adopted a flexible approach, alternating between coercion and conciliation, in its attempt to maintain control over its disparate work force.

Coercion at the Mines

One of the corporation's most important operations during the war, and one in which a largely homogeneous work force was employed, was its mining division. In response to military requirements in Europe, South Africa had agreed to provide the British government with 40,000 tons of iron ore per month from Iscor's own iron mine at Thabazimbi, almost double its normal output.[47] It was imperative that production not be disrupted, and, owing to the mine's isolated location in the northern Transvaal and its black migrant work force, the mine managers felt that they could take drastic steps to ensure worker productivity without fear of disrupting production.

The new demands for increased production at Thabazimbi quickly strained the ability of the management to provide housing and adequate care for the black workers. The number of miners jumped from 667 in February 1940 to two thousand in May 1941, while their housing, consisting of crude iron buildings, was not expanded proportionately.[48] These accommodations, termed "not satisfactory" even before the increase in employment, quickly became intolerable.[49] By May 1941, 2,504 cases of illness, including typhoid fever and pneumonia, had been reported in a six-month period. The mine averaged forty desertions per month—which on an annual basis amounted to one quarter of the work force.[50] Clearly, mine management needed to change its policies if order and efficiency were to be maintained.

But the corporation, beset by production targets and cost constraints, was more concerned with restraining its employees than with improving the conditions of their employment. The superintendent of the Thabazimbi mine, C. J. N. Jourdan, claimed to be thoroughly disgusted with his black workers and complained in graphic terms of their misconduct. Writing to Iscor's general works manager, Frederick Meyer, in 1942, Jourdan charged that his black employees were planting an "evil root and branch which is besmirching our beautiful and peaceful countryside. . . . It is disgusting to see strings of natives in all stages of drunkenness reeling and rolling up our beautiful avenue from 4 P.M. onwards on a Sunday evening, many of them tattered and torn as a result of fights, others bleeding and again easing themselves on the road as they waddle along and we are powerless to prevent this."[51]

In their attempts to control black workers, Jourdan and his white subordinates—against Meyer's stated wishes—often used corporal punishment. Such measures were, however, counterproductive. The inspector of native laborers, I. P. O'Driscoll, criticized the "terroristic activities" of the white supervisors and argued that "these assaults must eventually affect adversely the mine's labour supply and might be regarded as a predisposing cause of many . . . desertions."[52] In response to such criticism, Jourdan argued that more rather than less control over the workers was necessary, and he proposed "to fence in the entire compound and the entry into and the exit therefrom of all Natives will be controlled at a small office to be erected beside the gate."[53] Furthermore, he requested the establishment of a police station on the mine property, because "owing to the lack of any arrangements for . . . punishment, [the] employees without compunction absent themselves from work without leave or are drunk on duty, or refuse to work."[54] The superintendent of the mine hoped thereby, as many companies had done in the past, to prevent the black workers from leaving the compound, especially in search of liquor, and, if that was not possible, to have them punished severely with government sanction.

The government complied, providing even greater supervision over the mine's black workers, although the workers continued to protest against their conditions of employment. The Native Affairs Department proclaimed Thabazimbi a "labour area," necessitating regular review by a department official whose principal duty was to collect fees and taxes from black workers, amounting to approximately £5,000 per year.[55] Iscor proceeded with building its new, fenced-in compounds and police station, and in January 1944 the native commissioner commented that the police "had a very deterrent effect on the excessive beerdrinking and fights on the mines [and] the officials have proper control over persons, including employees, entering or leaving the compound."[56] Nevertheless, one year later the black miners took the unprecedented step of going on strike to protest their low wages and poor working conditions.[57] The strike was quickly put down by force, and many of the workers were dismissed. Control was maintained at the mine, but the price of such control was an unstable, ever-changing, and disgruntled work force.

Conciliation on the Factory Floor

Forceful methods of labor control that were effective at mines in remote parts of the country were not readily transferable to the corporation's Pretoria plant. At Thabazimbi, Jourdan could risk firing an employee who resented his working conditions; there was little training involved, and, as the native commissioner noted, "hundreds of Natives were waiting outside the Compound for work."[58] At Pretoria, however, Iscor employed a much wider range of workers: highly skilled foreign artisans and semiskilled local whites under union agreements as well as many black workers who performed jobs requiring training on specialized machinery.[59] None of these workers was easily replaced. Furthermore, at the Pretoria plant, unlike at the Thabazimbi mine, production was already unsettled due to problems in obtaining supplies essential for operation. In addition, plant production often shifted from one type of steel to another due to military requirements. At Thabazimbi, Iscor suffered from no such changes in the production process, simply mining iron ore on a continuous basis. The corporation could ill afford one more uncertainty at Pretoria—a high labor turnover accompanied by long training periods—to disrupt the essential production of steel billets for its partners and for South Africa's war effort. With most other factors of production in flux, Iscor's management needed stability in the factory work force.[60]

Early in the war van der Bijl subjected Iscor's most skilled workers to strict legal controls. With the outbreak of hostilities, highly trained white artisans were in great demand by the armed services as well as the mining and engineering industries. In consequence, men could pick and choose their jobs. Van der Bijl quickly moved to control the mobility of these workers. At van der Bijl's request in his capacity as director general of war supplies, Prime Minister Smuts in March 1941 placed all artisans in the country under the supervision of the controller of industrial manpower. The controller had the power to fix standard conditions of employment throughout the country and also to direct men to work at certain firms. Iscor soon benefited from the new regulations, as the controller of industrial manpower gave the corporation the highest priority for obtaining men due to its pivotal role in defense production.[61] Although some disputes arose, these workers were forced by threat of legal sanctions to accede to the arbitration of their grievances and were prohibited from striking.[62] Their wages were set relatively high, however, to compensate for official control, and as a result the Pretoria plant's general manager, Frederick Meyer, tried to keep their numbers as low as possible.

These regulations did not apply, though, to a large number of Iscor's artisans who were German and were considered to be enemy aliens subject to internment after the declaration of war on Germany in September 1939. Rather than lose these workers, Meyer established a separate workshop for them to perform important repair work on Iscor plant.[63] In a tenuous situation, the Germans proved easy to control and relatively cheap to employ, prompting the Iscor Board of Directors to continue operation of their workshop even after the war.[64] Thus, throughout the war Iscor, benefiting from the support of state officials, enjoyed relative peace and stability in its relations with its most skilled white workers.

But skilled workers were still relatively scarce during the war, and Iscor became more dependent upon its semiskilled, or operative, labor, especially at the rolling mills where the steel billets were produced. These workers were mostly local whites who had some training in operating the rolling machines that produced Iscor's billets. Although not highly trained, these men were responsible for manufacturing the bulk of Iscor's products during the war. Van der Bijl and Meyer had already tried to replace these whites with blacks prior to the war, believing that the blacks would prove a more malleable and cheaper work force. They had succeeded in filling 60 percent of the factory positions with blacks. Nevertheless, at the outbreak of the war the white operatives still held pivotal positions on the factory floor. They were neither under the direct control of the government as were the artisans, nor were they denied official recognition as were the black workers. Van der Bijl could not invoke government power against them, while Meyer had to respond to their demands for better conditions and higher wages. Under wartime conditions of strained supply and shifting production, these workers began to enjoy an increasing leverage over Iscor's management, which they were able to translate into greater job security.

Indeed, in 1941 the white operatives went on strike at the rolling mills over the issue of job security. The strike began when Meyer laid off one shift of men at the heavy rolling mill. He had shut down the blast furnaces for maintenance and, since he could neither produce nor import enough steel to keep the mills working at full production, he fired the men. In protest, the other two shifts went on strike, bringing to a standstill the plant's major productive division, where all of the billets for Iscor's partners were produced.[65] One hundred men were involved in the strike, and they demanded that Iscor guarantee their hours of work and hence their take-home pay.[66] Meyer claimed that this was impossible due to wartime difficulties in supplies and furthermore argued that the workers had no right to strike. He rebuked and threatened the workers, stating that "if these men on strike leave Iscor they will be going back to unskilled work as they are not artisans but rollers and should not take up the attitude of striking."[67] The workers ignored Meyer and continued their stoppage.

Unable to enforce his threat, Meyer had to give way. Facing the reality of firing one hundred men, retraining new employees, and running the risk of concerted action by the other operatives at a time when national demands for strategic steel products were intense, Meyer reached a compromise with the workers. He took the then extraordinary step of establishing an unemployment insurance fund for the operatives. In cooperation with their union, the South African Iron and Steel Trades Association, Iscor contributed equally with the employees to create the Iscor Daily Paid European Employees Lay-Off Wages Insurance Fund.[68] Thus, these workers were guaranteed their wages even if management had to dismiss them due to production problems. Acknowledging that he could not easily replace these men, Meyer in effect had to agree to increase the security of their position.

But while Meyer made considerable compromises to placate white operatives, he soon moved to undermine their position at the important rolling mills, essentially by "deskilling" the labor hierarchy at those divisions. In 1944, the Iscor Board of Directors decided to leave the Industrial Council for the Engineering Industry and establish a separate council exclusively for Iscor. Meyer, as the corporation's representative to the new body, soon succeeded in fashioning a labor agreement that radically altered the work force. The new agreement reflected not only an increase in the number of all employees at the mills, due to the successful completion of plant extensions, but also a significant shift in the conditions of employment for white operatives, including their level of training and the wages they would receive.

While the white operatives' union was satisfied that standard wages for whites throughout Iscor increased, from a median level of 1s. 10d. per hour to 2s. 4d. per hour, it acceded to the creation of a group of new positions— all of these in the mills where plant production was centered—which averaged only 1s. 6d. per hour, equal to new trainees' wages. Furthermore, to receive the standard wages detailed in the new labor agreement, white employees had to spend a considerably longer period in "training," at lower wages, than they had under the old agreement. In previously established jobs, the increased training period was commensurate with the growth in wages, reflecting about a one-third increase in both, thus really offering no gain for the workers involved. And in the new positions at the mills, the least skilled of all positions at Iscor, workers had to wait 450 shifts for their basic wages rather than the 200 shifts previously set as the corporation's standard training period.[69] Thus, Iscor delayed payment of higher wages to its long-standing employees while creating less skilled—and less expensive—positions for its new employees. While Meyer had agreed to the use of white operatives on the factory floor, he had also found a way to make them less expensive to hire and more easily replaceable.

Under these circumstances, Iscor began to hire more and cheaper white workers as, for the first time in the corporation's history, white employment began to rise faster than black.[70] Between 1934 and 1940 the percentage of white workers had dropped steadily from 55 percent of the total number of men employed to 38 percent.[71] By 1944, with Iscor's total labor force more than doubled, whites comprised 49 percent of the corporation's employees.[72] Only a small part of the white work force—13 percent—was skilled, as most of the growth in white employment took place in operative positions.[73] Through a mixture of legal controls, conciliation, and

deskilling, Meyer had finally given Iscor the appearance of being committed to the old policy of "civilised labour," yet without fundamentally raising the corporation's production costs or weakening its position at the
hands of organized labor.

At much the same time, the mid- to later war years, Iscor's Board of
Directors became increasingly concerned about the consequences of relying on considerable amounts of black labor in the steel plant. At the beginning of the war three unions had claimed to represent black workers in the
engineering industry, and one, the Non-European Confederation of Iron,
Steel, and Metal Workers' Union, continued throughout the war to press
claims for higher wages for blacks.[74] Wartime inflation hit black consumers hardest and spurred demands for higher wages in all industries.
Nevertheless, Smuts refused to recognize the black unions.[75] Even without
official recognition of the unions, however, constant worker demands
prompted Meyer to raise the wages of the general laborers—black factory
workers—four times, nearly doubling the hourly rate.[76] Indeed, even at the
end of 1944 the general business manager had complained to the Iscor
Board of Directors about the rising cost of black labor as one of the corporation's principal problems in accumulating any profit.[77] Unable to mollify
black demands as they could those of white workers through union-nego-
tiated compromises over conditions of labor, Meyer (with van der Bijl's
approval) chose to raise black wages, as well as to depend on white workers to a greater extent, to ensure peace and productivity.

Despite the growth in white labor, Iscor maintained its production cost
per unit until the end of the war. Although production costs had initially
jumped at the beginning of the war, once the ratio of white employees
began to rise there was no further erosion in the corporation's profits. This
was partly due to the fact that while the growth in white employment was
dramatic compared to the corporation's prewar attempts to decrease the
number of white workers, the bulk of the factory work force remained
low-paid black workers. And although the new white workers earned far
more than any blacks, they still earned significantly less than the skilled
workers, whose numbers were not increased in proportion to the entire
work force. Moreover, the expansion in Iscor's overall production created
economies of scale that offset increased labor costs. Thus, Iscor's labor
policies succeeded in stabilizing production at its mills as well as protecting the corporation's financial position.

Escom and Black Demands

While Meyer largely avoided confrontation with black factory workers
at Iscor, managers at Escom and the vfpc were forced in 1944 to deal

much more directly with the problem of controlling black factory workers. At that time, black workers at the power stations along the Rand went on strike in protest against their low wages. Under the terms of van der Bijl's agreements with VFPC, the private company operated all of these stations and, in reasoning consistent with the historical development of the VFPC, these workers were governed by the same laws regulating mine workers. During the war, however, black workers at the stations were engaged in military production, and many performed tasks similar to those in other engineering workshops. Yet their wages were much lower, in conformity with those in the mining industry. As Deborah Posel argues generally for urban African workers during this period, low wages rather than unemployment were the major problem under inflationary wartime conditions: "This mixture of desperation and disaffection proved explosive," and African workers continually protested their situation throughout the war, even at the government-owned power stations.[78]

Discontent at the power stations had first emerged in November 1942, when the government raised the minimum wage for blacks working in urban industries but specifically excluded mine and power-station workers. Responding to the inflation that wracked the country, hitting urban areas hardest, Wage Determination No. 105 more than doubled the minimum wage for unskilled black workers in the Johannesburg area. Workers in the gold mines and at the power stations, however, were specifically excluded from the provisions of the wage determination. The mining industry had argued successfully that because their workers were housed in compounds and supplied with food, they were insulated from the effects of inflation and therefore had no need for a pay raise. But the families of these workers, in the words of the workers' union representatives, could barely survive on the "small margin between their earnings and the cost of living . . . in the native territories or the rural districts."[79]

Demanding an increase in their wages, the power-station workers threatened to go on strike in January 1943. The general manager of the VFPC, T. G. Otley (who had succeeded Bernard Price in 1936), agreed to meet with the employees to hear their grievances. Otley had been with the VFPC for years and had himself "scabbed" during the 1914 strike, being later rewarded with an increase in his salary.[80] Otley was hardly sympathetic to the employees' demands, and he determined that "no concessions could be made in the way of pay on the grounds that their wages were adequate for the type of service rendered and the conditions under which they worked."[81] In response to this decision, the employees at the company's main Rand engineering workshop at Rosherville went on a hunger strike to bring home the seriousness of their grievances. As a consequence, Prime Minister Smuts promised to initiate a government inquiry into their wages in order to judge if the wage determination should be extended.[82] In the meantime, the workers agreed to wait for the government's findings before taking further action.

But the government commission spent more than a year investigating the situation, with the result that the power-station workers went on strike in protest. The chairman and the secretary of the African Gas and Power Workers' Union, Gana Makabeni and D. K. Mfili, respectively, had been working to convince the commission of the workers' right to higher wages, and they counseled the union members against striking. Their pleas went unheeded, and in December 1943 they warned the government that the workers would strike if the commission's report were not issued immediately. By the middle of January 1944 the workers were pressing for a strike against the recommendations of union officials, who wanted to continue negotiations.[83] Acting without the sanction of their union, more than two thousand workers at five of the VFPC-operated stations scattered along the Rand and in Vereeniging simultaneously went on strike for higher wages on 21 January 1944. Beginning at 1 A.M., two hundred black workers at the Brakpan station went on strike, demanding higher wages. By 6 A.M. the black workers at Simmer Pan and Rosherville, the other two Rand stations, were also on strike, and by 1 P.M. the VFPC notified the government that the workers at the two stations in Vereeniging were also out.[84] All of the VFPC-owned stations as well as Escom's Klip and Vaal stations were affected, leaving only Escom's Witbank station untouched.

With five of the six power stations servicing the Rand out on strike, South Africa's gold-mining industry as well as most of the country's defense and engineering operations faced the threat of being closed down. While the workers hoped to take advantage of the situation and exercise strong leverage against the company and the government, they found that their strategy had already been anticipated and was quickly countered. Over the course of the previous month, December 1943, Otley and the minister of mines, C. F. Stallard, had agreed that the government would provide the company with the necessary workers in the event of a strike. In consequence, as soon as the strike began, the government dispatched the Native Military Corps to the power stations and succeeded in preventing any disruption in service.[85] The company was well satisfied with the situation, believing that the strike "would fizzle out in the course of a few days."[86] Smuts, however, saw the use of troops as a temporary measure and, while promising police protection for any strike breakers, refused to keep the soldiers at the power stations for more than one day.[87] The Chamber of Mines likewise refused to provide any temporary labor, and Otley was forced to negotiate with the workers or risk shutting down the stations.[88] He succeeded in persuading the workers to wait for the government report in the hope that its conclusion would bring them higher wages.[89]

The strike sent a powerful message to the government concerning the future of the black urban work force. These workers, migrant laborers brought in from rural areas on short-term contracts, had quickly grasped the inequities of their pay situation as compared to that of other industrial workers and did not accept the injunction that, as black migrant workers, their pay should logically conform to that of black miners. The plight of rural Africans was becoming increasingly difficult at this time, with over-crowding in the Native Reserves and a nationwide drought in 1942 inten-sifying problems. These black migrant workers and their families were entirely reliant on their urban wages and could not live with the fiction that the families were self-supporting in the reserves. Their desperation and anger had quickly been transformed into action, much to the surprise of white officials. Indeed, without assistance from the union organization, they had successfully staged a strike at five different facilities, involving large numbers of workers. As the South African manufacturing industry developed and rural conditions worsened, the government could expect more such protests from black workers who refused to be treated as harshly as the black miners were. Moreover, it was inevitable that black miners would themselves follow the lead of their peers in the manufactur-ing industry and likewise rebel.

But the government was not ready to acquiesce to the demands of black workers in the electricity industry, especially so long as any rise in wages inevitably had direct consequences for the price of power charged to the gold mines. When the members of the Witwatersrand Mine Natives' Wages Commission recommended meeting worker demands for higher wages, the government rejected their findings out of hand.[90] The crux of the matter, as put by the government mining engineer, H. S. H. Donald, was "the capacity of the mining industry to contribute a sufficiently large sum to Revenue Account." Any diminution in gold revenues would undercut the government's finances, and, as Donald stated flatly, "It has become increasingly apparent for some years that the interests of the state in the gold mines are considerably greater than the interests of the sharehold-ers."[91] Not only would the electricity company pass on an additional £70,000 in costs to its mining customers, but such pay raises could also prompt similar action at collieries adjacent to the power stations—adding another £200,000 in costs.[92]

Smuts agreed that the mining industry was central to the issue of black wages at the VFPC's power stations and paradoxically invoked an Afrikaner nationalist metaphor in asserting that "the mining industry is so to speak 'the ark of the covenant.'"[93] In other words, nothing could be done that would in any way impinge on the cost structure of the mines. Otley went along with this argument, conjuring dark images of what was to come if a line were not drawn, preferably at any attempt to raise wages in his company's industry. Forecasting that the vfpc employees were only the "spearhead of attack," he boldly offered to "fight the issue out with them—numbering as they do only 2500/2600 native employees—rather than run the risk of having to do battle with the 300,000 or more natives employed in the Mining Industry at a later date."[94] The government accepted his recommendation to "disregard the findings of the Commission as far as they apply to the vfp natives."[95]

The black union leaders turned to the white South African Trades and Labour Council to present their case.[96] Although Labour Council representatives met on behalf of the black workers with Prime Minister Smuts regarding implementation of the commission's recommendations, nothing was done, a development that caused no surprise to Otley, who believed that the white unionists were "not, in his opinion, genuine in their desire that [wage increases for black workers] should be carried out."[97] Indeed, during the strike the white workers had stayed at their power-station posts, stopping short only of "doing work normally carried out by natives."[98] Receiving no satisfaction from Smuts or the Labour Council, union leader Dick Mfili tried to rally support among the workers, and unrest among the employees continued through to the end of the war. Such protest action had only limited effect since Otley, believing that the union leaders were out of step with their followers and were "undoubtedly causing serious unrest among our Native employees, who otherwise would be perfectly content with their lot," had the most outspoken workers sacked.[99] While the system of outright labor repression had been shaken and had proven costly, it still held sway at the power stations throughout the war.

Although Smuts refused to deviate from the traditional treatment of African workers inside South Africa—an assumption of no skills, no permanence, and no individual importance—the power-station strike exemplified changing circumstances that the South African state would be forced to recognize. Industries in the country's cities were growing during the war years, and their labor needs were attracting rural Africans, who by 1946 outnumbered whites in the cities. The urban industries could easily draw upon the growing numbers of impoverished rural Africans for their work force, but the migrant labor model, which argued for low African urban wages because Africans drew support from the rural areas, could not be sustained. And protests and disruptions of production were less tolerable under increasingly demanding methods of production, which required at least semiskilled work to be performed by low-paid African workers. As industrial development increased and industries and work forces came into close geographical proximity on the Rand, the likelihood of organized and extensive labor agitation grew. Indeed, by 1946 the Rand had erupted in an industrywide strike by Africans in the gold-mining industry, putting the lie to their supposed acquiescence.

While Smuts may not have endorsed the structural reorganization of the South African work force, or even any significant reform, van der Bijl and his managers, particularly H. J. van Eck, learned some valuable lessons from the power-station strike. First, it appeared that isolation of workers would be a more effective strategy in stemming unrest. Otley, for example, noted that "our natives employed at Witbank remained at work. . . . I think, due that [sic] being nearly 100 miles away from Johannesburg they were less subject to outside influences."[100] Second, it appeared that unions, rather than being the nemesis of employers, as Otley and others often argued, could in fact be used to defuse worker agitation, often heading off profit-threatening strike action. After all, the African Gas and Power Workers' Union had consistently counseled moderation in the face of worker demands for action. The lessons of the power workers' strike were not lost upon van der Bijl and his successors, who in turn began to formulate policies of industrial decentralization and union cooperation to ensure industrial peace.

Toward the end of the war, van der Bijl began to address the reorganization of the industrial work force despite Smuts's lack of guidance. He moved quickly to establish the groundwork for a stable labor supply at Vecor by proposing the wholesale use of operatives at the new plant. In fact, the general manager of the new concern, O. J. Hansen, formerly at Iscor, stated in 1945 that without the use of the operatives "it will be almost useless to carry on with the proposed establishment of the Works." He requested the controller of industrial manpower to sanction the "training as soon as possible [of] machinists specialised in one or other type of machine," who would be paid on a bonus system.[101] The chief inspector of labor at the Department of Labor agreed with Hansen, stating that "the whole success of this venture hinges upon the availability of labour," and he proposed that the department put pressure on the artisanal labor unions to accept the new class of operatives.[102]

Van der Bijl also began to move Iscor's and Escom's operations away from the unrest-prone labor markets of the Rand and Vereeniging into remote areas, where labor could be more easily controlled. When the commission again began to build stations following the war, it invariably chose isolated locations, shipping its labor in from the reserves. Likewise, Iscor located all of its postwar extensions south of Vereeniging, creating an entirely new town, Vanderbijlpark. Unable to scatter its factories in isolated areas, Iscor created instead a "company town" directly under its control. Through a combination of new financial and marketing arrangements and new labor policies, the state corporations during the war had radically altered their strategies for survival and, ultimately, the very nature of state economic intervention.

The Industrial Development Corporation

Nowhere was the change in the state corporation policies better exemplified than in the operations of the youngest state corporation, the Industrial Development Corporation. Also chaired by van der Bijl, the IDC was established in 1939 to lure overseas investment capital into local ventures. The third state corporation was brought into being with none of the controversy marking the inception of Iscor and Escom, although it fundamentally embodied a far closer relationship between the government and private business. The IDC was to fund the establishment of private, not state, corporations in partnership with private businessmen. At the time of the IDC's founding in 1939, this approach conformed to van der Bijl's hopes of closer cooperation with private capital. During the war years, however, the expansion of the IDC was constrained by the unavailability of plant as well as of investment capital, and the IDC's managing director, H. J. van Eck, worked at studying the long-term potential of import substitute industries in South Africa.[103]

By the end of the war van Eck had completed plans for the establishment of several private industrial ventures, including the manufacture of textile yarns, food yeast, paper (pulp), and masonite.[104] All of these ventures were to be established by the IDC in cooperation with foreign firms, and in one case with the Anglo-American Corporation, but they were not allowed to enter into a marketing partnership. Learning from the experiences of Escom and Iscor, van der Bijl required that the private partners invest funds and get dividends but not have a share of the new markets. Furthermore, all of the new industries established by the IDC were to have a monopoly of production and supply within South Africa, their sole competition coming from imports.[105]

Van Eck was also well aware of the importance of labor to any incipient industry, and in the case of the only enterprise that he actually brought to fruition during the war years, the textile yarn industry, he opted for production by rural black workers over urban labor. He was familiar with the potential problems in using black factory workers. He had been a member of the Iscor team negotiating with the 1936 Industrial Conciliation Board that had dealt with white union protests over the use of blacks in the factory. Therefore, he commissioned the IDC's technical adviser, A. Cornish-

Bowden, to prepare a study of all of the factors concerning labor in the textile industry. The resulting memorandum, "Location of the Cotton and
Wool Spinning Plant," was based on the premise that "the textile industry
must be considered in the spinning and weaving stages at any rate, to be
almost entirely a native industry." Cornish-Bowden advised that "the
locality must be such that labour conditions in existing industries in the
area are not upset by such a policy," that is, by the use of black operatives
in the factory. Therefore, he recommended that the industry should move
to the rural areas rather than ship black migrant workers into the already
industrialized cities. Some rural locations were discounted, however, especially those near white farms, because the new industry "would create
competition with farm labour. This is deemed undesirable in consideration
of the present state of the farming community." The ideal location, according to Cornish-Bowden, would be in an area with "a settled native population in the vicinity upon which to draw, and a larger hinterland of native
reserves, etc., which can be drawn upon in the future and in which products can be marketed." Under these conditions, the workers would not be
"transient and a tradition of life-long employment can be built up
amongst the population in the area. Natives must not always be wanting
to return to their kraals." Rather than give the impression that such a location might also be used to improve the economic conditions of the black
community, he ended his memorandum with the injunction that "it must
be remembered that our job is first and foremost to promote efficiency in
the spinning and weaving of cotton and wool. To mix this job too inti-
mately with the broader issue of the national development of the natives
is undesirable in that it will detract the attention of the management from
the issue of industrial and technical efficiency."[106] Using black rural workers was good business, not social policy.

By 1944 the IDC was prepared to make a decision concerning the location of the textile plants and, following Cornish-Bowden's suggestions,
placed them next to large Native Reserves. Noting the low wages at Uitenhage, as opposed to Port Elizabeth, in the eastern Cape near the Transkei
and Ciskei reserves, van Eck urged the corporation's Board of Directors in
1944 to establish its wool-processing industry there. He went even further
with the cotton-spinning plant, to be established in King William's Town,
"within the native territories on land to be leased from the Native Trust,"
which he touted as providing "industrial employment for native families
in their home area and an alternative livelihood for those natives who are
unable to get adequate support from the soil."[107] The Native Trust agreed
to build "a model settlement village" nearby, which would both draw in
workers and relieve the IDC of the cost of housing. Van Eck favored the use
of black operatives and the assurance of a vast labor pool, both of which

could be secured by locating operations in the rural areas near the homes of workers.

The war years had created opportunities for the industrial expansion of South Africa that van der Bijl had envisioned. Yet the war had also exposed the serious contradictions inherent in such development. With an unlimited market for their goods, local manufacturing saw their net output more than double, constrained only by access to supplies.[108] By the end of the war van der Bijl could foresee the local manufacture of industrial machinery to fuel further economic growth. However, the expansion of industrial capacity had only come about through the enrichment of private partners, a trend that would lead to high local costs for development and eventually to a renewal of successful foreign competition for local markets. And such competition would again raise the question of lowering labor costs and the differing dilemmas of control over white and black workers. In order to continue South African industrialization, costs would have to be brought under control either by cutting private profits or by formulating a successful model of labor control—or both. It remained to the government to devise strategies, already underway at the state corporations, to attempt to solve the contradictions of South African industrialization.

CHAPTER SIX

The State Corporations and Apartheid

In the years immediately following World War II, South Africa experienced a crisis that is most widely known for its political repercussions and the introduction of the dramatic legal mechanisms for enforcing racial separation known as apartheid. These changes, however, were not entirely of political origin but were brought about by profound economic and social transformations. For the first time in the country's history, manufacturing accounted for the largest share of output, eclipsing both agriculture and mining. At the same time, Africans were moving into cities in unprecedented numbers, constituting a majority in the urban areas by 1946.[1] These developments focused attention on unresolved long-term problems in South Africa: the country's economic growth was still dependent on the participation and labor of disenfranchised and low-paid black workers. Even the new industries that could provide jobs for white South Africans needed to employ blacks if they were to make a profit. These contradictions were increasingly addressed by politicians in the postwar period and eventually led to decisive policies intended to nurture successful industrial development, ensure white access to the rewards of such development, and maintain control over the African workers who made it all possible.

In the years after World War II the direction of South African economic growth appeared to change, with serious financial and social implications. Overall, the manufacturing sector experienced the greatest growth, surging ahead of mining for the first time. This growth was primarily accounted for by one industry, metals products, at the expense of other segments of manufacturing. For example, while metals production grew as a percentage of overall manufacturing output, food processing, textiles, and wood furniture all decreased in the decade following the war.[2] While this would apparently indicate a shift toward the production of industrial goods—those that could be used by other industries—and therefore evidence of an economy moving toward greater industrial self-sufficiency,

133

local metals production was matched by an unprecedented increase in imports of metals products.[3] In other words, local production was not meeting demand. In fact, it may have accounted for a dramatic increase in imports, as both the economist S. H. Frankel, and the next chairman of Anglo-American, Harry Oppenheimer, argued at the end of the war that manufacturing was not self–sufficient but was instead dependent on imported inputs of raw materials and machinery.[4]

As manufacturing output continued to grow after the war, so too did the country's balance of payments problems, leading to recurrent crises in fiscal 1948/49, 1953/54, and 1957/58.[5] The crises were averted in the short run through currency devaluations and restrictions on imports; in the long run the only answer was to increase exports. However, the two principal exports remained wool and gold, and while those products enjoyed healthy markets following the war, they did not reflect development toward a self-sustaining economy. The fear of many, again as expressed by Harry Oppenheimer, was that "far, therefore, from secondary industry offering an alternative to take the place of mining in our economy, the fact is that the prosperity of gold mining and the other primary exporting industries is a prerequisite and a condition of our industrial development. . . . Manufacturing industry will only be able to serve as a substitute for the wasting asset of our mining industry if it is able to increase substantially its contribution to our export trade." The only way to increase exports, argued Oppenheimer, was to reduce costs, and that required "greater efficiency and a large internal market."[6]

In South African terms, this prescription implied the creation of an African industrial work force and an African consumer market. Even in 1946 it appeared that Oppenheimer's solution might not be far off, as an unprecedented number of Africans moved into the cities, exceeding whites for the first time, and were employed in the manufacturing sector. The percentage of whites in such jobs continued to fall—a general trend, with some variations, since at least the 1930s—as more Africans became "production workers."[7] Africans entering the cities could provide cheaper labor for manufacturing industries as well as a large local consumer market, apparently the answer to the country's efforts to become economically self-sustaining. The only problem would be how to protect white benefits in the face of expanding African participation in the economy and the production of the country's wealth.

The growing contradictions between desired expansion and control forced all South African politicians to address the future economic role of urban Africans. Two opposing approaches to these problems were presented by the dominant white parties, Smuts's United Party and D. F. Malan's Herenigde Nasionale Party (Reunited National Party—HNP). The Smuts government accepted that Africans in the cities were there to stay, while the HNP proposed strict separation in principle. Despite these substantive differences, neither party was able to formulate specific methods to achieve their principles.[8] Smuts was the first to offer a strategy for African urbanization, in the 1946 Native Laws Commission Report, known as the Fagan Report, which acknowledged that the African urban population was "a fact" and that total segregation was not feasible. Rather than accepting unrestricted African urbanization and its attendant political implications, however, the Fagan Report offered weak compromises, implying that Africans should voluntarily honor influx control provisions and remain in the countryside unless they were assured employment in the cities.[9] In other words, they could enter the cities to work, but for nothing else.

Alternatively, the Sauer Report, written by the HNP in 1947, demanded the removal of Africans from white urban areas while at the same time acknowledging that continued African integration into the economy was necessary to ensure growth.[10] The Nationalists wanted Africans to go on working for whites, just as did Smuts, but not necessarily in the cities. Both parties were reluctant to shut the door completely or, alternatively, to open it wide to a permanent urban African industrial work force, although both acknowledged the necessity of employing Africans in industry.

But the Nationalists were far more aggressive in arguing that the government, not private industry, should take control over the process of African urbanization, which they felt had thus far been dictated by private businessmen, equated with "foreigners." Although there were considerable divergences within the HNP on particular issues, fear over the general direction taken by the South African economy was expressed by L. J. du Plessis at the Volkskongres in 1939, when he stated that Afrikaners were no longer ready "to tolerate the destruction of the Afrikaner volk in an attempt to adapt to a foreign capitalist system, but to mobilise the volk to capture this foreign system and adapt it to our national character."[11] The economic interests of the volk were not uniform, however, and the HNP faced the same contradictions within its party as were faced at large: while Afrikaner workers feared losing their jobs to African workers, Afrikaner employers in both agriculture and industry needed cheaper black workers to increase their profits. Rather than achieve these goals though the interaction of economic forces, which they felt were weighted against Afrikaners, HNP politicians believed that direct government control would be necessary. In particular, the government should step in and control—and discourage—African urbanization.[12] While such control would certainly help farmers and white workers, its effect on urban industries was obviously a problem. The HNP was prepared to take bold steps to bring African economic integration under control, yet the party still could not reconcile segregation and economic development within a coherent program.

When the white voters turned to the Nationalists in 1948, Malan and his colleagues were given the chance to shape and control "this foreign system." However, they came to rely more heavily on previous government experience than on party rhetoric in formulating apartheid's economic structure. The Nationalists were faced with the task of implementing their contradictory goals of white economic prosperity and effective racial segregation. With the expansion of manufacturing industries, the role of African workers—on the shop floor, in the cities, and as possible consumers—could not be dismissed. How could control over the economy and over these crucial workers be effected within the parameters of exclusive white rule? Early in their administration, the new National Party rulers moved to gain undisputed control over all government instruments of power, including the state corporations. But rather than completely change the direction of state corporation policies, the apartheid ideologues instead learned from the experiences of these firms. Many of the subsequent economic policies implemented under apartheid were being formulated in fact well before 1948 by van der Bijl and his colleagues.

In the postwar period each of the three state corporations pursued distinct strategies to solve the dilemmas faced by the nation as a whole. None of the state corporations—Escom, Iscor, and the IDC—were immune from the problems faced by the rest of the South African economy: high inflation, a backlog of demand for imported machinery, political pressures from would-be white employees, and increasing demands from an urbanized black work force. The first step taken by van der Bijl at the end of the war was to move all three corporations toward monopoly control in their respective fields. He wanted to avoid the problems attendant on competition and private partnerships that had plagued the corporations during the war. These efforts presented the Nationalists with the type of control they wanted, even if it came at a price and under certain circumstances that they questioned.

It was the labor policies of the state corporations, however, that most clearly presented the new government with options for the future. Each state firm pursued unique strategies based on its individual history and nature of production, with strikingly varied rates of success. The IDC attempted the most innovative industrial restructuring, using African workers in factories requiring moderate capitalization. Van Eck employed Africans as operatives, semiskilled workers who could produce finished manufactured goods. The twist in IDC policies was that the corporation established its factories outside the urban areas, near Native Reserves, providing a possible answer to growing concerns over African urbanization.

Iscor, on the other hand, operated in the heart of the expanding industrial areas in the Vaal triangle (the Pretoria-Witwatersrand-Vereeniging region), employing both whites and Africans in a shifting industrial hierarchy. Drawing on urban Africans and attempting to balance the demands of African and white workers, Iscor policies addressed continued African urbanization. The answer at Iscor was to move to a labor structure defined solely by race without regard for skill, privileging white workers but still using blacks in critical aspects of production. Escom was an entirely different case and ultimately proved to be the most successful of the three. Expanding rapidly after the war, the commission increasingly mechanized operations and avoided employing workers other than technicians, at the same time moving out of urban areas and closer to the rural coalmines that fed its generating plant. Providing an ominous lesson for the continuing success of South African industrialization, state corporation policies foreshadowed various government attempts to enforce apartheid through industrial decentralization, job reservation, and increasing mechanization.

The Failure of Rural Industries

Following the war the IDC pioneered new policies intended to address long-range national social goals and economic development as the means to social stability. Chaired by H. J. van Eck, the IDC was heavily influenced by the findings of the Social and Economic Planning Council (SEC), which van Eck also chaired, and whose reports addressed the importance of industrial development as the solution to many of the country's growing social problems. In particular, the SEC favored the growth of consumer industries, which could lower the cost of living and provide large numbers of jobs, thereby defusing the increasing competition between blacks and whites for scarce resources. The industries van Eck chose to pursue through the IDC, notably textile manufacture, fitted SEC recommendations and relied more heavily on labor than capital, in particular on semiskilled operatives. The IDC established two textile factories, Fine Wool Products to produce woolen yarn and flannel and Good Hope Textiles to produce cotton cloth. The problem that would arise at both of the IDC factories was how to ensure a measure of control over labor costs—and the laborers themselves—in order to secure industrial success.

At first, IDC ventures into textile production enjoyed a natural monopoly as well as fulfilling national economic requirements. Although South Africa had a long history of garment and blanket manufacture, the materials required for clothing production, including cotton and woolen yarns, had to be imported, as there was no local processing industry.[13] During the war the IDC had established a small plant for scouring wool and had

ordered equipment for wool and cotton spinning. By 1946 its "textile project" represented by far the corporation's largest, and most rapidly expanding, investment, at a combined authorized level of £1,000,000.[14] The IDC
established two plants in partnership with foreign manufacturers for the
manufacture of cotton and rayon and a third on its own for the spinning of
woolen yarns. Hoping to satisfy the local demand for cloth, the IDC
appeared to be filling an urgent need in the South African economy.

But van Eck and his planning staff failed to appreciate the very significant level of competition involved in textile manufacture. Unlike steel
production or electricity generation, textile plants required relatively little
capital. For example, by 1950 the total value of seventeen textile mills
inside South Africa was only £5,393,073, compared to the start-up costs of
£5,000,000 and £8,000,000, respectively, at Iscor and Escom.[15] Furthermore,
as a basic consumer product, textiles—unlike steel or electricity, which
were used primarily by industry—enjoyed a flexible and expanding market.
As a result, competition on an international scale had been fierce for many
years, and it intensified after the war. Japanese textiles in particular threatened to flood the South African market at prices well below those at which
the IDC's Good Hope Textiles (established in 1946) and Fine Wool Products
(established in 1944) could compete. Japanese cotton sold for 13d. or 14d.
per yard, as against 24d. for the South African product, and Japanese wool
flannel sold for 14s. per yard, as against 25/6 for Fine Wool's product.[16] At
the same time as cheap foreign products competed for South Africa's market, local manufacturers, attracted by the postwar demand for clothing and
facing no large start-up costs, began production. By 1947 the IDC factories
had eight local competitors: three new cotton manufacturers (Frame, Hor-
rocks, and Dodds) and five new woolen manufacturers (Hex River, Tootal
Broadhurst, Fothergill, Union Spinning, and Cape of Good Hope).[17] To
make matters worse, all of the local manufacturers produced similar goods
rather than different types of textiles and vied for identical markets.[18]

Intense competition aggravated other problems van Eck encountered in
the textile industry by increasing the pressure to lower costs in order to
meet the competition. He soon discovered the very restricted limits the
IDC enjoyed in controlling costs in the textile industry. Unlike Iscor and
Escom, the IDC did not control the price or the manufacture of the raw
materials necessary for production. Rather than the long-term supply contracts for coal or the direct ownership of mines enjoyed by those state corporations, the IDC had to buy wool from South African farmers and cotton
from abroad, all at fluctuating world prices. It was therefore impossible to
plan production on the basis of stable prices, let alone to try to control
those costs. Indeed, the Board of Trade and Industries recommended that
the government support the local cultivation of cotton, to stabilize prices

as well as to save £3,000,000 in foreign exchange.[19] The position at Fine Wool was particularly acute, due to the instability of wool prices following the war and their rapid increase.[20] In 1947 the IDC Board of Directors decided to cut back on production rather than operate the factory using the currently expensive wool.[21] By 1950 raw wool cost 15/1 per yard of cloth produced, higher than the total price of the Japanese cloth.[22] The situation continued, with the price of wool steadily rising until 1952, when it began a slow and erratic decline.[23]

Furthermore, at the marketing end of textile manufacture, the new state corporation found itself face to face with a diffuse consumer market rather than the industrial customers with which Iscor and Escom dealt in bulk. The textile industry demanded an extensive marketing organization to distribute IDC products to consumers through various merchants scattered throughout the country. Fine Wool found it particularly difficult to compete with the large range of products put out by British manufacturers, with the result that British yarn accounted for nearly 75 percent of all consumer sales.[24] By 1953, Fine Wool, accepting that its own sales organization "was not entirely suitable to the class of customer with which it had to deal," sought to reach a marketing arrangement with the British firm of Patons and Baldwins.[25] The foreign firms, long dominant in the local market, had developed successful marketing organizations, which reinforced that dominance.

In short, low capital requirements made it relatively easy for the IDC to set up a textile industry, but just as easy for private competitors to set up their own operations. Moreover, local state and private producers had to face fierce competition from the booming overseas textile industry, particularly from Japan, which produced goods at prices no local manufacturers could match. Finally, textile production was not a simple matter of making one type of product for one type of customer but a highly complex structure of hundreds of different products for an equally variable market. The IDC could not easily dominate that market without an overwhelming advantage, one that van Eck hoped could be found in low labor costs.

The High Costs of Rural Labor

The IDC's plans for the establishment of the textile industry had been based on and partially motivated by a desire to use rural black labor, isolated from the industrial centers of South Africa. In 1942 the IDC's technical adviser, A. Cornish-Bowden, had informed the corporation's Board of Directors that "it is improbable that an economic [textile] industry can be founded in the Union upon any other basis [than native labour]."[26] In consequence, Fine Wool was located at Uitenhage with due regard for the local availability and lower wage rates of black workers as well as its proximity to the major source of wool in the country.[27] And Good Hope Textiles was established within a Native Reserve, at King William's Town, specifically for the purpose of using rural black workers.[28]

Almost immediately following the formation of Good Hope Textiles in 1946, however, the Textile Workers' Union, representing white and Coloured workers, raised objections to the IDC's rural-labor policy.[29] Indeed, the union had been trying since 1937 to reach a national wage agreement for the entire industry, and union officials believed that they were on the verge of such agreement when the IDC entered the picture. The union, as well as many employers, including Good Hope's and Fine Wool's competitors, insisted that the two new firms enter into the national agreement in order to reach some standardized wage for the industry.[30] The effect of a national agreement on these firms, however, would be to undermine completely the very rationale behind the IDC's establishment of the factories in remote areas, and for the next seven years the corporation fought all pressure to raise wages.

In combating union attempts to standardize wages in the textile industry, van Eck employed a strategy already used and found wanting at Iscor: to divide and isolate units within the industry. Under the terms of the Industrial Conciliation Act, employers were required to meet jointly with industrywide unions to determine common, equitable standards for work at all factories. Van der Bijl had earlier succeeded in freeing Iscor from having to abide by such arrangements, arguing that there were significant differences in the production process used at Iscor, and he had established a separate Industrial Council with Iscor as the sole employer. Meyer had encountered problems with this method once his white operatives expanded their union on a nationwide scale. Nevertheless, van Eck tried the same approach with the textile industry, convincing the minister of labor, C. F. Steyn, in 1946 to establish separate councils for fine cotton and worsted wool manufacture, areas of manufacture dominated by the new state concerns.[31]

But van Eck found himself faced with the same problem all over again the following year, when private firms announced their intention to enter these areas of production, thereby threatening Good Hope and Fine Wool not only with competition for the market but also with the likelihood of having to raise wages. Moving quickly, IDC officials conferred with the Department of Labor and the Wage Board to try to salvage the situation. In consequence, Minister Steyn simply exempted the IDC's cotton textile factory, Good Hope Textiles, from the provisions of both the Wage Act and the Industrial Conciliation Act.[32] The minister in fact had the power to exclude any geographic area from implementation of a wage determination, and especially so if the area lay within a Native Reserve.[33] Thus, the King William's Town location proved especially beneficial to the IDC.

But the IDC soon discovered the limits of its control over workers even under the seemingly ideal conditions enjoyed at King William's Town. The work force was made up primarily of black males, barred from official union representation in the African Textile Workers' Union—an unregistered union claiming to represent more than seven hundred of the nearly one thousand black operatives at the plant—and now excluded from the protection afforded through government-imposed wage determinations.[34] The factory was located near the site of a new black township, Zwelitsha, built by the Department of Native Affairs specifically to house workers from the Good Hope plant. The workers were housed at no expense to the firm and, because of the rural location, ideally isolated from the direct influence of a larger working class. In fact, everyone in Zwelitsha was dependent upon Good Hope, since it was the only employer in the area. As the factory's managing director, Robert Cowan, put matters, "Zwelitsha cannot live without the Good Hope Textile Corporation." The company recruited young black males between 16 and 20 years old, preferably those with a minimal education because, in Cowan's words, "They are more apt in learning and better usually as a worker, with less education." Without recognized unions or even workers' councils, the factory management relied on "boss-boys who are intelligent and loyal to us who act as spokesmen" when communicating with the workers. Nevertheless, at the same time as having a highly dependent and strictly regulated black work force, Good Hope suffered from an enormous turnover rate of more than 100 percent causing, in Cowan's view, a considerable amount of "wastage" in training and production. Indeed, the company had spent more than a year training the first shift of weavers at the plant (twice as long as it should have) as a result of the high turnover rate at the factory.[35]

Although the company attributed the turnover to "tribal customs," low wages were a more likely cause. The company had set wages at levels prescribed by the IDC based on "the minimum economic requirements of an unskilled, inexperienced male Native in this reserve area."[36] Because the factory was the only industrial employer in the reserve, however, the method of determining wages was arbitrary at best. As Cowan explained, the company's only real responsibility to the township was issuing "economic wages so that they can pay economic rents for the houses."[37] Yet in 1950 Good Hope's wages were the lowest in the entire textile industry, averaging £1/9/5 per week, compared to £3/2/– on the Rand in Benoni.[38] Such wages were far too low to support a family even in Zwelitsha. With rents and service charges in the new township ranging up to £2 per month, twice the cost of housing in the government's only other experimental rural township, most black inhabitants could not make ends meet.[39] But the company was not prepared to raise its wages in the face of competition from Japanese cotton textiles.[40]

As a result, many workers simply left the reserve to find more lucrative employment on the Rand, and the others who stayed went on strike against the company. When the workers struck in June 1951, their main protest was at the low wages paid, a similar complaint being made by the company's trainees, who struck at the same time.[41] When another strike was threatened in March 1952, Good Hope managers were unresponsive. Since they could not sell their product, they were not too concerned about work stoppages, as officials at the Department of Labor noted: "Mr. Kushke of the IDC recently stated that the Cotton Textile Industry was almost at a standstill in that no orders were being received and consequently the factories were manufacturing for stock only. For this reason it would seem that employers in the industry would not be very much concerned if they had to close their factories for any reason whatsoever."[42] Again in November 1952 the workers went on strike, this time in conjunction with the countrywide Defiance Campaign launched by the ANC. The workers stayed on strike for one month, and more than two hundred were jailed.[43]

The IDC was finally forced to abandon its attempts to create a pliable work force within an African community. In 1952 the IDC's Board of Directors admitted that Good Hope's wages were insufficient to support a family and that "the average native could barely afford to live in the Township."[44] Not long after, the board decided to abandon plans for Zwelitsha as a "model settlement" for black industrial workers and their families and instead began to construct "huts" for single males on company property; families would be required to live, and to support themselves, elsewhere.[45] Acknowledging failure in its attempts to create an ideal labor force at King William's Town, the IDC turned to traditional methods of containing production costs by seeking total control over its workers.

At Fine Wool the IDC faced a different situation with a racially divided operative work force that could not be isolated from the national industry. At least 40 percent of Fine Wool's workers were classified as Coloured and therefore entitled to official union representation. These workers, unlike those at Good Hope, were represented by the predominantly white Textile Workers' Union, which resented the lower wages paid to Coloured employees at Uitenhage by comparison with white and Coloured workers elsewhere. Indeed, Fine Wool refused to abide by an old wage determination for the industry (No. 55 of 1937), using Iscor's argument that the processes involved were quite different. The company also refused to work within an Industrial Council for worsted manufacturers, which could reach negotiated wage settlements.[46]

The IDC's rationale for establishing the industry in Uitenhage had been to avoid paying wages at the national level. Shortly after Fine Wool started production in 1946, leaders of the Textile Workers' Union submitted a list of demands to the company, specifically for higher wages, and at the beginning of 1948 requested a formal Conciliation Board hearing of their grievances.[47] The company and the union then entered into direct negotiations in May 1948. The company agreed to institute a bonus system and higher wages for its senior grade employees, mostly whites, while lowering apprentice rates and lengthening training periods for Coloured and black employees. In this manner, the company kept its basic wages for the bulk of the work force—Coloureds and blacks—much lower than those set by the other firms.[48] The agreement pleased the union but drew the ire of rival manufacturers, who were bound by Industrial Council agreements. Nevertheless, the minister of labor allowed Fine Wool's separate agreement to stand, protecting the racial hierarchy in the labor force while allowing the IDC to isolate its black and Coloured workers.[49]

But the firm's black and Coloured workers pressured the union into renewed negotiations. The union's position with these workers was seriously undermined as a result of the special agreement with management, leading to the resignation of all black workers (unofficially represented) as well as a number of the Coloured females who worked in the factory.[50] In consequence, the union insisted on further Conciliation Board hearings, but the company refused to raise its wages to the level agreed upon by the other manufacturers.[51] Union negotiators argued for a higher basic wage to no avail, complaining that the requirements for earning the bonuses were set too high for a significant number of employees to reach. Even two years later, with the firm still operating under the 1948 agreement, the union charged that no employees had yet reached the company's top pay grade.[52] The firm was feeling equally hard pressed, however, and the managing director complained in May 1950 that due to foreign competition and high capital costs, labor costs "must [drop] or we are bust." His attitude to any wage increases was, "Over my dead body."[53]

Fine Wool was rewarded for its tenacity in 1952 when a new national labor agreement with the union recognized wage differentiation on a geographical basis, thus opening the door to individual agreements between the firms and the union concerning wages.[54] Area differentiation of wages was the cornerstone of van Eck's plans for the company, otherwise he would not have argued for its establishment in Uitenhage. When another Conciliation Board hearing was called to meet the workers' grievances, company management enjoyed a certain amount of added leverage because of the new agreement and concluded an agreement that the IDC Board of Directors found very advantageous.[55] In return for agreeing to increase the basic wage, Fine Wool management obtained the union's acquiescence in "labour loading," that is, requiring the weavers to operate more than one loom at a time.[56] In the long run, this could significantly cut labor costs as well as increase control over a smaller work force; alternatively, labor loading also increased the company's reliance on the semi-skilled weavers. Nevertheless, the IDC Board of Directors—controlling 93 percent of Fine Wool shares—was pleased that significant wage increases had been resisted, because "it was of great importance that the principle of area differentiation in wage rates would be recognized."[57]

Although the company was successful in negotiating the terms of employment at the factory, it failed to appreciate the inadequacy of area differentiation for its black workers. In 1949 the African Textile Workers' Union, affiliated to the Textile Workers' Union but lacking official government recognition in any negotiations, warned that wage determinations as well as Industrial Conciliation agreements concerning blacks "made by European workers in their own interests cannot possibly be satisfactory to African and mostly low paid workers."[58] Indeed, at Fine Wool the managing director admitted in 1950 that there was "more than a fairly high labour turnover rate" among the 350 black workers—60 percent of the work force—at the plant, a serious problem considering that it took between three and six months to train each weaver.[59] The previous year, van Eck had speculated that conditions at the nearby Uitenhage location would indeed undermine worker stability. "He had felt somewhat concerned during his recent visit to Uitenhage regarding the living conditions of the native and coloured employees working in the Fine Wool Products factory. . . . Greater stability in their home lives and the development of a sense of social responsibility would undoubtedly have a desirable effect on the efficiency of the workers."[60] By 1952 van Eck reported to the IDC Board of Directors that there was a serious threat of strike at the plant and that the "labour situation was still difficult." As at Zwelitsha, the problem lay in the cost of living in Uitenhage, where, van Eck said, "The position . . . was serious."[61]

Despite Fine Wool's limited victories over its work force, the company could not overcome its high costs—especially for raw wool and for retraining labor—and was in serious financial trouble by 1952. The Board of Trade and Industries had noted in 1950 that the company's board meetings were used primarily "to decide how to raise more money when the losses are exposed at the end of each year."[62] While the IDC had been subsidizing the company's shortfall each year, by 1952 van Eck decided to try to cut his losses and search for a foreign firm interested in buying up the IDC's Fine Wool shares.[63] By 1953, however, with the search unsuccessful, the company's debts amounted to nearly £1,000,000, almost half the factory's worth, and there was no relief in sight.[64]

At the same time, van Eck was more successful in establishing other industries near Native Reserves that required only unskilled African workers with minimal training. In 1948 the IDC took the first steps to establish plants for the manufacture of pulp for paper and rayon near government timber plantations in Zululand. During World War II the Union Corporation first approached the IDC to finance a paper mill based on the utilization of local timber.[65] After some investigation, a site for the industry was chosen near the Kwambonambi eucalyptus plantations in Natal, where "the propinquity of a Native Reserve [would] ensure an adequate unskilled labour force."[66] In 1950 the IDC was again approached, this time by British and Italian firms, to assist in the financing of a rayon pulp mill also using eucalyptus from Kwambonambi. The Board of Directors immediately reiterated its judgment that the "propinquity to Native Reserve Territory" was a prime drawcard, adding that "tree-planting by natives in the territory might be encouraged as a ready market for the timber would have been created."[67] Likewise, the Department of Native Affairs "had shown great interest in the possibility of arranging for natives in some of the Zululand Reserves, at present leading a precarious existence, to plant eucalyptus in those areas which were unsuitable for other agricultural activities."[68] Thus, impoverished blacks living in Native Reserves could provide cheap labor for the processing of government-controlled timber.

The only obstacle to the development of either scheme was high capital costs. In fact, the costs were so high—initially estimated at £2,500,000 for the paper project and £6,000,000 to £7,000,000 for the rayon enterprise—that there was some difficulty in raising funds.[69] Still, the high capital requirements kept out competitors—unlike in the cotton and woolen textile industries—leaving the local market open. Furthermore, the capital was to be spent on heavy machinery and highly technical equipment that would obviate the need for operative labor, the companies relying primarily on local black labor to cut down the trees and foreign technicians to supervise processing. The government's only request was that some of the pulp be used to develop a South African rayon manufacturing industry and thereby promote local industrialization. After its experience with cotton and woolen textiles, however, the IDC never pursued rayon manufacture, and even by 1970 all rayon pulp produced inside South Africa was exported.[70] Both of the new enterprises sold their goods to industrial consumers to manufacture into either boxes or rayon cloth, avoiding more complicated marketing arrangements. Thus, they escaped many of the problems encountered by the IDC's textiles enterprises, including those involved with competition, marketing, and labor.

The IDC's postwar experiences clearly demonstrated the limits of labor coercion in South African manufacturing. The textile factories, especially

Good Hope, were designed to take the maximum advantage of local labor supply. Wages were kept low and strikes quickly put down, reflecting a considerable amount of control over the work force. But such control could not extend to ensuring the stability of the work force. Both Good Hope and Fine Wool suffered high turnover rates, which were unacceptable in industries requiring up to six months' training for the operative workers entrusted with valuable machinery. The pulp plants, however, were far more successful, as they employed unskilled workers who could easily be replaced with little disruption in production or profits. While it became obvious at the textile firms that the rural areas could not sustain black workers on minimal wages, driving them to find better wages in the cities, such a predicament did not affect tree planting or harvesting. In a society where the bases of black economic and social security were constantly reduced and undermined, minimal wages could not foster stability among any black work force, whether in the cities or the countryside. Rural industries could lower wages for unskilled workers, but they could not ensure a stable or docile work force.

Iscor: Market Control and Production

Rather than attempt to forge a new industrial labor structure, officials at Iscor could not escape the preexisting structure shaped by war, politicians, workers, and a never-ending search for profits. As a result of shifting policies at the steel corporation since 1936, Iscor straddled divides between the use of black and white operative workers, as well as between state and private financial partnerships. In the postwar years the corporation would come under increasing political pressure to jump off the fence and abandon both private partners and black workers, especially due to its prominent position in the midst of the country's booming urban and industrial centers on the Rand and in Vereeniging. Iscor officials were in no position to revolutionize South African industrialization but rather had to find new ways to deal with the outcome of the previous decade's developments.

The Search for Monopoly Control

In the immediate postwar years van der Bijl tried to consolidate Iscor's position through its powerful advantage as the sole local producer of steel during a period of acute worldwide shortage. The destruction wrought by the war thoughout Europe had crippled production there, and all available American and British steel was needed for the task of rebuilding Europe. Steel was also needed inside South Africa for construction projects delayed during the war and now essential to keep the economy running smoothly.[71] In the face of these competing international and local demands, steel imports dwindled while becoming prohibitively expensive.[72] In consequence, only half of the local orders were filled, 80 percent with Iscor steel and the remainder with high-priced and scarce imports.[73]

Van der Bijl took advantage of the corporation's position to alter the terms of trade it enjoyed with its customers as well as to limit the number of companies with which it dealt. Controlling the market allowed the corporation to cut down on its production of raw and semifinished steel products and to begin concentrating on the finished goods.[74] In particular, the corporation reduced its production of billets—unformed shapes of raw steel—switching instead to structural sections and sheets. Iscor's longtime partners, however, still received preferential treatment; Stewarts and Lloyds, for example, obtained 51,000 tons of Iscor billets out of a reduced total of 61,000 tons produced in 1947 by Iscor.[75] Another old associate, Dorman Long, received nearly half of Iscor's production of structural sections. And most of Iscor's sheets were sold indirectly to the mines for use in ventilation piping and for roofing, while well over half of all Iscor rails likewise went to the mines. Besides these important private customers, Iscor also met the demands of the government, setting aside a modest amount of sheets and reinforcing steel for the National Housing Project and the remainder of Iscor's rails as well as a large order of raw pig iron for the railways.[76] Aside from these customers, Iscor's steel was sparsely allocated to merchants throughout the country, leaving many manufacturers to their own devices.

In addition to the advantages of Iscor's postwar marketing situation, the corporation had gained an immensely important private partner, the Anglo-American Corporation. As a result of Anglo's takeover of the Lewis and Marks firm in 1945, Anglo became Iscor's principal partner in its major subsidiaries, including the Union Steel Corporation, African Metals (Amcor), and Vanderbijl Engineering (Vecor), a project van der Bijl had initiated jointly with Ernest Oppenheimer.[77] Furthermore, Iscor—as did Escom—depended upon Anglo's Witbank coalmines for a great deal of its coal.[78] There were numerous advantages for Iscor in the new situation, among them the fact that Anglo would probably not raise its coal prices to businesses in which it held investments. More important, van der Bijl recognized that Anglo, unlike the often nearly bankrupt Lewis and Marks, could be counted on for investment capital. With the market under his control and Oppenheimer by his side, van der Bijl prepared to turn Iscor into a steel monopoly.

But van der Bijl still needed significant government support to secure market control into the future. In particular, he wanted to ensure that the corporation could expand production far beyond supplying local steel firms. His plans required sums of money far in excess of what he could expect from Oppenheimer, and he needed access to government funds to realize his plans. He won Smuts's approval to build two new plants at Vanderbijlpark, but official approval did not guarantee sufficient funds; van der Bijl received only £15,000,000, less than half of what he needed. By the beginning of 1947 he had to report that costs were rising even higher, as a result of postwar inflation, leading to a serious capital shortfall.[79] He embarked on a long search for additional government funds in order to effect his plans for a steel monopoly.

But in the postwar years both the Smuts government and the new National Party government could not—and would not—provide van der Bijl with the funds for his grandiose partnerships with private manufacturers.[80] In the immediate postwar years Smuts and his cabinet were concerned over the cost of several development projects that had been postponed during the war, with the result that the minister of finance, J. H. Hofmeyr, opposed any further increases in the state budget. In fact, rather than provide Iscor with more money, Hofmeyr warned van der Bijl to keep his prices low, so as to offset the inflation that was hurting the other projects.[81] Government support for Iscor reached its nadir, however, in June 1948 when the National Party government came to power, intent upon keeping a tight rein on the corporation. The new government, headed by D. F. Malan as prime minister, was deeply concerned with fiscal austerity and faced a serious balance of payments crisis caused by the high demand for expensive imports. It could hardly face the massive expansions envisioned by van der Bijl, which would require not only funds but also continuing imports of expensive machinery. The country's trade crisis was so acute that it was only averted in 1949 through devaluation of the South African currency, which slowed down imports.[82]

The Nationalist politicians were also deeply suspicious of van der Bijl, Iscor, and state corporations in general, and especially of state support for private firms connected either to mining houses or to foreign firms, van der Bijl's closest associates.[83] As soon as the new minister of economic development, Eric Louw, assumed office, he informed Iscor's deputy chairman, P. V. Gawith, that he wanted to be "fully and timeously informed regarding matters of importance in connection with Iscor's affairs and developments."[84] The new government was intent on "capturing this foreign system," as L. J. du Plessis had charged nearly a decade before.[85]

Mistrusting the immense powers wielded by van der Bijl and resentful of the automony he had achieved, Louw spearheaded an investigation into van der Bijl's tenure as chairman of Iscor over the previous twenty years. In particular, the new minister suspected that van der Bijl had used his position to promote his own ambitions though his increasingly public associations with Oppenheimer.[86] It was true that van der Bijl had cultivated relationships with private businessmen and, following the war, had enjoyed an especially close friendship with Ernest Oppenheimer. Together they had arranged the establishment of Safmarine as a private ocean freight company in 1946, with van der Bijl as chairman and including Oppenheimer, Menell (of Johannesburg Consolidated Investment), and even "Bomber" Harris of Royal Air Force fame on the board of directors.[87] Van der Bijl's connections with the representatives of mining capital and the British military were understandably resented by the Nationalist government, which espoused avidly anti-British and antimining rhetoric.

When Louw issued his threats, however, van der Bijl was critically ill, in and out of hospitals for treatment of cancer. Nevertheless, Louw chose this time to exert his power over the ailing executive, informing him while in hospital that the renewal of his tenure as chairman, which had become routine over the years, would be held over until consideration of "the position in general" could be completed.[88] The new government viewed both van der Bijl and his state corporations as antagonists in a battle over state economic control.

True to his word, Louw commissioned a complete investigation into the corporation's business, which resulted in the cutoff of further funds for subsidiary development. Both Louw and N. C. Havenga, the minister of finance, were suspicious of any further investments on Iscor's part that they deemed not strictly in the state corporation's interests.[89] Shortly after taking office in June 1948, they instructed the undersecretary of commerce, J. N. Theron, to study the question and largely followed his recommendations, which included pulling Iscor's money out of Usco and Amcor while limiting future investment in Vecor. Theron argued that such investments benefited the private companies far more than Iscor, referring to Iscor's new partner, Anglo-American.[90] Anticipating Theron's report, the cabinet informed Iscor's board in September 1948 that the corporation could not invest further sums in any companies without government approval.[91]

But limitations on Iscor's activities were eased once the government exerted its prerogative of control, and following van der Bijl's death. When he died in December 1948, van der Bijl was succeeded as chairman of Iscor by the corporation's general works manager and the man responsible for increasing the number of white operatives in the corporation's factory, F. W. Meyer. Although Meyer was not considered as dynamic or talented as some of the other officials at Iscor, he had considerable experience in the industry as well as close personal connections with the new party in power. Meyer had in fact been present at the 1939 Volkskongres and was rumored to be a member of the Broederbond.[92] With the corporation under a modicum of "control" by the volk, the government report finally submitted by Theron recommended that the cabinet agree to let the corporation raise the money necessary for the extensions to its own plant—by then, £9,100,000 was needed—by way of debentures and loans.[93] In June 1950, the debentures were sold, primarily to Barclays Bank, and Iscor was finally able to go ahead with its plans.[94]

The corporation went even further and, in a startling departure from financial policy, Iscor's Board of Directors in 1952 decided to use the corporation's reserve funds, normally invested in government stocks and bonds and for emergency use, to regain through the purchase of stocks a controlling interest in both Amcor and Vecor.[95] Iscor later went on to acquire the source of one of the corporation's most important supplies, coking coal, when it purchased the Durban Navigation Colliery in 1956.[96] The new government was not entirely opposed to Iscor's continuing partnerships with private capital—not even mining capital—so long as the Nationalists felt that they had some control over such partnerships.

Under Meyer's chairmanship, Iscor succeeded in producing most of South Africa's steel. The new Iscor steel works at Vanderbijlpark brought the corporation's total production capacity up to 1,000,000 tons in 1952, exceeding the country's prewar demand.[97] By 1955 the corporation produced 70 percent of the country's requirements.[98] Basing production at the new plant on the installation of a modern continuous strip mill, all of the country's requirements for flat rolled products—plates, sheets, tube strip, and tinplate—could be manufactured there while the old Pretoria plant concentrated on the remainder of the steel products demanded inside the country. Indeed, the corporation had assured itself of a market at Vanderbijlpark, where the local subsidiary of Stewarts and Lloyds consumed the majority of steel sheets in the country for use in the manufacture of tubes and pipes. And the corporation's plates fueled production at nearby Vecor, which in turn manufactured heavy machinery for Iscor as well as the mining and manufacturing industries. The old plant at Pretoria catered primarily to the railways and merchants on the Rand who supplied engineering firms.[99]

Van der Bijl's plans to expand Iscor's market control were largely successful, turning the state corporation into the country's major supplier of steel. Market dominance included a significant measure of continuing cooperation with private firms, but the corporation had improved its leverage through its massive expansion of production and by obtaining significant support from Anglo-American. Van der Bijl succeeded in achieving market dominance with the support of private businessmen instead of the government protection so feared by private businessmen at Iscor's inception.

The Cost of Labor Control

But all of these successes in achieving market control set in train changes at the corporation that undermined control over labor costs. Shifting production priorities from fewer to more finished goods at the corporation placed greater emphasis on white skilled workers, who were no longer under the wartime control of the government. These artisans were now in great demand throughout the country, not only to control particularly delicate operations but also to maintain and repair the machinery upon which production depended. At the same time, the white operatives, while not as crucial to production, were becoming more assertive in demanding higher wages. While previously dependent exclusively on Iscor for employment—their union operating only at the state corporation—they began to gain both a greater awareness of their position as well as enhanced bargaining power when their union expanded for the first time after the war to represent workers at other firms.[100] And the position of the white operatives gained increasing political significance—before as well as after the Nationalist victory in 1948—with these workers epitomizing the contradictions of sustained economic development and continuing white political dominance. At the same time as Iscor demanded increasing funds from the government for the expansion of plant, corporation officials could not ignore these workers in staffing plans for the expanded facilities. Once again the corporation found that changes in production altered carefully arranged labor relations.

Beginning immediately after the war, the principal struggle at Iscor was between white artisans and white operatives over skill or race as the defining measure in the industrial labor hierarchy. The white operatives were especially vociferous, and in January 1947 Meyer was forced to modify the labor agreement he had so carefully framed during the war, raising operative wages in the training periods and reducing the number of shifts necessary before those workers could move into higher positions.[101] Admitting that the work carried out by these workers had changed substantially in response to production demands at Iscor, Meyer went on in 1949 to raise the basic rate for some positions by as much as 30 percent.[102] The artisans, however, feared that these concessions and the recognition that operative jobs were requiring increased levels of skill would undermine their elite status, and they argued that they deserved a commensurate raise in wages.[103] Meyer rebuffed their demands in 1949 on the grounds that he would no longer sanction any demands by white workers—artisans or operatives—for higher wages.[104] Nevertheless, the white workers called Meyer's bluff as they had in 1941 and, threatening to go on strike, won considerable wage concessions.

In June 1949 the operatives demanded a formal dispute, invoking the machinery of the Industrial Conciliation Act, and succeeded through arbitration in obtaining wage increases for plant hands and operatives, totaling an additional annual cost of at least £125,000 for the corporation.[105] And Meyer was forced in 1951 to raise the operative wages again, to a level equal to that throughout the industry, when a new Labor Agreement for the rest of the industry was negotiated by the private firms.[106] At the same time, the artisans were dissatisfied with the concessions made to the operatives, and in 1952 the Amalgamated Engineers' Union led a strike. Meyer could hardly afford to lose these workers, most of them foreigners recruited overseas in 1950 in the face of serious shortages of skilled workers.[107] As a result, the dispute with the Amalgamated Engineers' Union quickly went to arbitration, and the workers won significant wage increases.[108] Both groups of white workers, politically important South Africans and technically valuable foreigners, had to be placated and were protected in a modified wage hierarchy, which valued race but not entirely at the expense of skill.

The fate of Iscor's black workers was less clear. The decision to privilege the white operatives on the basis of race rather than skill opened possibilities for the use of Africans on the factory floor with jobs defined by their race rather than the skills involved in their work. As a consequence, the figures for black workers continued to rise, from 10,000 in 1950 to 11,600 in 1955, with approximately only 2,000 of those employed at the Thabazimbi mine.[109] Nevertheless, the board was quick to point out to the government in 1950 that since Iscor's inception its total wage bill amounted to £33,000,000, only £7,500,000 of which went to Africans.[110] In other words, no matter how many Africans were employed, whites were reaping the primary financial benefits of employment.

Even so, a significant number of Africans were employed on the factory floor, as before and during World War II, though classified only as "general labourers," the corporation's generic category for all African workers. These jobs—as with the position accorded the white operatives and artisans—would command a wage based on race rather than skill; in fact, skill could be considered irrelevant to wage level. In such capacities, they performed jobs that could rightfully be considered at least semiskilled , yet their title and pay were defined by the color of their skin. With approximately nine thousand white employees and nine thousand African employees (those not at Thabazimbi) in 1955, Iscor could claim a large white operative work force assisted by a significant number of general laborers on the factory floor. When the corporation had attempted to introduce general laborers onto the factory floor before the war, it had actually had to remove white workers and move Africans in, thus provoking a public scandal. In the postwar period, new factories could be organized around such racial proportions, and the white operatives, enjoying increasing prestige and wages at any rate, failed to raise the issue of doing away with African workers altogether on the factory floor.

Iscor continued to enjoy protected markets, and showed mounting profits, throughout the 1950s. A huge increase in production occurred in 1951 when Iscor's new plant at Vanderbijlpark came into operation, and in the following eight years sales more than doubled. Still, in 1958 personnel costs represented the corporation's largest single item of cost associated with production. Labor turnover remained high until Iscor established a training center for operatives, described as follows: "School boys of school-leaving age will be trained and introduced gradually into the industrial way of life. Investigations are also being conducted to provide special hostel accommodation," implying the presence of a racially mixed group of operatives.[111] The following year, 1959, Meyer reported a significant decline in labor turnover and an increased profit for the corporation.[112] The only problems for Iscor in the 1950s were the gradual decline in local demand for steel and the specter of renewed competition from European and American producers. The corporation's success in the 1950s rested on nearly unlimited demand for its goods and the stabilization of its work force.

Policy solutions at Iscor were markedly more successful than at the IDC textile factories; however, they rested on precarious grounds. Iscor could control markets in a way that would have been impossible at the textile firms and thereby eliminated competition as one of its problems. The steel corporation, therefore, was under less pressure to cut labor costs, van Eck's principal problem, and had more flexibility in labor policies. Iscor's primary labor concerns were the result of political pressure not to compromise the position of white workers. While African workers could openly be employed as operatives out in remote rural areas and at wages commensurate with unskilled work, bringing them into the highly visible factories at Vanderbijlpark and Pretoria was far more complicated. The question of African operatives at Iscor embodied all of the contradictions South Africa faced in the postwar period: How could economic expansion continue with a disenfranchised work force? Iscor's answer was to maintain a labor hierarchy based exclusively on race rather than skill, in order to gird white control while leaving the door open for the concealed use of Africans in all sorts of jobs. The only problem in Iscor's solution was growing African dissent over such terms of employment.

Escom: Monopoly and Mechanization

Escom best exemplified the successful model of industrial enterprise among South Africa's state corporations. Because of the nature of electricity generation, largely a physical reaction set off by mechanical processes, power stations were capital-intensive operations reliant only on skilled technicians to operate the machinery and unskilled miners to produce the coal necessary at Escom stations. Once van der Bijl succeeded in buying out the VFPC and achieving monopoly control over the electricity market, the commission expanded production by relying on greater use of machinery and a diminution in labor. In the postwar period van der Bijl, with crucial support from the country's principal electricity consumers, the gold-mine owners, succeeded in securing Escom's control over its markets and its labor force.

Trading New Partners for Old

The key to Escom's successful growth was the takeover of the VFPC. So long as the private company controlled the Rand, the largest—and expanding—market for electricity in the country, van der Bijl had little room to build up Escom's distribution. The VFPC, instead of Escom, was reaping the surplus revenue that the commission could have used for capital development. Furthermore, the private company rejected any plans to link its supply system with the systems in outlying areas, while Escom's ultimate aim was to establish a national grid. So long as the VFPC controlled the market and Escom's access to consumers, van der Bijl was powerless to expand production in a systematic and cost-efficient manner.

Van der Bijl received crucial support in his efforts to purchase the VFPC from the private company's most important customers, the gold-mine owners. During the war, Ernest Oppenheimer, chairman of Anglo-American, determined that the legislative protections incorporated in the Electricity Act could not help the mining industry in the face of the complicated arrangements that allowed the VFPC to make huge profits from Escom's electricity. Due to Escom's dependence on sales to the VFPC, van der Bijl had agreed to allow the private company to profit from the sale of Escom electricity. And, as we saw in chapter 5, the VFPC had taken advantage of this arrangement during the war and made huge profits at the mine owners' expense. As a result, the cost of electricity to the mines per ton of ore milled grew 10 percent during the war and represented the largest single item of expenditure on stores by the mines.[113]

In the immediate postwar years the mine owners also began to feel the effects of inflation, their costs per ton of ore milled generally rising by 1s. 10d. per year, up from an annual increase of only 11d. per ton of ore milled before the war.[114] While their profit margin was shrinking, capital requirements for the development of new areas in the Orange Free State, where Anglo-American held a dominant position, were increasing. By 1947 capital issued on the new mines in the Free State had risen to £17,000,000, from only £4,000,000 in 1945.[115] Clearly, with a declining profit margin, rising costs, and increasing capital requirements, the mine owners were anxious to alleviate their problems. When it was revealed that the vFPC had accumulated well over £6,000,000 in profits during the war, the private company became the target of the mine owners' wrath.[116] Oppenheimer believed that the only way to bring electricity costs on the mines under some sort of effective regulation was to gain greater direct control over the supply of power.

Oppenheimer was well situated to extend his influence over electricity generation and supply through an expanding relationship that had been developing for some time between Anglo-American and Escom. In particular, when Anglo bought out the African and European Investment Company—the old Lewis and Marks firm—in 1945, it acquired most of the collieries that supplied coal to the power stations at Witbank and Vereeniging. Furthermore, Anglo (indirectly through the vFPC) was Escom's biggest customer, as it consumed more electricity on the Rand than any other mining operation.[117] By 1946, with Anglo one of the electricity industry's major coal suppliers as well as largest power consumer, Oppenheimer decided to use his company's leverage to forge an alliance with Escom against the vFPC.

Oppenheimer initiated his partnership with Escom by supporting van der Bijl's efforts to buy out the vFPC. He angrily set out the case for compulsory acquisition of the vFPC in a memorandum to the Smuts government that detailed the private company's financial machinations. Oppenheimer concluded his memorandum by claiming, "The v.f.p. policy is to demand their full 'pound of flesh' and any approaches by the Mining Industry to the v.f.p. for a revision [of prices] are doomed to failure. The only way in which an equitable state of affairs can be brought about is by Government intervention."[118] Oppenheimer believed that forced expropriation of the company by Escom would save the mining industry between £2,500,000 and £3,000,000 per year in reduced electricity costs.[119] Convinced by Oppenheimer's figures, the minister of economic affairs, S. F. Waterson, determined that the government could also benefit financially from a takeover of the vFPC, since greater profits on the mines would result in increased taxation revenue for the state. Although the government did not sanction state expropriation—a step that was essentially blocked by the opposition of the ECB—Waterson's approval was necessary to allow van der Bijl to raise money on the private market for financing the purchase of the vFPC.

After Waterson's approval was obtained, van der Bijl began negotiations in 1947 with the vFPC to purchase all of its operations in South Africa. He was assisted in presenting Escom's case by a representative of the gold industry, R. B. Hagart, who was a director of Anglo-American and a close associate of Oppenheimer's.[120] More important, Anglo supplied £8,000,000 of the final £14,500,000 paid by Escom to acquire the VFPC's operations. By purchasing the VFPC van der Bijl obtained not only the company's fixed assets but also the all-important supply contracts to the mines as well as contracts for the supply of coal from Anglo-controlled coalmines. The mines also gained an important concession from the company, obtaining a VFPC agreement to repay its consumers a total of £1,500,000 in back payments on the rebate that the company had discontinued during the war.[121] In June 1948—the same month that disgruntled Afrikaner farmers and urban workers elected to power an HNP government committed to the implementation of apartheid—a monopoly operation controlling both the production and supply of electricity in South Africa was finally established by Escom with the support of the gold industry.[122]

Escom's takeover of the VFPC system benefited both supplier and consumer. While Escom continued to charge the mines the same price per unit as had been charged by the VFPC, the mine owners were contractually assured a larger rebate—or share in the "surplus" profit.[123] Moreover, in 1952 Escom lowered the unit price of its electricity to the mines from 0.31d. to 0.144d., resulting in even further savings.[124] Meanwhile, the price of gold jumped 44 percent in 1949, leaving the mine owners in a comfortable position. For Escom, the takeover of the VFPC was likewise rewarding. While under the provisions of the Electricity Act the commission could not accrue outright profits, it could put money aside in a reserve fund "generally for the betterment of the plant."[125] In the five years following its purchase of the VFPC, Escom was able to transfer more than £2,000,000 from the fund for the general improvement of plant, up from a yearly average of less than £200,000 before the purchase.[126] Thus, both Escom and the mine owners benefited financially from their new partnership, though van der Bijl saw little of the success of his plans, as he died suddenly in 1948.

Lowering Costs: The National Grid

Most expansion of Escom took place under van der Bijl's trusted assistant, A. M. Jacobs, who as the new chairman began in the 1950s to build a nationwide system of power stations, to be linked together in a "grid" of electricity distribution.[127] Jacobs had worked at Escom since 1926, first as senior engineer and later as chief engineer. As chairman of the commission after 1948, he supervised the establishment of new power stations near the Orange Free State goldmines at Vierfontein and Taaibos as well as near railway lines at Hex River in the Cape. At the same time, he began to extend Escom's services to municipalities that were embarking upon post-war industrialization—with the help of another state corporation, the IDC—and power stations were planned near Durban, at Port Elizabeth, and at East London. By 1954 Escom owned power stations near all of the major industrial centers in the country, stations that spanned most of the white-owned land in the country with the exception of the northern Transvaal and the northwest Cape. As a consequence, in 1954 Escom began to link its stations, beginning with the Kimberley station—acquired from Anglo in 1947—and the Rand system, affording Kimberley the benefit of the much cheaper electricity generated at Anglo's own coalfields.[128] In the same year the Natal stations were likewise linked together.

From 1955, all major power stations were henceforth built in the eastern Transvaal, near the coalfields where electricity could be most cheaply produced, and their power was transmitted over an ever-widening net of links to the regional stations built in the 1950s. By 1969 the national grid was complete, allowing Cape Town for the first time to enjoy the benefits of cheap electricity generated on the Transvaal coalfields.[129] Thus, the grid system allowed Escom to use many of the smaller, older stations not especially close to coalfields primarily as distribution centers for the electricity that was generated so much more cheaply in the eastern Transvaal. When completed, the grid rationalized electricity supply in the country, allowing Escom to provide power as cheaply as possible.

But the grid system provided more than the rationalization of power generation; it also allowed Escom to minimize and isolate its labor requirements. At the new stations established in remote areas, the commission brought in migrant contract workers, housed them in compounds, and faced few labor problems. Indeed, the new, highly technical stations with mechanized pulverized fuel-firing of the furnaces were very capital intensive and needed few workers to operate them.[130] Even by 1959 the majority of the black work force remained on the Rand in the old VFPC stations, which were used increasingly as workshops and as the central controlling body for the entire grid.[131]

In its remaining urban stations, Escom continued to insist upon control over its labor as strict and effective as that exercised over the often nearby mine workers. Indeed, when the VFPC was bought out, Escom's commercial manager, Percy Furness, notified the ECB that Escom would leave station operation to the small VFPC subsidiary, the Rand Mines Power Supply Company (RMPSC), now wholly owned by Escom, because "it has been the Falls Company's policy for many years past to conform in the matter of remuneration and conditions of employment of its servants with the precedents set by . . . the Witwatersrand gold mining industry. . . . The mining industry is most anxious that such conditions should be maintained and the commission feels that this will be facilitated by the retention of the Rand Mines Power Supply Company as an operating company."[132] While Escom's managers were reluctant publicly to advocate such methods of labor control, they believed a private company could do so with less controversy—paradoxically, the exact opposite of Hoy's argument in 1920. Such control indeed proved effective in the face of continuing worker unrest. In 1960, when an ANC-sponsored "stay-at-home" swept through the country, Escom's urban stations, especially those on the Rand, were largely unaffected. Explaining matters to the secretary of Bantu administration and development, M. D. C. de W. Nel, Escom officials put the situation clearly: "The 'stay-at-home' strike urged on the Bantu had no repercussions among the commission's labour force employed in the Transvaal and Orange Free State, all of whom are provided with accommodation. . . . In the Cape, however, where no accommodation or feeding is provided only 1% of the 400 Bantu employed reported for duty . . . in Durban the large proportion of our labour force compounded were not affected by the agitation, but of the Bantu not housed many failed to report for work."[133] Thus the efficacy of compounds, under either Escom or RMPSC management, ensured Escom's continuing control over labor even in the urban areas where the numbers of blacks necessary for operations could not be reduced.

But despite the considerable control over costs that Escom achieved, the commission refused to provide subsidized electricity to rural areas, regardless of repeated government requests. As early as 1946 Smuts had proposed rural electrification, offering to subsidize the cost until Escom could make such supply affordable.[134] The only problem for Escom was that most rural electricity schemes in South Africa would never become self-supporting. Power to rural areas would be very expensive, requiring long-distance reticulation at high voltage (lower voltages not being suitable for long-distance transmission) and forcing farmers to obtain costly equipment to transform such electricity to voltages suitable for domestic use. Even by 1950, and under the best of circumstances, Escom's new chairman, A. M. Jacobs, advised the government that "such a cost of electricity is probably out of all proportion to the financial means of those [rural] towns, and therefore the majority of this cost would require to be met by the Government" on a recurring basis.[135] Such a situation would lead to government pressure on Escom to readjust prices—especially to the mining industry, which paid such low rates—in order to subsidize the rural supply. Escom continually made small attempts, usually through investigations, to develop a rural system, but it generally stalled on providing rural electricity despite the expansion of the grid system; even by 1959 only six thousand white farms in the country out of a total of approximately one hundred thousand were receiving electricity from Escom.[136]

Although Escom achieved a high degree of control over production by 1960, the commission nevertheless limited the benefits of its success to a small group of consumers. The commission secured its sources of coal through arrangements with its major customer, the Anglo-American Corporation, which would hardly wish to drive up Escom's costs. With regard to labor costs, increasing production and mechanization minimized dependence on labor, thereby further reducing the commission's expenses. And the market for power supply, a natural though limited monopoly, was greatly expanded through the purchase of the vfpc, again with the help of Anglo-American.

And yet South African electricity was still too expensive to fuel more than the essential needs of industry and the white population. Escom did not take the opportunity to use the industrial electricity market, overwhelmingly dominated by the mining industry, to subsidize and thus lower the costs of electricity to any other consumers, most notably blacks living in urban and rural townships. Taken together, mining and industry accounted for 71 percent of all Escom sales in 1960, and these figures do not account for Escom electricity sold by municipalities to industries, especially to the Iscor plant in Pretoria.[137] Furthermore, these sales were made primarily to two customers: the Anglo-American Corporation, Escom's partner and the largest mining company in the country, and to Iscor and its subsidiaries, which made up the bulk of the South African engineering industry. Escom, while enjoying the maximum amount of control possible over its industry, continued to reflect the overwhelming predominance of mining and state-supported industries in South Africa.

The Changing Face of State Corporations

By the mid-1950s the Nationalist government could begin to apply some of the lessons afforded by the previous decade of state corporation experience. All three state corporations had undergone significant transformations since the end of the war and had explored divergent strategies for success. As had become apparent during the war, private partnerships were problematic, but necessary if they could lead to an elimination of competition. Both Iscor's and Escom's partnerships with Anglo-American had proven extremely valuable, a fact acknowledged by the Nationalists despite their suspicion of mining capitalists. Even such powerful partners could not eliminate worries over costs, however, and all of the state corporations were faced with decisions over labor control. Resounding beyond the individual concerns of the firms, labor policies carried serious implications for the social construction of an industrialized South Africa. Not surprisingly, similar policies began to emerge on a national political level in subsequent apartheid legislation engineered by the Nationalists. The decreasing importance of the correlation between wages and race with skill that proved successful at Iscor was later mirrored in the Industrial Conciliation Act of 1956 and dubbed "job reservation." Efforts to move industries out of the urban areas and near to rural labor sources recurred variously as the Border Areas Scheme (in 1960) and (since 1971) as Industrial Decentralization.

Aside from national political policies, however, the lessons of state corporation experiences in the postwar period most directly affected the subsequent development of new state corporations. All of the state firms established after 1950 followed the most successful examples of state enterprise: Escom and the IDC's pulp factories. They sought control over their markets and raw materials, were situated in remote rural areas, and relied on highly technical processes that required a work force split between a small group of technicians and a large number of unskilled workers. They not only resembled the older state corporations but also mirrored the most successful industry in South Africa, the mining industry.

While the establishment of the first three state corporations had been attended by controversy and crisis, in the 1950s a new generation of state enterprises quietly entered the scene.[138] Shortly after taking office, the Nationalist government began to appreciate the power at its disposal in the form of the state corporations and used the IDC as its conduit for the establishment of additional corporations without the need for parliamentary approval of specific legislation. Under clause 3(a) of the Industrial Development Act—an amendment added in 1942 to allow the IDC to get on with the woolen industry in the absence of any private investors—the IDC was allowed to establish undertakings on its own, rather than simply to assist private entrepreneurs, as had been the original intention of the act.[139] The Nationalist government was eager to gain control over crucial industries and even supported some financial partnerships and arrangements with the powerful mining houses to establish large-scale monopoly industries. By 1951 a fourth and a fifth state corporation—the South African Coal, Oil, and Gas Corporation (Sasol) and the Phosphate Development Corporation (Foskor)—were established by the IDC, and they were to dwarf all of the corporation's previous undertakings.[140]

Despite its unconventional establishment, Sasol's historical background paralleled that of Iscor. Private entrepreneurs had tried throughout the 1930s to float a company to produce oil from coal but consistently lacked sufficient capital, finally turning to the government for support. While Smuts agreed to consider the matter, no action was taken before the war.[141] Following the war, the government continued to study alternatives for promoting such an industry, establishing licensing procedures, regulations and protection via the Liquid Fuel and Oil Act (Act 49 of 1947), reminiscent in intent of the earlier Iron and Steel Encouragement Act of 1922. Nonetheless, capital was still lacking, and in April 1950 the minister of economic affairs, Eric Louw, finally proposed that the IDC raise a £15,000,000 loan for Anglo-Transvaal to enable the company to begin production.[142] This plan was quickly withdrawn due to anticipated parliamentary criticism of such close government ties with the mining company if this IDC transaction became public.[143] Within the year, the IDC instead bought out Anglo-Transvaal's interest in the proposition and began the establishment of an industry to manufacture oil from coal under the express control of the cabinet. In short, a state corporation had been established to produce what was perceived as a strategic commodity following the failure of private capital to do so.

Initially, Sasol was funded through the IDC, largely due to uncertainty over the actual operation of the industry. While oil-from-coal processes that had been tested and proven in Germany and the United States were to be used by Sasol, a fully operating oil-from-coal industry had not yet been established anywhere in the world. Neither the IDC nor the government's technical advisers had a clear idea of exactly how much capital would be necessary to get the operation going on a sound basis, and none knew what sort of a profit could be expected. In the past, Parliament had insisted on the offer of state corporation shares—by Escom, Iscor, and the IDC—to the public, and regardless of the fact that neither Iscor nor the IDC had ever attracted a significant number of private shareholders, private participation had been established as a feature of the state corporations. It was doubtful that Sasol could be approved by Parliament as a state corporation without such a stipulation. Van Eck agreed with the new Nationalist government that such a course would prejudice the interests of the new industry and could undermine its success. Private shareholders naturally expected dividends, which could drain funds necessary for development in the initial phases of production. Furthermore, raising money on the private market through loans or debentures could submit the company to heavy interest payments even before production was initiated, a fate that had befallen Iscor in its early years. Financially, it was far more beneficial to accept funds from the government via the IDC as either low-interest loans or share capital. Also, the government could more effectively keep the price of Sasol's petrol as low as possible—just as it was pressing Iscor to keep down its prices—if it was the sole shareholder.

Thus, the IDC agreed to establish the industry with government funds, concluding that this course would provide necessary flexibility for the industry:

In the establishment of a new key industry it is essential, in its initial stages, to maintain the greatest flexibility in the constitution and capital structure of the organization so that the door is left open for the organization to assume the form of a public utility such as for example, Escom or the Rand Water Board, at a later date should this be found desirable. . . . Flexibility is therefore highly desirable and only after the presently proposed unit is in full operation will it be possible finally to determine the most suitable basis upon which to develop the industry.[144]

The capital requirements of the industry did indeed grow, from the 1951 estimate of £18,000,000 to £33,000,000 by 1953, with even the minister of finance, N. C. Havenga—representing the sole shareholder—complaining that "[I am] very disappointed that s.a.s.o.l.'s capital requirements have increased to such an extent and would probably not have approved of the scheme had [I] visualized that the cost would reach such dimensions."[145]

In the case of Foskor, the government was even more concerned about the effect of private development on the fate of the industry. Like oil, phosphate necessary for the manufacture of fertilizer in South Africa was considered to be essential for the nation's survival. Indeed, Havenga believed that this project was more important even than Sasol.[146] All of the phosphate used in South African fertilizer was imported, and during the war it became evident that overseas supplies were undependable and often expensive. Local phosphate deposits had been discovered at Palaborwa, and the Anglo-American Corporation—on behalf of its chemical company, African Explosives and Chemical Industries (AE&CI)—had been negotiating for control of the property. The government—specifically Ministers Louw (Mines and Economic Affairs), Havenga (Finance), and le Roux (Agriculture)—had decided, however, that the deposit was too important to "national interests" to allow private ownership and that the government should obtain the property. Once again there was some difficulty over the form of such ownership. As a mineral property, the phosphate deposit would have to be considered a state mine under government ownership, raising the possibility of eventual leasing as well as the use of white labor, which the Department of Mines called "neither economic nor wise."[147] The solution was not hard to find: following the example of Sasol, Foskor was established in 1951 by the IDC to develop the Palaborwa deposit.

Both the new state corporations were a far cry from the industries that van Eck had hoped to see the IDC establish at the close of the war. Instead of consumer-oriented industries that could help to lower the cost of living as well as provide jobs and develop skills among the unemployed—both black and white—these new industries followed the old: they were based on minerals (coal and phosphate), the production of industrial goods (oil and fertilizers), and the use of highly skilled (technical) workers and unskilled mine labor. The new corporations were patterned on Escom; however, they also reflected the organization of the dominant mining industry. As with Escom's workers, mine workers received minimal training, were easily replaced, and held little leverage in demanding higher wages or better conditions of employment. The key to success was to reduce the importance of individual workers, making them easily replaceable and therefore subject to the corporations' dictates. This was difficult at Iscor and the IDC textile mills, where so many workers were specially trained to keep the factories in operation. But at Escom mechanized production required less manual operation and only occasional attention from skilled technicians. Taking a page from these experiences as well as from the mining industry, van Eck abandoned the development of light manufacturing—originally intended to provide jobs and training—and turned instead to industries in which labor costs were minimal. The result was the development of industries closely resembling mining, based on cheap, unskilled, and strictly controlled labor.

State Enterprise and Apartheid

By 1960 South Africa's state corporations were firmly implanted in a socioeconomic system that carefully protected the interests of both the white electorate and the dominant mining industry at the expense of the African majority. The mine owners were no longer threatened by government-supported industries—such as Kruger's—in which they now held a measure of control through investments and close business relationships. Nor were their methods of labor control questioned through the activities of the state corporations, which instead emulated mine labor practices. And white workers, while not absorbed en masse into state factories, nonetheless had jobs reserved for them at the top of the labor hierarchy within the state corporations, and they also benefited from the general expansion of industrial activities in obtaining jobs. The IDC in particular exemplified the expansion of the mines' model of industrial success— dependent upon disenfranchised workers—throughout the economy. Established to move South Africa away from reliance on the mining industry, the state corporations were instead modeled on the most successful industries inside the country: the mines.

CHAPTER SEVEN

Toward Privatization

How does the history of the state corporations explain the paradox, raised in the Preface, of dominant state enterprise in an aggressively capitalist society? By the 1970s there were eight major state corporations, while at the same time the South African government was avidly attacking (both verbally and physically) neighboring Angola for coming under Marxist "socialist" rule.[1] Is this a difference between rhetoric and reality or is there a consistency in these apparently contradictory positions?

Judging from the history of state enterprises in South Africa, there is a consistency in the government's seemingly hypocritical positions. Simply stated, South African governments have always tried to promote the private accumulation of capital, and it is the restriction of such accumulation, not the means used to effect such goals, that is the focus of attacks on socialism. The state corporations have intervened to control market forces in an effort to encourage private accumulation. Successive governments have been able to use the state corporations to produce goods and services and to structure local markets, prices, and employment. The purpose of these activities was seldom the accumulation of capital by the government—even though some government offices, such as the SAR, benefited—but rather the lowering of costs to private industries. Governments were thus capable of assisting select groups through the state corporations, reflecting the country's predominant social and economic forces. In twentieth-century South Africa those forces have invariably been represented by the white community and been underwritten by the country's mineral wealth. The state corporations have reflected and reinforced the relationship between white political and economic power.

Throughout most of the period covered in this study, South Africa's state corporations struggled to achieve success that was defined by the provision of lowered costs to private industry. Whether as adjuncts to the railways or as wholesalers of their products, Escom and Iscor in their early histories both worked to lower charges to those who shipped goods on the railways or purchased electricity and steel from private companies. In establishing these state firms, the South African government was combating what was perceived as the long-term dangers of dependence on private monopolies and cartels, in the form of the VFPC and the European steel cartel. It was believed that customers would suffer from rising prices under the control of private monopolies. Indeed, the imperative of lowered costs proved so strong that state corporations consistently found ways to avoid or ignore political pressures to employ expensive white workers. While the general purpose of state corporation activities was to protect white economic power, individual white workers were to benefit indirectly through the growth of private industries, not directly through state employment.

Even under the Nationalist government, which intended to capture the local economy for the volk, state corporations have continued to pursue lowered industrial costs and to sidestep the problems of white workers. Aside from Iscor, which employs a large number of white (as well as African) factory workers, all of the state corporations engage in production that requires a relatively small technical staff (white workers) in conjunction with a large unskilled work force (African workers). The one state foray into labor-intensive production—the IDC textile mills—attempted to use African workers rather than whites and quickly abandoned the effort, as labor costs were still too high to produce a competitive product. Since the 1950s the state corporations have further abandoned attempts to come to grips with the use of either black or white production workers, and they instead rely on highly technical processes to produce goods in capital-intensive industries. The results have been the provision of important industrial materials and services—oil (Sasol), phosphate (Foskor), aluminum (Aluminium Corporation of South Africa—Alusaf), shipping (Safmarine)—at reasonable prices.

After achieving a high level of success in lowering costs to local industries, why were these state enterprises suddenly slated for "privatization" in the late 1980s by the South African government? On 5 February 1988 President P. W. Botha announced government plans to sell the state corporations to private businessmen, apparently ending more than sixty years of state enterprise inside the country. The announcement was made toward the end of a decade that had been trying for South Africa: the gold price had fluctuated between $613 (1980) and $359 (1984) per ounce, foreign loans ($14 billion) had been withdrawn by international lenders, sanctions had been implemented by the United States and the European Economic Community, the rand had depreciated to a low of 37 U.S. cents, and internal unrest had prompted the government to enact a state of emergency for more than five years. Under these conditions, should not the state corporations have been used as valuable resources to bolster the economy? Or had it become impossible for the government to continue to finance the state enterprises? In the face of what would undoubtedly lead to a political crisis over white rule, had the government finally heeded liberal calls to let natural economic forces do away with apartheid, or was it quickly transferring these resources to the exclusively white private sector before an African government could gain control? Had the white government simply panicked in the face of multiple crises and tried to obtain quick capital through the sale of the state firms? What could lead the government to relinquish resources that had proven valuable for most of this century and to abandon policies of direct economic intervention?

The move to privatization was not the radical departure from previous policies that it appeared. In fact, the state corporations had been moving away from intervention in production and toward control over market forces since 1960. At that time the IDC started backing away from establishing any further state enterprises and instead worked as a conduit for government investment in private enterprises. Its programs included the Export Finance Scheme (1960) to subsidize South African exports, the Border Areas Development Scheme (1960) to finance industries near the African "homelands," and efforts at "rationalisation" that merged firms in the same industry under IDC-sponsored holding companies like Feltex (wool, 1965), Sentrachem (chemicals, 1967), DaGama Textiles (cotton cloth, 1968), and Ferrovorm (engineering, 1970). These efforts certainly represented a continuing and deepening involvement of the state in the private economy, but they also signaled a change in methods and a greater reliance on the private sector to take responsibility for production. In this light, privatization does not appear revolutionary, so long as it does not lead to increased prices for products.

And serious governmental concern over rising production costs inside South Africa had indeed preceded President Botha's announcement of privatization. In 1985 the government issued a White Paper on Industrial Development Strategy that questioned efficiency in local industries, asking "whether it was still feasible to develop manufacturing industry mainly on the basis of involving more resources rather than raising their productivity."[2] The state corporations loomed large in such concern, as by 1980 nearly 70 percent of South Africa's total net investment was consumed by the public sector. The government concluded that manufacturing industries, and especially the state corporations, needed to restructure their operations to become more efficient and competitive. The state corporations had absorbed an extremely large amount of capital: Escom's capital expenditures in 1982 alone equaled nearly 42 percent of the country's available savings.[3] And private businessmen increasingly came to view the state corporations as unfairly dominating capital markets to the disadvantage of the private sector.[4] By the mid-1980s they were becoming the focus of government and private concern.

Escom in particular came in for heavy criticism as "the largest capital investment in South Africa."[5] Indeed, by 1985 Escom's assets were valued at more than R30 billion, equivalent to one quarter of the market value of all shares on the Johannesburg Stock Exchange.[6] The commission had undergone an intensive program of expansion, increasing its total assets more than ten times in the 1970s—part of a program (in the wake of the cutoff of Iranian oil) to reduce dependence on fuel oil used to run power generators in rural areas. Between 1972 and 1982 the length of rural power lines more than doubled (from 25,000 to 52,000 miles), while the number of farms supplied with electricity grew ninefold (to 53,467 farms, from only 6,000 in 1959).[7] As a result, Escom provided electricity to half of the white farmers in South Africa at subsidized rates; at the same time, the mining industry still enjoyed the lowest charges for electricity.[8]

Nevertheless, by 1984 the government criticized Escom efficiency and recommended the complete restructuring of the commission into a downsized, profit-oriented operation. A White Paper on the country's electricity supply proposed to overturn sixty years of Escom orthodoxy: "The objective of providing an abundant supply of electricity at cost price wherever a demand exists in South Africa should be discarded."[9] Officials began to fragment Escom's overall structure, so as to create smaller units for possible future privatization. In particular, Escom created "strategic business units," smaller operational units within the commission, for the purpose of increasing accountability and efficiency. Escom chairman Johan Maree raised the possibility of gradually selling off parts of Escom's distribution system while retaining its generating plant, thereby returning the commission to its pre–World War II position as a retailer of electricity. In this way, Escom could cut back on costs and increase revenues while retaining control over its assets—the old policy that had worked so well for van der Bijl.

Under the government's privatization efforts, the only state corporation that was fully privatized was also the most troubled: Iscor. Although the corporation presented a relatively minimal drain on local capital compared with Escom, it consistently struggled to find markets and lower its costs. Iscor was the only state corporation to operate a fully integrated plant, which had led to recurrent crises over labor and its costs throughout the years. By the 1980s Iscor had also been hard hit by international competition, which could no longer be controlled through the sort of comprehensive marketing agreements van der Bijl had fashioned. And even by the

1980s the country's internal markets for steel had failed to expand sufficiently to ensure the corporation local sales. As a result, Iscor had come to
depend on exports of nearly 40 percent of its output in order to reach economic scales of production, remaining primarily a manufacturer of semi-
finished goods in a highly competitive international market.[10] When iron
and steel was included in the U.S. embargo on South Africa in 1986, the
corporation lost an important market.[11]

Not long after enactment of the trade embargoes, the South African
government began a publicity campaign to ready the South African public
for the privatization of Iscor and forecast a 20 percent increase in profits
in the year to come. The public, as the *Financial Mail* later commented,
"overlook[ed] the fact that steel is a rust-belt industry no matter where the
mills are located," and the share issue was sold out, for a total of R3 billion.[12] Yet in less than six months, with earnings well below the corporation's rosy forecast, share prices tumbled. Throughout 1990 and the first
half of 1991, sales revenue continued to fall in response to closed and soft
foreign markets, and the corporation was forced to cut dividends to private
shareholders.[13] Iscor was no more able to overcome competition and high
costs under private ownership than under state ownership.

Whatever the reasons for attempted privatization, its enactment
ignited historical concerns over the relationship between the state and the
economy, and in April 1990 the government reversed its position: "Many
of the State enterprises currently acting as monopolies may not be priva-
tised at all."[14] The steel corporation's failure to meet anticipated successes
reinforced the traditional perception that the state had established industries which private capital correctly believed could not produce sufficient
profits, and the government found investors wary of further share issues.[15]
White workers employed at the state corporations as well as in other state
offices began to fear for their jobs—believing that privatization and attendant pressure for profits would favor African workers—and publicly
protested through their unions. And the African National Congress,
preparing for negotiations with the government over the opening of political power to blacks, strongly opposed the transfer of the state corporations
to the private sector prior to a new political dispensation. Indeed, any new
government would want to continue using the state corporations to promote, control, and direct the local accumulation of capital toward new
constituent groups. The continuities in state corporation history were not
only the result of persistent concerns over costs; they also reproduced
powerful forces in transition and not yet fully changed within South
African society.

South Africa's state corporations have reflected many of the tensions
inherent in the country's history of exclusive white political and economic

power. Rather than representing political or economic forces in a simplistic fashion, these institutions have operated in response to a variety of pressures. They were caught between the political need to support the white community and the economic imperative to protect the mining industry. They sought to develop the local economy while encouraging continued foreign investment and involvement. And they forged important partnerships with private businessmen while pioneering useful economic policies for politicians. These tensions will continue into the future in new forms under an African government working to undo years of discrimination. They are not abstract generic institutions that can reproduce apartheid—or the Asian "miracle"—through the adjustment of a few policies. They will continue to shape South Africa's economic priorities, and they will also provide useful clues to the nature of social change in the future South Africa.

Notes

Preface

1. Davies et al., "Class Struggle," 10. Belinda Bozzoli also cast state corporations in a similar light, symbolic of the victory of national capital over imperial capital in the 1920s. See Bozzoli, *Political Nature of a Ruling Class*, 224.

2. Adam and Giliomee, *Ethnic Power Mobilized*, 164.

3. Christie, *Electricity, Industry, and Class*, 3, 205.

4. As John Lonsdale pointed out in relation to South Africa in the nineteenth century, "the process of articulation bore a double character, political and economic. But it was not a divided, dual character. Each dynamic worked upon the other, not strictly opposed, but not smoothly functional either." Lonsdale is referring not to the articulation of modes of production but to approaches to the interpretation of history, "a different form of articulation, humanist-materialist rather than one or the other. It begins to look like history again, a constant and uncertain struggle between political creativity and economic fate." See Lonsdale, "From Colony to Industrial State," 76, 77.

5. John Iliffe, book review of Saunders and Smith, 144. This is in contrast to the 1970s, when there was an active scholarly debate over the nature and workings of the state.

6. See especially Bozzoli, *Political Nature of a Ruling Class*; Clarke, "Capital, Fractions of Capital, and the State," 32–75; Davies, *Capital, State, and White Labour*; Davies et al., "Class Struggle," 4–30; Innes and Plaut, "Class Struggle and the State," 51–61; Wolpe, "Capitalism and Cheap Labour Power," 425–56. The most thorough but narrowly focused (in terms of state interests) research efforts were provided by Greenberg and Yudelman: see Greenberg, *Race and State in Capitalist Development*, and Yudelman, *Emergence of Modern South Africa*.

7. See Simons and Simons, *Class and Colour*, 535, 561; Lipton, *Capitalism and Apartheid*, 142; Nattrass, "Wages, Profits, and Apartheid," 88.

8. See Papers of the Industrial Manpower Commission, BC825, University of Cape Town.

Chapter 1: State Corporations and History

1. Amsden, *Asia's Next Giant*; Evans, *Dependent Development*.

2. The economist Ben Fine criticized efforts to build a general theory of public enterprise in Britain and proposed an alternative: "In this framework of analysis, as in the [current] synthesis, there are (different) underlying economic forces at work but these are now inseparably linked to broader social influences that are able to accommodate a role for class and other conflicts at the economic and political levels. Thus, whilst the proposition of no general theory of nationalised industries is accepted in the light of the complexity of the influences at work, there is an emphasis on a broader set of factors than those of the synthesis and with a different understanding of those that are considered in common." Fine, "Public Enterprise Economics," 139.

3. Wade, *Governing the Market*, 179; Jones, *Public Enterprise in Less Developed Countries*, 41.

4. Wade, *Governing the Market*, 99–100. Wade also offers an interesting explanation of Taiwanese government goals in pursuing certain economic strategies: "The state has been able to check the automony of these groups [businessmen, workers, foreign firms, and banks] as they have subsequently grown, and thereby found it easier to maintain its own autonomy," p. 275. In other words, he argues for a Taiwanese state that is autonomous from local and foreign businesses as well as labor. For most researchers, presupposing an autonomous state is both questionable in real terms and arid in theoretical terms.

5. Amsden, *Asia's Next Giant*, 301.

6. *Ibid.*, 291.

7. See Evans, *Dependent Development*, 89 and my chap. 3.

8. See Hughes, *Networks of Power*, for discussions of the various interests involved in pricing, distribution, and ownership of various electricity systems in London, Berlin, Chicago, and California.

9. Evans, *Dependent Development*, especially chaps. 3 and 5 and p. 225.

10. See my chap. 4.

11. Wade, *Governing the Market*, 180, 185.

12. Amsden, *Asia's Next Giant*, 324.

13. *Ibid.*, 5.

14. As Amsden states, "The Korean government has a policy with respect to every conceivable aspect of economic development except labor relations. Responsibility for labor relations within the government bureaucracy has largely been left to the Korea Central Intelligence Agency or to the police." Amsden, *Asia's Next Giant*, 324.

15. Cardoso, "Dependency and Development."

16. O'Donnell, *Modernization and Bureaucratic Authoritarianism*. See also Seidman, "Labor Movements."

17. Burawoy, *Politics of Production*.

18. After facing labor repression throughout the postwar era without benefit of union representation, in 1973 workers in private manufacturing industries in Durban erupted in protest that later spread to other industrial areas, eventually leading to the legalization of African trade unions in 1979 in an effort to bring black workers under some control.

19. For South Africa see my chap. 5. For Japan see Smith, *Political Change and Industrial Development*, and Tsurumi, *Factory Girls*. The similarities in the conditions of employment, both involving contracts and dormitory dwelling, as well as the reactions of these workers, are striking considering the differences between the two societies. Nevertheless, it is clear that in each case the work force was composed of those categorized as subordinate and susceptible to such exploitation.

20. Gerschenkron, *Economic Backwardness*, 9.

Chapter 2: Mine Owners and the State, 1886–1918

1. See Wilson and Thompson, eds., *Oxford History of South Africa*, vol. 1, 424–35. On the nature of the *Volksraad* see *ibid.*, p. 365. With regard to the Voortrekker economy, with its mix of subsistence and market-driven forces, see Neumark, *Economic Influences*, arguing that one of the principal motivations for the Great Trek was a desire to obtain more land for commercial stock farming to supply the growing Cape market.

2. Wilson and Thompson, *Oxford History of South Africa*, vol. 1, 420–21.

3. Letter from the Executive of the Republic of Lydenburg, dated 3 April 1860, reprinted in du Toit and Giliomee, eds., *Afrikaner Political Thought*, 227.

4. See Wagner, "Zoutpansberg," 327–37.

5. See Wilson and Thompson, *Oxford History of South Africa*, vol. 1, 438–42, and vol. 2, 281–83, and Delius, *The Land Belongs to Us*.

6. Wilson and Thompson, *Oxford History of South Africa*, vol. 1, 441–42.

7. See Arndt, *Banking and Currency Development*, 93–117, on the ZAR's various attempts to establish a secure currency; and on the chronic weakness of the ZAR administration, Delius, *The Land Belongs To Us*, 147–49.

8. Trapido, "Reflections on Land," 352.

9. See Delius, *The Land Belongs To Us*, 181–212.

10. *Ibid.*, 246.

11. See Arndt, *Banking and Currency Development*, 118, and Houghton and Dagut, *Source Material on the South African Economy*, 337.

12. On land speculation and the growth of "notables" see Trapido, "Reflections on Land," especially 354–58.

13. Henry, *First Hundred Years of the Standard Bank*, 59–60.

14. Kruger was one of the leaders of the Transvaal uprising against the British in 1881, won election as president in 1882, and assumed the office in 1883. See his entry in de Kock, ed., *Dictionary of South African Biography*, 448–49.

15. Gordon, *Growth of Boer Opposition to Kruger*, 36. On state expenditures and revenues see Houghton and Dagut, *Source Material on the South African Economy*, 337.

16. A number of other nations also turned to such means in the early twentieth century, including Turkey, India, Brazil, Mexico, and Korea. For Germany and Japan see Henderson, *State and the Industrial Revolution in Prussia*, and Smith, *Political Change and Industrial Development in Japan*.

17. Imperial Blue Book, *Report of the Transvaal Concessions Commission, 19 April 1901, Part III, Appendix of Documents*, "Agreements under the Industrial

Scheme of 1896," D.1., "List of Existing Concessions." These industrial concessions were modeled on mining concessions granted in the 1860s and 1870s, the first in 1860 to an H. Austin, who received the sole right to explore and develop a particular tract of land for mining purposes, Concession to H. Austin, July 1860, 55/R3915/60, TABA.

18. See Richardson and Van-Helten, "Gold Mining Industry," 18.

19. Imperial Blue Book C.9093, *Report on Trade, Commerce, and the Gold Mining Industry of the SAR, 1897*, carton 11, Leyds Archive, TABA; Houghton and Dagut, *Source Material on the South African Economy*, 274–75; Richardson and Van-Helten, "Gold Mining Industry," 19.

20. Kubicek, *Economic Imperialism*, 21–25.

21. Tabulated from Frankel, *Capital Investment in Africa*, 95.

22. On state revenues see Imperial Blue Book C. 9093, *Report on Trade, Commerce, and the Gold Mining Industry of the SAR, 1897*, carton 11, Leyds Archive, TABA; and Houghton and Dagut, *Source Material on the South African Economy*, 337–38.

23. For population figures see Houghton and Dagut, *Source Material on the South African Economy*, 286–90; Wilson and Thompson, *Oxford History of South Africa*, vol. 1, 425; and Marais, *Fall of Kruger's Republic*, 1.

24. Richardson and Van-Helten, "Gold Mining Industry," 21. For a dramatic contrast consider that in 1841, "when 24,000 emigrants left [Britain] for Canada and 14,500 for Australia and New Zealand, only 130 went to the Cape." For the quote see Frankel, *Capital Investment in Africa*, 51.

25. Imperial Blue Book C. 9093, *Report on Trade, Commerce, and the Gold Mining Industry of the SAR, 1897*, carton 11, Leyds Archive, TABA.

26. For dividend figures see Frankel, *Capital Investment in Africa*, 95; for ZAR revenues see Houghton and Dagut, *Source Material on the South African Economy*, 337–38.

27. Imperial Blue Book C. 9093, *Report on Trade, Commerce, and the Gold Mining Industry of the SAR, 1897*, carton 11, Leyds Archive, TABA.

28. For extensive discussion of the political ramifications of the rise of gold mining, and of Kruger's policies, see Marais, *Fall of Kruger's Republic*.

29. Gordon, *Growth of Boer Opposition to Kruger*, 37.

30. For varying opinions on the relative commodisation of Boer agriculture in the late nineteenth century, see Bundy, *South African Peasantry*; Keegan, *Rural Transformations*; and Morris, "Development of Capitalism."

31. On these speculators see Trapido, "Reflections on Land," and idem, "Landlord and Tenant."

32. Imperial Blue Book, *Report of the Transvaal Concessions Commission, 19 April 1901, Part I, Part II, Minutes of Evidence, and Part III, Appendix of Documents*, D.1.

33. On the NZASM see Van-Helten, "German Capital"; van der Poel, *Railway and Customs Policies*; and Gordon, *Growth of Boer Opposition to Kruger*.

34. This concession was not particularly profitable, largely because it did not have a monopoly and other banks had already entrenched themselves in the Transvaal. See Arndt, *Banking and Currency Development*.

35. The RCE did not have a monopoly on electricity generation—another power-supply company was formed in 1897 by a different mining group—but it did remain the largest operation, supplying twelve mines. See Imperial Blue Book, *Report of the Transvaal Concessions Commission, 19 April 1901, Part III, Appendix of Documents*, "Report on the Rand Central Electric Supply."

36. See the opinion of the State Attorney (J. C. Smuts) regarding the Dynamite Concession, 20 October 1898, Smuts Papers, A1, vol. 96, no. 3, TABA; Cartwright, *Dynamite Company*; Gordon, *Growth of Boer Opposition to Kruger*; and Marais, *Fall of Kruger's Republic*.

37. For a summary of mine owners' criticisms of the concessions policy see *Report of the Transvaal Concessions Commission*, written by the occupying British administration in 1901. On the origins of the South African War and the role of Kruger's concessions see Marks and Trapido, "Lord Milner and the South African State," 50–80, and Kubicek, *Economic Imperialism*.

38. Hobson, *War in South Africa*, 93. The dynamite concessionaires finally built a local factory in the Transvaal in 1898, though they did not begin production at that time. The Chamber of Mines attempted to enlist state support in making an offer to buy the factory but was turned down by the concessionaires. See Percy Fitzpatrick to J. C. Smuts, 31 January 1899, Smuts Papers, A1, vol. 96, no. 9, TABA.

39. Milner to Joseph Chamberlain, 8 November 1901, quoted in Denoon, *Grand Illusion*, 37.

40. Frankel, *Capital Investment in Africa*, 154.

41. See Denoon, *Grand Illusion*, for a thorough discussion of Milner's plans.

42. See van Onselen, *Studies in the Social and Economic History of the Witwatersrand*, vol. 1, 63.

43. See Van-Helten, "German Capital," 14; Cartwright, *Dynamite Company*, 115–16; and Transvaal Chamber of Mines, Annual Reports, 1895, 1910.

44. Imperial Blue Book, *Report of the Transvaal Concessions Commission, 19 April 1901, Part II, Minutes of Evidence*, 24.

45. *Ibid., Part I*, 23.

46. On railway policies see in general van der Poel, *Railway and Customs Policies*.

47. For a complete history of these efforts and strategies see Jeeves, *Migrant Labour*.

48. Evidence presented to the Mining Industry Commission, testimony of A. W. K. Pierce, 19 September 1907, 17/08, vol. 9, LA. Pierce had also worked as manager of the African Concessions Syndicate (see below). See also testimony of Hans Charles Behr, Consulting Mechanical Engineer, Consolidated Goldfields, 26 May 1909, and testimony of David Gilmore, Consulting Mechanical Engineer, Randfontein Mines, 9 June 1909, evidence presented to the Power Companies Commission, vol. I, C40. For further discussion of the connections among labor policy, mechanization, and electrification, see Christie, *Electricity, Industry, and Class*, 5–23.

49. Testimony of David Gilmore, Consulting Mechanical Engineer, Randfontein Mines, 9 June 1909, evidence presented to the Power Companies Commission, vol. I, C40.

50. Union of South Africa, *Union Statistics for Fifty Years* (Pretoria, 1960), p. L35; South African Chamber of Mines, Annual Report, 1975.

51. Three gold mines had also built their own small power stations. See Christie, *Electricity, Industry, and Class,* 17–22.

52. Lionel Phillips, managing director of Central Mines, argued that purchasing power from another company would relieve his own concern of the heavy costs involved in setting up an electricity station. See Phillips to J. Wernher, 30 March 1908, printed in Fraser and Jeeves, eds., *All that Glittered,* 188.

53. Imperial Blue Book, *Report of the Transvaal Concessions Commission, 19 April 1901, Part III, Appendix of Documents,* "Report on the Rand Central Electric Supply."

54. General Electric had in August 1897 taken over the original concession granted in July of the same year to the Simmer and Jack mine. See the Articles of Association of the General Electric Power Company, 26 August 1897, 6330, 5220/97, SS.

55. For a thorough discussion of the economics of production and the history of electricity see Hughes, *Networks of Power.*

56. Charles Rivers Wilson, Rand Central Electric, to Patrick Duncan, Colonial Secretary, 5 January 1906, and Lance and Hoyle to Commissioner of Mines, 15 February 1906, MNW 846, 1934/26; Charles Rivers Wilson, Rand Central Electric, to Lord Selbourne, 12 January 1906, ps19/2/06, GOV 973.

57. "Private Draft Ordinance to Grant Certain Rights and Powers to the African Concessions Syndicate, Ltd., for the Transmission and Generating of Electrical Energy or Power upon and within Certain Areas," July 1906, CS 656/8130.

58. General Manager, Standard Bank, Cape Town, Report, 18 April 1906, GMO 3/1/45, Standard Bank Archives. Emil Rathenau, founder of the AEG, has been described as the "inventor of the principle of market creation through investment financing" and regularly obtained bank credits to provide electrical machinery to utilities in exchange for investment shares. See Hughes, *Networks of Power,* 179–81.

59. Curtis to Colonial Secretary, 9 July 1906, CS 656/8130. Numerous municipalities that generated their own electrical power also objected to the proposed legislation on the grounds that it would infringe on their rights. See for example, Town Clerk, Krugersdorp, to Colonial Secretary, 11 July 1906, and Extracts from Minutes of Special Meeting of the Johannesburg Town Council, 25 July 1906, CS 656/8130.

60. See, for example, General Manager, Standard Bank, Cape Town, to London Board of Directors, 1 and 8 August 1906, GMO 3/1/46, Standard Bank Archives.

61. Final Agreement between government and Rand Central Electric, 1 November 1906, 1934/26, MNW 846.

62. R. Solomon to Transvaal Secretary, 5 December 1906, CS 656/8-8130.

63. See the correspondence of van Hulsteyn, Feltham, and Fry, representatives of the African Concessions Syndicate, to the Johannesburg Town Council, 25 July 1906, and Executive Council Resolution No. 2249, 28 November 1906, CS 656/8130.

64. General Manager, Standard Bank, Cape Town, Report, 24 December 1906,

GMO 3/1/46, Standard Bank Archives. The adjectives quoted, from English newspapers, are reprinted in Christie, *Electricity, Industry, and Class*, 30. See also pp. 31–32 for details on the floating of the VFPC.

65. General Electric shareholders also received £50,000 in cash. The transaction first involved the sale of GE to the African Concessions Syndicate, which then became incorporated into the VFPC. For details see Memorandum re Sale of General Electric Company to African Concessions Syndicate, Ltd., 1907, enclosed with VFPC to Minister of Mines, 30 April 1910, 1934/26, MNW 846.

66. For details of the transaction see Memorandum dated February 1907 contained in 1934/26, MNW 846. On the director's comments, See Christie, *Electricity, Industry, and Class*, 32. The VFPC also dealt with another potential rival, the entrepreneurial firm of Lewis and Marks, by agreeing to establish its power station in Vereeniging near the latter's collieries and nascent industries and to hand over twenty thousand shares and a seat on its board, in exchange for Lewis and Marks's not proceeding with plans for electricity generation. See Christie, *Electricity, Industry, and Class*, 32, and Mendelsohn, *Sammy Marks*, 220–21.

67. VFPC to Power Undertakings Board, 24 August 1910; Power Undertakings Board to Minister of Mines, 20 October 1910, ECB 56.

68. In his study of the South African electricity supply industry, Renfrew Christie argues that the VFPC was primarily a cover for German interests otherwise locked out of the Rand by British manufacturers, and he claims that "the AEG and the German banks were effectively buying their way into the British Colony of the Transvaal." Christie, *Electricity, Industry, and Class*, 31. This sentiment certainly worked to the advantage of the power company, which needed such eager investors. It is not true, however, that the German banks were entirely locked out; Siemens and Halske was involved with RCE. Furthermore, the German firms were the most advanced producers of electrical machinery in the world; "in contrast, on the eve of World War I the leading British electrical manufacturers as a group produced less heavy electrical machinery than either of the two leading German firms." Hughes, *Networks of Power*, 232.

69. See the evidence of W. A. Harper to the Power Companies Commission, 2 June 1909, and that of Professor Georg Klingenberg, 7 June 1909, vol. 2, C40. For further details of the complex negotiations see also Christie, *Electricity, Industry, and Class*, 32–36.

70. See Christie, *Electricity, Industry, and Class*, 39.

71. Transvaal Electrical Energy Bill, 1909, No. EE 2/09, LEG CO 19.

72. Petition in Opposition to Transvaal Electrical Energy Bill 1909 from Municipal Council of Johannesburg, Minutes, Municipal Council of Johannesburg, 16 June 1909, EE 22/09, LEG CO 19.

73. See the evidence of Michael Dodd, Transvaal Coal Owners' Association, 10 June 1909, Power Companies Commission, vol. 3, C40.

74. See *Report of the Power Companies Commission*, TG 13/1910, 1.

75. Other issues investigated by the commissioners included the extent of AEG (meaning German) control over electrical production, the location of power plants and the resulting impact on local water supplies, and the implications of electrification and mechanization for white employment.

76. See Frankel, *Capital Investment in South Africa*, 56, 107–08, 111–18.

77. See *ibid.*, table 12, between pp. 82 and 83, for operating statistics, 1897–1937, and Wilson, *Labour in the South African Gold Mines*, 157.

78. On the developing state-capital relationship see Yudelman, *Emergence of Modern South Africa*, 59–78.

79. Phillips to F. Eckstein, 7 May 1910, quoted in Christie, *Electricity, Industry, and Class*, 43.

80. See Frankel, *Capital Investment in Africa*, 56, 95, 152, and Yudelman, *Emergence of Modern South Africa*, 77.

81. Transvaal, *Report of the Power Companies Commission*, TG13/1910.

82. *Ibid.*, 26.

83. See the Transvaal Power Act, No. 15, 1910. For the point of view of one municipality opposing monopoly see Pretoria Town Council Resolution, 1910, CS 868/15227–17. For discussion of the input of the gold magnates, particularly that of Lionel Phillips of the Corner House group, to the proposed legislation, see Christie, *Electricity, Industry, and Class*, 43–45.

84. On Power Board actions see GME to Secretary for Mines, 16 April 1912, 742/12, MNW 109, and GME report on engineering branch, 6 June 1912, mm1657/12, MNW 124. In 1922 Bernard Price, general manager of the VFPC, testified to the Mining Industry Commission that, "For all I know they [the mining groups] have no holdings today." Evidence of Price, Mining Industry Commission, 5 June 1922, vol. 1, p. 2046, K161.

85. The quotes are from Mendelsohn, *Sammy Marks*, 221. For discussion of power generation in the rest of the world see Hughes, *Networks of Power*, especially chaps. 8 and 14.

86. See Imperial Blue Book, *Report of the Transvaal Concessions Commission*, parts 1 to 3, for full details.

87. Frankel, *Capital Investment in Africa*, 56–57, 381, 383–84.

88. De Kock, ed., *Dictionary of South African Biography*, vol. 5, 610.

89. "Ground Plan of Pretoria Workshops," *Souvenir of the Visit of the Members of the Rand Engineering and Chemical Societies to the Locomotive, Carriage, and Wagon Repair Shops of the CSAR, Pretoria, 1904*, Collection A1269f, University of the Witwatersrand Library. Union of South Africa, *Report of the Select Committee on the Scrap Iron Agreement* (SC9–12), May 1912.

90. Testimony of the Transvaal Iron and Steel Company, vol. 1, and testimony of R. B. Ballantine, vol. 2, Transvaal Customs and Industries Commission, November 1907, C33. *Report of the Customs and Industries Commission* (TG6–1908), no. 25, vol. 10, LA. Union of South Africa, *Report of the Select Committee on the Scrap Iron Agreement* (SC9–12), testimony of Sir Thomas Rees Price, 30 April 1912, pp. 104–05.

91. Draft Agreement between CSAR and Department of Mines, no date, mm2615/09, MNW 385.

92. Colony of the Transvaal, *Memorandum re the Iron and Steel Industry* (TG30–1909), by GME Robert Kotze, 8 March 1909; Harbord to Agent General for the Transvaal, 30 September 1909, mm1139/09, MNW 1145.

93. Agent General for the Transvaal to the Minister of Mines, 1 October 1909, mm1139/09, MNW 1145.

94. "Transvaal Government Notice No. 127 of 1910 on Iron and Steel Manu-

facture in the Transvaal," in *Report of the Select Committee on the Scrap Iron Agreement* (SC9–12), Appendix A.

95. See Kubicek, *Economic Imperialism*, 141–47, for a description of General Mining's origins and activities.

96. Kotze to Secretary for Mines, 27 May 1910, mm811/10, MNW 5.

97. Edgar Allen and Company to Donald Campbell, 2 March 1910, mm811/10, MNW 5.

98. Kotze to Secretary for Mines, 7 July 1910, mm811/10, MNW 5. Gilbert Walker to Kotze, 2 August 1910, and Kotze to Secretary for Mines, 22 April 1911, mm1504/10, MNW 13.

99. For an exhaustive life of Marks and his various business operations see Mendelsohn, *Sammy Marks*.

100. See *ibid.*, 220–21 and chap. 5 in general.

101. GME to Secretary for Mines, 6 April 1911, mm839/11, MNW 53; Inspector of Mines, Natal, to GME, 13 July 1911, IP 178/3; testimony of Kotze, 23 April 1912, printed in Union of South Africa, *Report of the Select Committee on the Scrap Iron Agreement* (SC9–12), 21.

102. See Richards, *Iron and Steel Industry in South Africa*, 34.

103. Testimony of William Wilson Hoy, General Manager, SAR, 23 April 1912, *Report of the Select Committee on the Scrap Iron Agreement* (SC9–12), Appendix G, "Draft Agreement to be Entered into with the Union Steel Corporation (of South Africa), Ltd."

104. Richards, *Iron and Steel Industry in South Africa*, 36; emphasis in original.

105. Quoted in *ibid.*, 39; emphasis added by Richards.

106. Robert Kotze to Secretary for Mines and Industries, 20 December 1913, mm4107/13, MNW 167.

107. Department of the Interior to Minister of Mines, 8 October 1912, mm3093/12, MNW 147; "Cheap Skilled Labour," *Rand Daily Mail*, 11 October 1912; "Standard Wage Vereeniging Dispute," *Transvaal Leader*, 12 October 1912; "On Sammy Marks' Job," *Sunday Times*, 13 October 1912.

108. Mendelsohn, *Sammy Marks*, 229; W. W. Hoy to Secretary for Mines and Industries, 12 March 1915, mm584/13, MNW 167.

109. Richards, *Iron and Steel Industry*, 51; "Report on the Mining, Iron, and Steel Works . . . by the Commission of Experts of the Gutehoffnungshutte," 15 December 1924, p. 65, Annexure 203–1927, Parliamentary Library; Union of South Africa, *Select Committee on Railways and Harbours, Seventh Report (Memorandum of Agreement Between Minister of Railways and Harbours and the Pretoria Iron Mines Limited)*, SC5B–20, p. 54.

110. Hoy to Secretary for Mines and Industries, 12 March 1915, mm584/13, MNW 167; Usco to Prime Minister Botha, 8 February 1916, mm3394/15, MNW 306.

111. Kotze to Secretary for Mines and Industries, 29 April 1916, mm4107/13, MNW 167.

112. Richards, *Iron and Steel Industry*, 51. See also the letter from Usco in 1916 stating that it could not meet all the SAR's needs, Usco to Prime Minister Botha, 8 February 1916, mm3394/15, MNW 306.

113. Hoy to Secretary for Mines and Industries, 4 June 1917, mm2147/17, MNW 385.

114. Scientific and Technical Committee to Secretary for Mines and Industries, 13 June 1917, S 5/1.

115. Secretary for Mines and Industries to Secretary, Scientific and Technical Committee, 8 June 1917, BIS 165.

116. Taxes on the gold-mining industry rose from £1,045,067 in fiscal 1913–14 to £1,290,877 in 1917–18, even though there was no corresponding increase in sales. See *South Africa Yearbook* (Pretoria, 1918), 568, 789. When the government opened up new mining areas on the East Rand in 1916, the mining industry foresaw massive new developments that could only be hindered by continuing taxation and the wartime limitation of capital markets. Furthermore, other sources of capital disappeared during the war, as the South African and British governments prohibited trade with enemy subjects and froze approximately £25,000,000 in investments by Germans on the Rand. See Kubicek, *Economic Imperialism*, 22.

117. General Manager, Standard Bank, Cape Town, Report, 18 December 1916, GMO 3/1/61, Standard Bank Archives.

118. Industrial Development Company, Chairman's Report, 14 August 1917, BC294A43.37.1, Duncan Papers, University of Cape Town Library.

119. W. W. Hoy, "Memorandum on the Iron and Steel Industry in South Africa," 16 August 1917, P8/89, SAS 1062.

120. Hoy to Kotze, 26 June 1918, BIS 381.

121. For the figures see Frankel, *Capital Investment in Africa*, 107–08. The figures for exports as a percentage of national income are for the 1920s. For a full series of figures on the value of exports and on the contributions of major economic sectors to the national income see *Union Statistics for Fifty Years*, pp. N4–5, S3.

122. See Yudelman, *Emergence of Modern South Africa*, chaps. 2–4, for an insightful discussion of these issues.

123. Quoted in Christie, *Electricity, Industry, and Class*, 52.

Chapter 3: The Creation of the State Corporations

1. *Union Statistics for Fifty Years*, pp. N4–5; Frankel, *Capital Investment in Africa*, 150–51, 208.

2. Freund, "Social Character of Secondary Industry," 81; emphasis in original.

3. On the Bambatha uprising see Marks, *Reluctant Rebellion*; on the ordering of the black population see van Onselen, *Studies in the Social and Economic History of the Witwatersrand*, vols. 1 and 2.

4. See Walker, *History of Southern Africa*, 554, 558–63; Yudelman, *Emergence of Modern South Africa*, 108–10.

5. Yudelman, *Emergence of Modern South Africa*, 98–103.

6. Among the Afrikaners there were two notable exceptions to this generalization about poverty, the wine farmers of the western Cape and the maize farmers of the Transvaal, who found a lucrative market for their goods on the mines and gained political control of the country through, first, Het Volk and, later, the South African Party. See Garson, "Het Volk," and O'Meara, *Volkskapitalisme*, chap. 1.

7. Yudelman, *Emergence of Modern South Africa*, chap. 4 in general.

8. *Ibid.*, 134–35. See also Johnstone, *Class, Race, and Gold*, 94. For statistics of gold-industry dividends see Frankel, *Capital Investment in Africa*, 95.

9. See Wilson, *Labour in the South African Gold Mines*, 46, 157.

10. See Yudelman, *Emergence of Modern South Africa*, 138, for the quote, and 136–44 for the issue of the low-grade mines—which he aptly points out was as much a political question as an economic one—in general.

11. General Manager, Standard Bank, Cape Town, Report, 29 November 1916, GMO 3/1/60, Standard Bank Archives.

12. *Idem*, 1 May 1917, GMO 3/1/61, Standard Bank Archives.

13. IDC to Secretary for Mines and Industries, 26 January 1917, IP 128/1; Industries Section, Cape Town, to High Commissioner for South Africa, London, 23 May 1917, ICT 5/2/17. The Industrial Advisory Board in turn recommended the establishment of a Scientific and Technical Committee, again with members drawn largely from the private sector, to deal with all specialized issues, particularly those relating to research, and it was this committee that, as I discuss in chapter 2, recommended that the state not invest in Lewis and Marks's iron and steel enterprise. The board was replaced in 1921 by the Board of Trade and Industries.

14. "The Industrial Development of South Africa," 17 September 1917, BIS 582.

15. Options examined included tariff protection, government purchase of existing operations, job training or other indirect measures, and even direct government investment. See "The Industrial Development of South Africa," 17 September 1917, Memorandum re "Encouragement of Industrial Development by the Government," 25 February 1918, Memorandum on "Forms of State Aid Other Than Tariffs for the Development of Natural Resources of South Africa," 24 June 1919, "Report on Forms of State Aid Other Than Tariffs," 17 March 1920, "State Aid Other Than Tariffs," 23 December 1920, and Caldecott to BIS re State Aid for Industrial Development, 6 June 1922, all in BIS 582.

16. Minutes, Meeting of Engineering Section, Scientific and Technical Committee, 30 April 1918, BIS 345; Memorandum by Advisory Board of Industry and Science on the Iron Industry, IP 178/12–19.

17. See, for example, Houghton, *South African Economy*, 116–23; Yudelman, *Emergence of Modern South Africa*, 240–42; Freund, "Social Character of Secondary Industry," 80–81.

18. *Union Statistics for Fifty Years*, pp. G6, 9; Wilson, *Labour in the South African Gold Mines*, 157.

19. *Union Statistics for Fifty Years*, pp. G7, 9. The manufacturing sector accounted for 90 percent of the jobs available in private industries.

20. *Ibid.*, pp. G6, 20, L3. White wages dropped steadily from 1915 through 1921 despite the growth in manufacturing. From statistics for 1918, white workers in manufacturing earned an average of £209 annually, while those employed in the mines received an average of £474. Wages for blacks in manufacturing and mining were much more comparable, with workers in the manufacturing industry getting an average of £38 per year and those in the mines getting £41.

21. *Official Yearbook of the Union of South Africa, 1910–1925*, no. 8 (Pretoria, 1926), 271; Wilson, *Labour in the South African Gold Mines*, 46.

22. On the poor-white problem and Afrikaner employment in the gold industry see Johnstone, *Class, Race, and Gold*, 61–62, 105; Yudelman, *Emergence of Modern South Africa*, 127–34; and Davies, *Capital, State, and White Labour*, 72–80. Bill Freund has pointed out that "white male unskilled workers played relatively

little part in practice in secondary industry." See Freund, "Social Character of Secondary Industry," 87.

23. Hertzog's and Smuts's careers often ran in parallel. Both studied law overseas, with Hertzog eventually becoming a judge in the Orange Free State and Smuts state attorney for the South African Republic. Both fought against the British during the South African War and rose to the rank of general. After the war both were members of the responsible governments in their respective provinces, and at Union both became members of Louis Botha's cabinet. Their careers diverged thereafter, however, as Hertzog became an ardent supporter of Afrikaner nationalism, while Smuts hewed closely to policies that favored the mining industry and South Africa's connections with Britain. Dan O'Meara has suggested that the difference in approach can be accounted for in some part by the fact that Hertzog's main constituents, Free State farmers, did not have the same close market connections to the gold-mining industry as did Smuts's Transvaal farmers. See O'Meara, *Volkskapitalisme*, 26–27. On Hertzog see van den Heever, *General J. B. M. Hertzog*, and on Smuts see Hancock, *Smuts*.

24. See the report of the House of Assembly Debates, *Cape Times*, 14–15 June 1917, and Notulen van het Derde Kongres, De Nationale Partij van de Kaap Provincie, 2 Oktober 1917, 1/2/2/1/1, PV346, Institute for Contemporary History.

25. See Yudelman, *Emergence of Modern South Africa*, 158, whose figures are derived from *Union Statistics for Fifty Years*, p. G18. Davies, *Capital, State, and White Labour*, 98, has slightly different statistics, collected from the official yearbooks and the annual reports of the Department of Mines, Labor Division.

26. *Union Statistics for Fifty Years*, p. G20; Wilson, *Labour in the South African Gold Mines*, 157; Yudelman, *Emergence of Modern South Africa*, 150.

27. Chamber of Mines statement quoted in Yudelman, *Emergence of Modern South Africa*, 150.

28. *Ibid.*, 149–51.

29. *Ibid.*, 154–55.

30. Quoted in Johnstone, *Class, Race, and Gold*, 62.

31. Quoted in Davies, *Capital, State, and White Labour*, 80.

32. Smyth to Minister of Mines and Industries, 15 April 1919, ICT 158/19.

33. Davies, *Capital, State, and White Labour*, 149.

34. See above. The railways, which had considered various schemes for the electrification of their lines as early as 1902, believed that the increased horsepower and the cost savings (particularly from reduced labor needs) by changing from steam to electrical power would not only increase its own revenues but also provide a great boost to the coal industry and to wheat farming in the form of lower transportation costs. Comparative cost figures estimated by the SAR were under steam: 7,024,763 miles, £132,814 in wages; under electricity: 4,841,707 miles, £58,500 in wages. Memorandum re "Electrification of Natal Main Line," 1912, P12/131, SAS 1081. See also CSAR, "Record of Reports and Negotiations in Connection with Proposed Electrification of Springs-Randfontein Section of Line," 1905, TKP 253; Minutes, Meeting in Connection with Railway Construction, 4 December 1919, mm2855/19, MNW 490; Merz and McLellan Report on Natal Electrification, 1919, P12/131/1, SAS 1083.

35. Brebner (Private Secretary to Botha) to Blankenberg, 31 December 1918, IP 373/1–19.

36. The quote is from Christie, *Electricity, Industry, and Class*, 81. Numerous reports on the financial advantages of electrification for the railways and by extension for the South African economy were produced by government-appointed overseas consultants between 1917 and 1920. See in particular Christie, 75–81; Merz and McLellan Report on Natal Electrification, 1919, P12/131/1, SAS 1083; and Hoy to Kotze, 26 June 1918, BIS 381.

37. See in general Jacobs, *South African Heritage*. On his appointment see the original recommendations, 28 March 1918, ICT 22/18; Smyth to Minister of Mines and Industries, 5 September 1917, vol. 7, A583; report of the House of Assembly Debates, *Cape Times*, 7 May 1919; and Minutes of a Meeting of the Board of Industry and Science, 7–9 January 1920, BIS 706. Van der Bijl's book, published in 1920 by McGraw-Hill, was kept in print until 1940.

38. The first of van der Bijl's statements, made in 1921, is reprinted in Christie, *Electricity, Industry, and Class*, 77. The Prime Ministers' Archives, which Christie used for his research in the 1970s, were closed to researchers in the 1980s. The second statement is from letter by van der Bijl to Minister of Mines and Industries, 2 March 1923, mm1280/24, MNW 715.

39. On his preference for the private management of the electricity industry see van der Bijl's "Memo on the Draft Electricity Bill and Its Relation to the Economic Supply of Electrical Power," 4 April 1922, ECB mm3250/21.

40. Hoy to Government Mining Engineer, 17 May 1921, P4/14, SAS 1021. See also Memorandum of the Parliamentary Section of the SAR, 31 March 1920, P12/131/1, SAS 1083; Inspector of Labor, Natal, to Chief Inspector of Labor, 27 October 1920, mm3385/20, MNW 548.

41. Government Mining Engineer to Minister of Mines and Industries, 10 August 1921, P4/14, SAS 1021.

42. Document from Prime Ministers' Archives, quoted in Yudelman, *Emergence of Modern South Africa*, 143.

43. An exception was Pacific Gas and Electric, which had completed formation of a regional system in northern California by 1914. See Hughes, *Networks of Power*.

44. By 1921 the Hydro-Electric Power Commission of Ontario provided electricity to more than two hundred municipalities as well as directly to private consumers. It was cited by Hoy as a successful example of state regulation and production. See Union of South Africa, *Report of the Select Committee on the Electricity Bill* (SC7–22), p. 51, and Appendix D, "Memorandum on the Bill by the General Manager of the South African Railways and Harbours."

45. On the background to the proposed legislation see "Report of the Engineering Section of the Scientific and Technical Committee," 28 December 1918, BIS 428.

46. Draft of Electricity Bill, 25 February 1921, SAS 1021/P4/14. The drafting committee was comprised of officers from the Railway Administration, including Hoy, as well as officials from the Departments of Mines and Industries, Post and Telegraphs, and Irrigation. The government mining engineer, Sir Robert Kotze, was the chairman. Russel to Accountant, 6 October 1920, mm3216/20, MNW 53. The

particular officers entrusted to prepare the draft were technical officers in the SAR and the Department of Mines. See Minutes of the departmental drafting committee, Electrical Power Supply in Union, 8 October 1920, IP 373/1–19.

47. For figures on electricity output see *Union Statistics for Fifty Years*, p. L34. On Price's objection to the Electricity Bill, see his letter to the Undersecretary of Mines and Industries, 22 March 1921, Draft Electricity Bill, "Comments on Draft and Proposed Amendments," 18 April 1921, 42/–/–, STA 1.

48. Transvaal Chamber of Mines to Undersecretary of Mines and Industries, 6 April 1921, Draft Electricity Bill, "Comments on Draft and Proposed Amendments," 18 April 1921, 42/–/–, STA 1.

49. Yudelman, *Emergence of Modern South Africa*, 149.

50. See Johnstone, *Class, Race, and Gold*, 153–54, for discussion of correspondence passing between Hertzog and Cresswell in 1921 and 1922.

51. Smuts to A. Clark, 24 March 1922, reprinted in van der Poel, ed., *Selections from the Smuts Papers*, vol. 5, p. 115.

52. See the discussion of parliamentary debates in Davies, *Capital, State, and White Labour*, 79–80. The 1922 strike is best analyzed in Johnstone, *Class, Race, and Gold*, and Yudelman, *Emergence of Modern South Africa*.

53. GME to Secretary of Mines, 4 March 1921, IP 373/1–19; GME to Minister of Mines and Industries, 10 August 1921, P4/14, SAS 1021; Smyth to Kotze, 10 December 1921, IP 373/2–21; Draft Bill to Provide for the Supply and Control of Electricity, May 1922, P4/14, SAS 1021.

54. Hoy to Kotze, 30 May 1922, P4/14, SAS 1021.

55. Hoy to Kotze, 11 April 1921, P4/14, SAS 1021; "Comments on Draft Electricity Bill," 18 April 1921, 42/–/–, STA 1; Union of South Africa, *Report of the Select Committee on the Electricity Bill* (SC7–22), 3.

56. *Report of the Select Committee on the Electricity Bill* (SC7–22), 34.

57. See the evidence of Elsdon Dew in *ibid.*, 25.

58. W. S. Webber, SAP–Troyeville, and R. B. Waterston, Labour–Brakpan, were the members from the Rand.

59. Their fears were well-founded, as the SAR had come under considerable public scrutiny in 1921 when the auditor general discovered that the SAR regularly charged its capital outlays to the Depreciation Fund rather than to the Loan Fund, so as to avoid increasing its debts. See the report of the House of Assembly Debates, *Cape Times*, 19 and 28 April 1921; and Hoy to Railway Board, 25 August 1921, P4/14, SAS 1021.

60. See Price's testimony on this proposal in *Report of the Select Committee on the Electricity Bill* (SC7–22), 36, 43.

61. Price to A. N. Aikman, 16 January 1923, quoted in Christie, *Electricity, Industry, and Class*, 84.

62. See McColm to Hoy, 1 November and 1 December 1921, P12/131/1, SAS 1083; and *idem*, 8 and 10 July 1922, P4/14, SAS 1021. The Railways Construction Act of 1922 contained the provision for SAR power stations.

63. VFPC to Kotze, 26 January 1923, ECB 56/8/1.

64. Hoy to Minister of Mines and Industries, 16 February 1923, mm583/23, MNW 717. See evidence regarding the VFPC strike presented to the Mining Industries Commission, June 1922, vol. 1, K161.

65. Within months of its establishment the Electricity Control Board had itself been inundated with competing applications and requests, and it had called on the government to set up Escom as soon as possible. See Minutes, ECB, 7 February 1923, mm2565/23, MNW 676.

66. Memorandum by H. Warington Smyth, 16 February 1923, mm583/23, MNW 717.

67. For the exact provisions of the legislation see the Electricity Act of 1922.

68. Indeed, as the Electricity Bill neared passage, van der Bijl had written to Smyth, "I have great apprehensions about the ability of such a Commission to supply electricity in the most economical manner and . . . I don't quite see how we can go ahead with the Bill." Van der Bijl to Smyth, 7 June 1922, 42/–/–, STA 1.

69. Van der Bijl's ideas are well laid out in Jacobs' *South African Heritage*.

70. See the report of Smuts's 31 March 1922 speech to the House of Assembly reprinted in van der Poel, *Selections from the Smuts Papers*, vol. 5, pp. 118–35.

71. On employment conditions in the mines see Wilson, *Labour in the South African Gold Mines*, 46, 157, and Johnstone, *Class, Race, and Gold*, 137, 141; on manufacturing opportunities or lack thereof see *Union Statistics for Fifty Years*, pp. G6, 20; and on white unemployment and poor whites see Davies, *Capital, State, and White Labour*, 75, 160–62.

72. For the quoted descriptions see T. R. H. Davenport, *South Africa*, 256–57.

73. On government negotiations with Delfos and the role of Lionel Phillips see the minutes of the meeting of the Engineering Section, Scientific and Technical Committee, 30 April 1918, BIS 345; Memorandum by the Advisory Board of Industry and Science on the Iron Industry, 9 October 1919, IP 178/12-19; Hoy's speech to the House of Assembly, reported in *Cape Times*, 10 August 1920; and Inspection Report, Standard Bank, Pretoria Branch, 17 October 1919, INSP 1/1/262, Report of General Manager, Standard Bank, Cape Town, to London, 30 December 1919, GMO 3/1/63, and *idem*, 21 May 1920, GMO 3/1/64, all in the Standard Bank Archives. On Delfos and the nascent steel industry in general see Richards, *Iron and Steel Industry*, 56–68.

74. General Manager, Standard Bank, Cape Town, to London Board of Directors, 5 November 1920, GMO 3/1/65, Standard Bank Archives.

75. Memorandum by Advisory Board of Industries and Science on the Iron Industry, 9 October 1919, IP 178/12-19; Richards, *Iron and Steel Industry*, 69.

76. The British Trade Facilities Advisory Board did so on the grounds that a South African producer would compete with British steel makers. For information concerning the course of negotiations with the British government and British producers see South African Iron and Steel Company to Board of Trade and Industries, 30 March 1922, BTI 32/1; J. Leisk to Private Secretary to the Prime Minister, 11 May 1922, BTI 32/47/1; Delfos to South African Iron and Steel Company, 16 February 1923, and South African Iron and Steel Company to Delfos, February 1923, 25/–/–, STA 1; and Delfos to Creswell, 10 February 1927, BTI 32/47/12. On negotiations with other countries see Delfos to Tielman Roos, 4 December 1924 and 28 August 1925, and Niven to Creswell, 10 January 1925, 509, vol. 1, HEN 3248.

77. Delfos to Creswell, 10 February 1927, BTI 32/47/12.

78. Delfos to Tielman Roos, 28 July 1924, BTI 32/47/1.

79. At the time of the French occupation of the Ruhr, many of the German

steel firms were moving their assets out of the area for safekeeping and were interested in making investments elsewhere. Karl Sphilhaus to Delfos, 18 July 1923, BTI
32/47/1; Delfos to Creswell, 10 February 1927, BTI 32/47/12. At the same time,
however, the German steel industry was in the process of forming a cartel in cooperation with German manufacturers, and it was hardly in their interests to establish a new industry in South Africa. Before the South African report was final, the
firm withdrew support for the venture, begging poverty due to the heavy reparation
payments required by the French. See Feldman, *Iron and Steel*, 451–54. Delfos to
Tielman Roos, 28 July 1924, BTI 32/47/1.

80. Board of Trade and Industries Report on the Steel Industry, 23 June 1922,
and van der Bijl to Minister of Mines and Industries, 1 June 1922, 25/–/–, STA 1;
Kotze to Secretary of Mines and Industries, 8 July 1922, BTI 32/47/1.

81. "The Steel Industry and the Railways," *Cape Times*, 28 April 1924, P8/89,
SAS 1062.

82. Hancock, *Smuts*, vol. 2, p. 162.

83. Quoted in *ibid.*, 162.

84. Skeels to Fremantle, 2 October 1923, A608, vol. 14. Smuts's South African
Party did, however, retain control of the Senate. For two differing interpretations
on why the National Party was able to get out the Afrikaner vote see Stadler,
"Party System in South Africa," who stresses the importance of economic issues as
symbols for more fundamental nationalistic sentiments, and O'Meara, *Volkskapitalisme*, 31–35, who argues that such sentiments reflected the various class interests compressed within the NP, all of which were at odds with monopoly capitalism and British domination of trade.

85. Yudelman, *Emergence of Modern South Africa*, 232–33.

86. In 1925 the government established a levy to be used to promote the dairy
industry and also established the Fruit Export Board; in 1926 the Perishable Products Export Board was established and the Fahey sugar agreement drawn up to stabilize sugar prices. Wilson and Thompson, eds., *Oxford History of South Africa*,
vol. 2, pp. 137–38. As for the special treatment still accorded the mining industry,
part of the explanation lay with the continued political expertise of Lionel Phillips
and his successors in having their views heard. On 31 July 1924 Phillips wrote to
his son, "I made it my duty to cultivate the new masters [Botha and Smuts in 1906]
and, in the end, greatly modified the relations. You and Wallers will have to try to
get upon good *personal* terms with Hertzog, Beyers and Co. It is amazing what can
be done by *discreet* action. It is not necessary, nor would it be wise, to pretend to
agree with their politics, but personal discussions on material questions are infi-
nitely more effective if you can seek interviews in a quiet, friendly way than if
everything has to be formal or in writing. . . . Moreover, at a quiet lunch or dinner
at one's home, confidence is more easily established and the individual may *sound*
one [out] as to the effect of this or that measure (possibly floating in his brain then)
and one can point out its effects (if baneful) with success. Things are often done in
ignorance of the consequences, especially by politicians playing up to the gallery,
without the *intention* of harm." Quotations in original reprinted in Fraser and
Jeeves, eds., *All That Glittered*, 355.

87. William Martin argues that the 1925 Tariff Act marked a "significant
break" in government policies toward local industries. In particular, the act did sig-

nify a serious realignment of government policy toward imports with its attempt to break free from reliance on British suppliers. Furthermore, Hertzog concluded trade agreements with Germany in 1928 (granting most favored nation status) and in 1933 (a barter trade agreement). Martin's argument that the Tariff Act reflected a change in the attitude of the state toward industry, however, is more difficult to substantiate, because of the significant considerations given to mining and agriculture consumers. See Martin, "Making of an Industrial South Africa," 59–85.

88. See "The Industrial Development of South Africa," 17 September 1917, BIS 582, and Robert Kotze's remarks in Minutes, Board of Trade and Industries, 12 June 1922, vol. 1, BTI 32/7.

89. See Yudelman, *Emergence of Modern South Africa*, 221–29, for discussion of the Pact's legislative program.

90. Roos supported but refrained from participating in the 1914 rebellion; instigated but did not join the Vryheidsdeputasie that traveled to the Paris Peace Conference in 1919 to ask for South African independence; and, while not condoning the 1922 Rand Revolt, urged Afrikaners to refrain from serving in police action against the strikers. Hertzog's suspicions of Roos were substantiated in 1932 when Roos began negotiations to form a political coalition with Smuts, excluding Hertzog. See the entries on Roos and Hertzog in de Kock, ed., *Dictionary of South African Biography*, vol. 1. The quotation is from p. 373.

91. Roos to Beyers, 22 September 1924, BTI 32/47/1.

92. Delfos to Tielman Roos, 28 August 1925, 509, vol. 1, HEN 3248.

93. In parliamentary debate on the Electricity Bill in 1922 one prominent Nationalist politician, J. H. Munnik, had claimed that the minister of mines and industry "seemed to have tried to cover up very carefully the fact that the Government was now practically launching out on a State enterprise, which was nothing more than another branch of nationalisation." See the report of the House of Assembly Debates, *Cape Times*, 1 June 1922.

94. South African Iron and Steel Company to Minister of Mines and Industries, 10 December 1925, 509, vol. 1, HEN 3248.

95. Feldman, *Iron and Steel*, 456.

96. Memorandum by Director of Stores and Shipping, 16 March 1926, 509, vol. 1, HEN 3248.

97. See *Union Statistics for Fifty Years*, p. G15, and Wilson, *Labour in the South African Gold Mines*, 157.

98. "Report on the Mining, Iron, and Steel Works, Proposed by the South African Iron and Steel Corp., Ltd., by the Commission of Experts of the Gutehoffnungshutte," 15 December 1924, part 7, section 4b, "Consumption of Iron and Steel: By the Mines Including Witwatersrand," pp. 69–70, Annexure 203–1927, Parliamentary Library; Richards, *Iron and Steel Industry*, xxxii, table 14.

99. See Yudelman, *Emergence of Modern South Africa*, especially chap. 6.

100. Hoy to Smyth, 8 December 1925, P8/89/1, SAS 1065.

101. Colony of the Transvaal, *Memorandum re the Iron and Steel Industry* (TG30–1909), by GME Robert Kotze, 8 March 1909; Union of South Africa, *Report of the Select Committee on the Scrap Iron Agreement* (SC9–12), testimony of Sir Thomas Rees Price, 30 April 1912; "Memorandum on the Iron and Steel Industry in South Africa," by W. W. Hoy, 16 August 1917, P8/89, SAS 1062; SAR Memoranda

re Iron and Steel, 9 October 1924, P8/89 Part I, SAS 1062, and 17 August 1925, W8532/27/3, SAS 2301.

102. Smyth to Creswell, 10 February 1926, 509, vol. 1, HEN 3248.

103. "Memorandum on the Iron and Steel Industry in South Africa," by W. W. Hoy, 16 August 1917, P8/89, SAS 1062. In January 1925, Kotze had just finished a report on the development of mineral resources, in which he consistently steered away from direct government involvement or any action that would pass development costs on to consumers. See *South African Journal of Industries*, April 1925.

104. See Yudelman, *Emergence of Modern South Africa*, 230–31.

105. Delfos to Tielman Roos, 13 January 1925, 509, vol. 1, HEN 3248.

106. Memorandum by Creswell to the Cabinet, 16 February 1926, 509, vol. 1, HEN 3248.

107. *Union Statistics for Fifty Years*, p. G6.

108. The government mining engineer, Robert Kotze, was dismissed by Creswell in December 1926, and Hoy and Smyth both retired in 1928.

109. Upon coming into office, the Pact government replaced all the old board members and charged the new ones with revamping customs tariffs; the result was the 1925 Tariff Act. For the quotation see "Statement to Be Presented to the Economic and Wage Commission by the Board of Trade and Industries," 30 November 1925, BTI 439.

110. "Memo on Establishment in the Union of an Iron and Steel Industry, with Special Reference to the Report of the Gutehoffnungshutte on the Proposed Iron and Steel Works at Pretoria," by F. Meyer, pp. 40–41, 509, vol. 2, HEN 3248.

111. Clause 16(1)(f), of the "Bill to Promote the Development within the Union of the Iron and Allied Industries . . ." (A.B. 18–27), *Union Gazette Extraordinary*, 17 February 1927.

112. "Proposed Establishment of State Encouraged Iron and Steel Industry in Union," by GME Pirow, 27 January 1927, BTI 32/47/12.

113. General Manager to Bruwer, 21 February 1927, BTI 32/47/12. Creswell agreed to changes in the bill proposed by the SAR, introducing them verbatim during the hearings of the select committee. See *Report of the Select Committee on the Iron and Steel Industry Bill* (SC5–27), xix, xx.

114. *Select Committee on the Iron and Steel Industry Bill* (SC5–27), viii.

115. *Ibid.*, 69.

116. *House of Assembly Debates*, 2 March 1927, column 925; *Select Committee on the Iron and Steel Industry Bill* (SC5–27), xi, xxii.

117. The report commissioned from the German steel experts had originally recommended that the Rand mines be charged the highest prices of all customers in South Africa. In coming to a compromise Creswell reversed that recommendation, with Meyer testifying that he did "not think that there is any principle there as soaking it into the mines. You do not have one ex-works price only." See "Report on the Mining, Iron, and Steel Works . . . by the . . . Experts of the Gutehoffnungshutte," Annexure 203–1927, Parliamentary Library; and Meyer to Oppenheimer, in *Select Committee on the Iron and Steel Industry Bill* (SC5–27), 52.

118. *House of Assembly Debates*, 28 February 1927, column 809. See also *Select Committee on the Iron and Steel Industry Bill* (SC5–27), 100–05, for objec-

tions made by local manufacturers, led by the Federated Chambers of Industry, to Iscor's potentially harmful effect on local competition.

119. *House of Assembly Debates*, 2 March 1927, column 924.

120. *Minutes of Proceedings of a Joint Sitting of Both Houses of Parliament* (No. 2–1928, Joint Session), 30 March 1928. Authorization for such sessions was provided under Section 63 of the South Africa Act, 1909, and due to similar disagreements the sessions were also exercised in 1925 to consider the Official Languages of the Union Bill; in 1926 to consider the Mines and Works Act, 1911, Amendment Bill; and in 1927 to consider the Precious Stones Bill. Thereafter, the South Africa Act was amended to allow for the dissolution of the Senate 120 days following an election, at which time the government could nominate its own candidates, thus precluding an Opposition majority in the Senate.

121. See the evidence of C. T. Te Water, *House of Assembly Debates*, 28 February 1927, columns 848–49.

122. Smuts to M. C. Gillett, 6 December 1948, Smuts Papers 279/270, A1, TABA.

Chapter 4: Strategies for Survival

1. *Our First Half Century: 1910–1960, Golden Jubilee of the Union of South Africa* (Johannesburg, 1960), cited in Bozzoli, *Political Nature of a Ruling Class*, 224.

2. *Ibid.*; Davies et al., "Class Struggle," 10; Adam and Giliomee, *Ethnic Power Mobilized*, 164.

3. An exception in the literature is Seidman and Seidman, *South Africa and U.S. Multinational Corporations*. Through an examination of foreign involvement in South Africa's economy, the Seidmans have uncovered numerous links between the state corporations and private capital: "In intervening in the critical sectors of the South African economy, the parastatals have cooperated closely both with the domestic mining finance houses and with foreign-based multinational corporations" (p. 67).

4. Debates, House of Assembly, printed in *Cape Times*, 23 May 1922.

5. Debates, House of Assembly, 21 February 1927.

6. Under the terms of the Electricity Act, Smuts's government provided £8,000,000 for Escom's initial development, and thereafter the commission was to raise loans from the public through the issue of nonvoting stocks. Iscor was funded differently, through the issue of debentures and shares to the public; the government was responsible for buying the first half-million shares at £1 each but eventually purchased all shares and debentures because of a weak public response.

7. David Kaplan and Mike Morris have documented the change from white labor preference to black at Iscor but have failed to note the extent to which such a change affects their argument concerning Iscor's position vis-à-vis "national" capital. See Kaplan and Morris, "Labour Policy in a State Corporation." Alternatively, while Renfrew Christie has explained in great depth the connections between Escom and the privately owned VFPC, including the fact that Escom-owned stations were run by the VFPC, which used repressed black labor extensively, he still views Escom as a promoter of white labor and sees state efforts to

develop the electricity industry as geared toward the replacement of black work-ers with whites. See *Electricity, Industry, and Class,* especially 95–96.

8. Escom confidential memorandum, 28 November 1923, mm3396/23, MNW 687.

9. See chap. 3.

10. The municipalities, especially those of Johannesburg, Cape Town, and Dur-ban, had strongly opposed the Electricity Bill and fought to guard their rights. For example, see General Manager, SAR, to Government Mining Engineer, 11 April 1921, P4/14, SAS 1021.

11. See Secretary of Mines to all Ministers, 5 August 1924, mm1649/24, MNW 722; Department Memorandum of Meeting between Minister of Mines and Indus-tries and H. J. van der Bijl, 5 March 1925, mm1288/24, MNW 717.

12. The VFPC held a license to supply electricity on the Rand, which expired in 1948. Under the provisions of the Electricity Act, Escom could expropriate the com-pany at that time in exchange for reasonable compensation. On the contracts entered into between the mining companies and the VFPC see "A Descriptive List of Contracts Entered into by the Applicant in the Transvaal," VFPC to Power Undertakings Board, 13 August 1910, ECB 56.

13. See chapter 3 for discussion of the debate surrounding the bill and of the VFPC's satisfaction at preventing the immediate establishment of Escom upon pas-sage of the Electricity Act.

14. VFPC to ECB, 26 January 1923, ECB 56/8/1.

15. VFPC pamphlet, September 1925, mm2137/25, MNW 795.

16. Escom objection to VFPC application, 17 September 1923, mm583/23, MNW 717.

17. Minutes of Water Court Hearing re Witbank Station, p. 52, 7 January 1924, mm1172/24, MNW 711.

18. Memorandum by Secretary of Mines re VFPC application, 16 February 1923, General Manager, SAR, to Minister of Mines and Industries, 16 February 1923, H. J. van der Bijl to Minister of Mines and Industries, 30 May 1923, mm583/23, MNW 717.

19. VFPC to ECB, 26 January 1923, ECB 56/8/1.

20. Van der Bijl to Kotze, 9 June 1923, mm583/23, MNW 717.

21. Escom objection to VFPC application, 17 September 1923, mm583/23, MNW 717.

22. See Christie, *Electricity, Industry, and Class,* 105–07.

23. Escom-VFPC Agreement Relating to Generating Station at Witbank, 5 July 1924, mm1367/24, MNW 717; evidence of Bernard Price, 26 November 1931, Low Grade Ore Commission, vol. 5, K34.

24. VFPC license, 1910, 1934/26, MNW 846; Chamber of Mines private cables concerning negotiations with VFPC, 9, 15 January and 1 February 1924, mm1367/24, MNW 717.

25. ECB Annual Report, 1934, 507/5, HEN 3239.

26. "Supply of Electricity to Industries in Johannesburg," 13 September 1921, IP 373/2–19.

27. SAR Electrical Engineer to General Manager, SAR, 23 September 1921, P4/14, SAS 1021.

28. Evidence of Bernard Price, Low Grade Ore Commission, 26 November 1931, vol. 5, K34; ECB Annual Report, 1932, 507/5, HEN 3239.

29. Escom to Minister of Mines and Industries, 16 January 1925, mm1288/24, MNW 717.

30. Escom Report, 22 October 1924, Administrator of the Transvaal to Johannesburg Town Council, 1 December 1924, mm1288/24, MNW 717.

31. Confidential Escom memo, 28 November 1923, mm3396/23, MNW 687.

32. Minutes of Meeting between Escom, Johannesburg representatives, and Minister of Mines and Industries, 4 March 1925, Department Memorandum re same Meeting, 5 March 1925, mm1288/24, MNW 717.

33. H. J. van der Bijl to Johannesburg Town Council, 12 October 1925, mm1288/24, MNW 717.

34. Interestingly, the Electricity Supply Act, passed four years after South Africa's Electricity Act, also created a Central Electricity Board to construct and operate the grid that was modeled after Escom. As Thomas Hughes says, apparently unaware of Escom's existence, "The board concept was more original than the technical aspects of the Grid. A public corporation that was able to raise its own funds, the CEB was organized and administered by government-salaried managers and engineers who were not part of the civil service. . . . The CEB was eligible for financial guarantees from the Treasury to aid it in raising funds, but these came from the sale of interest-bearing, nonvoting stock to the public." Hughes, *Networks of Power*, 354.

35. Escom Report on Power Station at Salt River, Cape Town, 9 July 1924, mm3285/23, MNW 685.

36. Escom Report on Electrical Undertaking in Durban, 1 October 1925, mm2402/25, MNW 800.

37. Department of Justice to Secretary of Mines and Industries, 9 January 1923, mm469/23, MNW 657; Minutes ECB meeting, 7 February 1923, mm2565/23, MNW 676.

38. A. C. McColm to Secretary of Mines and Industries, 6 February 1924, mm1367/24, MNW 717.

39. The municipality preferred to have a guaranteed price rather than to take the power at cost. Agreement between Escom and the Durban Corporation, 21 April 1925, mm2402/25, MNW 800.

40. Secretary of Mines and Industries to all Ministers, 5 August 1924, mm1649/24, MNW 722.

41. Escom Annual Returns, 1927/28, ECB 81/2.

42. SAR Memorandum, 20 December 1928, F18037/1, SAS 413.

43. On the increasing costs of electrification, coupled with a decline in the coal trade in Natal, which together undermined the economic rationale for the SAR's grandiose schemes, see SAR Report on the Electrification of the Maritzburg-Glencoe Section, 13 July 1925, mm1711/25, MNW 785; Hoy to Minister of Railways and Harbors, 19 May 1927, mm1711/25, MNW 785; Coal Consumption at Power Stations, 1928–29, mm2177/29, MNW 994; SAR to ECB, 6 July 1929, F18037/1, SAS 413; Escom statistics, January–November 1931, BTI 47/4; Union of South Africa, *Official Year Book of the Union of South Africa, 1934–1935,* (Pretoria, 1936), 715; *Report of the Committee of Inquiry into the Base Mineral Industry,* 1940, vol. 4, p. 34, K14.

44. On More's complaints see the extracts from *Hansard* re Escom, 25 March 1929, and SAR to ECB, 6 July 1929, F18037/1, SAS 413.

45. Under the terms of the Electricity Act, Escom was entitled to government loans only until 1930; after that time it would have to appeal to the public for additional funds through bond sales. See van der Bijl to Minister of Railways and Harbors, 10 February 1930, F18037/1, SAS 413.

46. Secretary of Finance to Secretary of Mines and Industries, 15 May 1930, 508/3, vol. 1, HEN 3244. Although contractual obligations prevented the VFPC from passing on its increased costs in higher charges, it could reduce the percentage of "surplus profit"—a variable rate between 25 and 50 percent—that it shared with the mines.

47. Escom Memorandum re SAR Annual Report (1930), pp. 9–10, quoting General Manager, 4 February 1931, mm47/2, MNW 1122.

48. L. P. van Zyl Ham had succeeded Herbert Warington Smyth in 1928. Secretary of Mines and Industries to Minister of Mines and Industries, 24 July 1930, mm1623/30, MNW 1031.

49. See van der Bijl's testimony printed in *Report of the Select Committee on the Iron and Steel Industry Bill* (SC5–27), pp. 69–70.

50. Secretary of Mines to Escom, 23 July 1930, 7 November 1930, BTI 47/4; Minister of Mines and Industries to Escom, 12 December 1930, and Draft Amendment to Electricity Act, 1930, mm1623/30, MNW 1031.

51. Van der Bijl to Secretary of Mines, 12 November 1930, BTI 47/4.

52. Departmental Memorandum to Minister of Mines and Industries, 27 November 1930, mm1623/30, MNW 1031.

53. General Manager, SAR, to Minister of Railways and Harbors, 5 March 1931, F18037/1, SAS 413. Cape Town's consumption at Salt River was covered under the "interchange" and later "pooling" arrangements, and it never counted in the station's official consumption figures. This served to give the SAR a claim to higher consumption percentages than were actually the case.

54. Cape Town City Council to Minister of Mines and Industries, 6 August 1931, mm47/5, MNW 1122.

55. From 1928 national income, imports, and exports had fallen yearly, reaching a low in 1932. General Manager, SAR, to Minister of Mines and Industries, 14 June 1932, mm47/2, MNW 1122; Secretary of Mines to Minister of Mines and Industries, 8 February 1932, mm47/5, MNW 1122; *idem*, 29 June 1932, mm47/2, MNW 1122. In the face of ministerial disapproval, More withdrew the SAR's application for control over the power stations and retired as general manager. See Secretary of Mines to ECB, 12 October 1932, mm47/2, MNW 1122.

56. The stations were Salt River (Cape Town), Congella (Durban), Colenso, Witbank, and Sabie. See Escom's Annual Reports for 1927 and 1932.

57. See Escom, Annual Returns, 1932, ECB 81/2; ECB Annual Report, 1932, 507/5, HEN 3239; Electrical Superintendent to General Manager, SAR, 19 September 1932, mm47/5, MNW 1122.

58. The statistics are from Yudelman, *Emergence of Modern South Africa*, 251–52.

59. See Record of Discussions re VFPC license, 11 December 1933, ECB 56/0;

van der Bijl to Government Mining Engineer, H. Pirow, 29 December 1933, mm68/3, MNW 1136.

60. See ECB to Secretary of Commerce and Industries, 17 April 1934, 507/4, HEN 3238.

61. For statistical returns of the VFPC's profits see Christie, *Electricity, Industry, and Class*, 108–09.

62. Government Mining Engineer to Secretary of Mines, 30 April 1934, mm68/2, MNW 1135.

63. ECB to Secretary of Mines, 16 November 1933, mm68/2, MNW 1135; Record of Discussions re VFPC license, 11 December 1933, ECB 56/o.

64. ECB Annual Report, 1934, 507/5, HEN 3239.

65. Escom to ECB, 15 July 1936, ECB 72.

66. Report on the Work of the ECB (1938), 507/5, vol. 1, HEN 3239; Report on the Work of the ECB (1939), ECB 171.

67. Escom to Secretary of Commerce and Industries, 24 February 1939, 508/3, vol. 1, HEN 3244.

68. Escom, *Annual Report*, 1939. Total production in 1939 was 6.5 billion kwh. See *Union Statistics for Fifty Years*, p. L34.

69. See *Union Statistics for Fifty Years*, pp. L34, 35.

70. *Ibid.*

71. No duties on steel had been enacted under the 1925 Tariff Act, in order to allow in at low cost an important industrial input. After 1928 the government refrained from enacting a steel tariff in response to parliamentary criticisms that such protection would foster an inefficient state industry.

72. Van der Bijl's statement is from his May 1932 address to the Economic Society of South Africa, excerpted in Richards, *Iron and Steel Industry*, 293–94; emphasis in original.

73. "Report on the Mining, Iron, and Steel Works, proposed by the South African Iron and Steel Corp., Ltd. by the Commission of Experts of the Gutehoffnungshutte," 15 December 1924, Annexure 203-1927, Parliamentary Library. F. Meyer, the government adviser on the steel industry, relied heavily on the German report in his report to the Board of Trade and Industries. See his "Memorandum on the Establishment in the Union of an Iron and Steel Industry," 3 May 1926, 509, vol. 2, HEN 3248.

74. The GHH estimated £5,500,000 as being necessary; van der Bijl thought at least £7,000,000 had to be found. See the Memorandum from van der Bijl to Iscor Board of Directors, 1929, Iscor Library.

75. *Ibid.*

76. Iscor Memorandum on Establishment of Works at Pretoria, February 1931, mm66/2, MNW 1132.

77. Quoted in *South African Mining Year Book* (Johannesburg, August 1934), p. 67.

78. South Africa, *Report of the Select Committee on the Iron and Steel Bill* (SC5–27), 79, 87.

79. Minutes of Meeting between Board of Trade and Industries and H. J. van der Bijl, 29 November 1932, 32/2/3, HEN 457.

80. J. H. Dobson to Secretary of Mines, 20 March 1931, 32/1/1, vol. 3, HEN 454.

81. H. J. van der Bijl to Minister of Mines and Industries, 6 June 1932, 32/2/3, HEN 457.

82. Minutes of Meeting between Board of Trade and Industries and H. J. van der Bijl, 29 November 1932, 32/2/3, HEN 457.

83. H. J. van der Bijl to Minister of Finance, 4 August 1933, 32/2/3, HEN 457.

84. Memorandum from H. J. van der Bijl to Iscor Board of Directors, 1929, Iscor Library.

85. *Iron and Steel Industry Act*, Sections 15(2) and (3). See also Agreement between Railway Administration and Iscor, Sections 1 and 4, 14 April 1934, Annexure 665–1934, Parliamentary Library.

86. Richards, *Iron and Steel Industry*, appendix 7–(4).

87. *Ibid.*, appendix 3.

88. Minutes of Meeting between Board of Trade and Industries and representatives of Iscor, SAR, and Department of Commerce and Industries, 12 December 1934, 509/6, vol. 1, HEN 3260; Notes of Meeting between representatives of Iscor and SAR, 7 June 1935, 509/6, vol. 2, HEN 3260.

89. Iscor memorandum on the Establishment of the Works at Pretoria, February 1931, mm66/2, MNW 1132. The African and European Investment Company was owned by the firm of Lewis and Marks, which also owned the coal mine at Vereeniging supplying the VFPC station.

90. Minutes, BTI Meeting, 25 and 28 January 1930, 32/1/1 vol. 1, HEN 454; First Report of Iscor Directors, August 1928 to December 1929, February 1930, mm 66/2, MNW 1132; General Manager, Cape Town, to London Board of Directors, 2 May 1930, GMO 3/1/90, Standard Bank Archives.

91. A previous request for a loan to build a sheet plant at Iscor had met with considerable criticism from the government and left van der Bijl wary of any similar maneuvers. See Secretary of Commerce and Industries to Minister of Commerce and Industries, 29 November 1933, 32/2/3, HEN 457; Minutes, Iscor Board of Directors, 21 June 1934, 509/8, vol. 1, HEN 3261.

92. SA Bolts and Nuts to Department of Commerce and Industry, 20 December 1938, 509, vol. 3, HEN 3248.

93. Iscor, *Address of the Chairman to the Shareholders*, 28 April 1935.

94. Usco to Secretary of Mines, 9 July 1931, 32/2/1, HEN 457; Steel Sales Company to Secretary of Commerce and Industries, 20 October 1936, 32/1/4, HEN 455; Inspection Report on Vereeniging Branch, 18 November 1939, INSP 1/1/384, Standard Bank Archives.

95. Usco to Department of Commerce and Industries, 20 December 1938, 509, vol. 3, HEN 3248.

96. Minutes, Iscor Board of Directors, 9 April 1935, 509/8, vol. 1, HEN 3261; Minutes of Iscor Board of Directors, 21 November 1935, 509/8, vol. 2, HEN 3261; Inspector of Factories to Divisional Inspector, 5 August 1939, CF2/1/1, ARB 2005.

97. General Manager, Cape Town, to London Board of Directors, 23 December 1938, GMO 3/1/122, Standard Bank Archives.

98. Minutes of Iscor Board of Directors, 20 July 1938, 509/8, vol. 3A, HEN 3262.

99. General Manager, Cape Town, to London Board of Directors, 21 April 1939, GMO 3/1/124, Standard Bank Archives.

100. See van der Bijl to Minister of Labor, 23 April 1930, mm2464/28, MNW 934.

101. Government Mining Engineer to Minister of Mines and Industries, 21 August 1930, mm66/3, MNW 1133.

102. JCI was formed in 1889 by Barney Barnato, who used profits from diamond mining in Kimberley to buy into the gold-mining industry on the Rand. Minutes, Iscor Board of Directors, 25 October 1934, 509/8, vol. I, HEN 3261; Minutes, Iscor Board of Directors, 11 July 1935 and 28 August 1935, 509/8, vol. 2, HEN 3261.

103. Minutes, Iscor Board of Directors, 3 September 1936 and 28 April 1937, 509/8, vol. 2, HEN 3261.

104. Secretary of Commerce and Industries to the Minister, 24 January 1936, 509/27, HEN 3276.

105. A. C. McColm to Minister of Commerce and Industries, 28 December 1935, 509/27, HEN 3276; Minutes, Iscor Board of Directors, 18 June 1936, 29 October 1936 and 25 August 1937, 509/8, vol. 2, HEN 3261; Minutes, Iscor Board of Directors, 23 February 1938, 509/8, vol. 3A, HEN 3262.

106. Iscor, *Address of the Chairman to the Shareholders*, 1935, 1939.

107. Report attached to correspondence from H. J. van der Bijl to Minister of Commerce and Industries, 21 November 1934, CI34, MED 8.

108. For discussion of the impact of these events on South Africa, see Richards, *Iron and Steel Industry*, chap. 8, "The International Background and the International Steel Cartel."

109. Figures quoted refer to 1935. Iscor to Minister of Commerce and Industries, 11 May 1936, 32/1/3, vol. 1, HEN 455.

110. BTI to Iscor, February 1935, CI34, MED 8; BTI to Minister of Railways and Harbors, 16 February 1935, 32/21/4, vol. 1, HEN 460; Notes re Meeting between Ministers of Finance, Railways and Harbors, Commerce and Industries, and BTI, 1 July 1935, 32/21/3, HEN 460.

111. Memorandum re the Fifth Union-German Payments Agreement, with charts attached showing the values of South Africa–German trade, 1932–33, 24 June 1938, CI77, MED 14.

112. Department of Commerce and Industries to Iscor, February 1935, CI34, MED 8; Report on Railway Rates on Iron and Steel Products by Secretary of Commerce and Industries, 18 May 1935, 32/21/3, HEN 460; Department Memorandum re Steel Sales Company Products, 25 July 1935, 509/3, vol. 2, HEN 3254.

113. H. J. van der Bijl Memorandum outlining Agreement with European Steel Producers to Minister of Commerce and Industries, 23 March 1936, 32/1/3, vol. 1, HEN 455; BTI to Minister of Commerce and Industries, April 1936, CI34, MED 8.

114. Richards, *Iron and Steel Industry*, appendix 7.

115. *Ibid.*, xli.

116. Gold Producers' Committee to Iscor, December 1939, 32/5/1, vol. 3, RHN 462.

117. Unlike Escom, Iscor could accumulate profits that were to be passed on to shareholders through dividends. When Iscor used such funds to finance expansion, the government, as practically the sole shareholder, offered only muted criticisms. Minister of Commerce and Industries to H. J. van der Bijl, 23 August 1934, CI34, MED 8.

118. Minutes of Meeting between BTI and A. C. McColm, 7 November 1936, 32/21/4, vol. 1, HEN 460.

119. Evidence presented by A. C. McColm, July 1938, Committee of Inquiry into the Base Mineral Industry, vol. 7, K14.

120. Reference to 1934 action in Secretary of Mines to Iscor, 6 November 1941, mm37/60, MNW 1119.

121. Government Mining Engineer to Minister of Mines and Industries, 21 August 1930, mm66/3, MNW 1133.

122. Iscor to Minister of Mines and Industries, 19 May 1931, mm66/2, MNW 1132.

123. Secretary of Mines to Minister of Mines and Industries, 24 December 1929, mm2464/28, MNW 934; Minutes of Iscor Construction Committee, 2 December 1932, 509/4, vol. 1, HEN 3258.

124. Minutes of Meeting between BTI and H. J. van der Bijl, 19 December 1932, 32/2/3, HEN 457; Minutes of Meeting between BTI, H. J. van der Bijl, and A. C. McColm, 16 October 1933, 509/6, vol. 1, HEN 3260.

125. Minutes, Iscor Board of Directors, 21 July 1933, 509/6, vol. 1, HEN 3260.

126. Minutes, Iscor Board of Directors, 13 October 1933, 509/8, vol. 1, HEN 3261.

127. Inspection Report on Vereeniging Branch, 31 January 1935, INSP 1/1/359, Standard Bank Archives.

128. Minutes of Meeting between BTI and H. J. van der Bijl, 19 December 1932, 32/2/3, HEN 457; Iscor employment chart, July 1934, CI34, MED 8.

129. Minutes, Iscor Board of Directors, 3 January 1934, 509/8, vol. 1, HEN 3261.

130. Minister of Commerce and Industries to H. J. van der Bijl, July 1934, CI34, MED 8.

131. Minutes, Iscor Board of Directors, 20 December 1932, 509/4, vol. 1, HEN 3258.

132. BTI Memorandum re Iscor, 4 February 1933, CI39A, MED 11; Minutes, Iscor Board of Directors, 26 May 1933, 509/4, vol. 1, HEN 3258; Minutes, Iscor Board of Directors, 26 July and 22 November 1934, 509/8, vol. 1, HEN 3261.

133. Minutes, Iscor Board of Directors, 22 November 1934, 509/8, vol. 1, HEN 3261.

134. Answer prepared in response to question from House of Assembly, 4 February 1936, 509, vol. 3, HEN 3248.

135. Minutes, Iscor Conciliation Board, 28 April 1937, LC1052/173/2, ARB 571.

136. Divisional Inspector of Labor to Secretary of Labor, 28 May 1935, LC1052/154, ARB 567.

137. South African Boilermakers, Ironworkers, and Shipbuilders Union to Minister of Labor, 20 May 1935, LC1052/154, ARB 567.

138. Minutes, Iscor Conciliation Board, 16 August 1937, LC1052/173/2, ARB 571.

139. "Stryd Tussen Staalwerkers en Ou Vakunie Duur Voort," *Die Vaderland*, 5 August 1936.

140. Undersecretary of Labor to the Secretary, 25 January 1937, LC1052/173, ARB 570.

141. Sums Lent by Iscor, etc., by Secretary of Commerce and Industries, 8 September 1939, 509/8, vol. 3A, HEN 3262.

142. Iscor, *Annual Report, 1936, Balance Sheet.*

143. Department of Labor memorandum, 27 August 1937, LC1058/121–1, ARB 1103; Affidavit of I. L. Walker, Secretary of Labor, re Case Giles et al. v. Hofmeyr et al., 3 November 1937, LC1052/173, ARB 570.

144. Secretary of Labor to Undersecretary, 9 March 1937, Divisional Inspector of Labor to Secretary, 9 April 1937, LC1052/173, ARB 570.

145. Minutes, Iscor Conciliation Board, 30 June 1937, Report of Shirt Sleeve Committees appointed by Conciliation Board, 15 July 1937, LC1052/173/2, ARB 571.

146. Report of Shirt Sleeve Committees appointed by Conciliation Board, 15 July 1937, LC1052/173/2, ARB 571.

147. Minutes, Iscor Conciliation Board, 10 August 1937, LC1052/173/2, ARB 571.

148. Report of Iscor Conciliation Board, 3 September 1937, LC1052/173, ARB 570.

149. During the proceedings of the Conciliation Board the Industrial Council had rapidly reformed itself and, after private consultations, published a new agreement, with the official approval of the minister of labor, J. F. H. Hofmeyr, covering wages and conditions of employment for the entire industry, including unskilled workers and those not party to the agreement. This agreement, which cemented a labor structure consisting of skilled white workers and unskilled blacks, was binding on Iscor and its employees, whatever the outcome of the Conciliation Board, and could not be reversed without approval of the entire council. See Chief Clerk C Division to Acting Secretary of Labor, 17 July 1937, LC1052/173, ARB 570.

150. Department of Labor Memorandum, 27 August 1937, LC1058/121–1, ARB 1103.

151. "Blanke Werkers by Yskor op Groot Skaal deur Naturelle Vervang," *Die Transvaler*, 9 April 1938.

152. Minutes, Iscor Board of Directors, 21 October 1938, 509/8, vol. 3A, HEN 3262.

153. Iscor Memorandum 2 November 1938, CI34, MED 8; Minutes, Iscor Board of Directors, 23 November 1938, 509/8, vol. 3A, HEN 3262.

154. See Iscor, *Address of the Chairman to the Shareholders*, 1934–1938, for figures.

155. See Frankel, *Capital Investment in Africa*, 114–18, and Yudelman, *Emergence of Modern South Africa*, 241, 252, 255.

156. See *Union Statistics for Fifty Years*, p. S3.

157. *Ibid.*, p. L34.

158. *Ibid.*

159. See Richards, *Iron and Steel Industry*, 300–02.

160. *Ibid.*, 304.

161. Webster, *Cast in a Racial Mould*, 45.

162. *Union Statistics for Fifty Years*, pp. G6, 15; Wilson, *Labour in the South African Gold Mines*, 158.

163. Wilson, *Labour in the South African Gold Mines*, 158.

164. *Ibid.; Union Statistics for Fifty Years*, pp. G6, 15.

165. *Union Statistics for Fifty Years*, pp. L32, 33.

166. The Iscor employment chart of July 1934, CI34, MED 8, has 55 percent of Iscor's workers as white; Richards, *Iron and Steel Industry*, table 8, facing p. 270, has whites as 58 percent of the work force.

167. Richards, *Iron and Steel Industry*, xxxix–xli. Richards was quoting in part from speeches made in Parliament at the time of Iscor's establishment. Emphasis in the original.

168. *Ibid.*, 300.

169. *Ibid.*, xlix, lii, lxi.

170. Frankel, *Capital Investment in Africa*, 114–18. Frankel had already estimated in 1930 that at least 50 percent of all government and provincial revenues in South Africa were derived directly and indirectly from the Rand gold mines.

171. *Ibid.* Frankel's tax estimates were for gold industries in the United States and elsewhere.

172. *Ibid.*, 136–37.

173. See the letters of the General Manager, Standard Bank, Cape Town, to London Board of Directors, 18 and 21 April 1939, GMO 3/1/124, Standard Bank Archives.

Chapter 5: War and the Transformation of Industry

1. Lewis, *Industrialisation and Trade Union Organisation*, 90.

2. Posel, *Making of Apartheid*, 26.

3. *Ibid.*, 27.

4. Van der Bijl to Smuts, 7 September 1942, 3/82, MED 24.

5. "Extract from the Report of the Rural Industries Commission," 8 April 1940, 3/35, vol. 1, MED 22.

6. Smuts to Minister of Commerce and Industries, 14 October 1939, 514/1/1, vol. 1, HEN 3324.

7. Minutes, Select Committee on Industrial Development Bill, 11 April 1940, Annexure 441–1940, Parliamentary Library.

8. Van der Bijl to Smuts, 7 September 1942, 3/82, MED 24.

9. "Discussions of the Agricultural and Industrial Requirements Commission on Labour and Related Topics," 1939–1941, Papers of the Industrial Manpower Commission, Bc 825, University of Cape Town.

10. Stratten to van der Bijl, 1 July 1943, MED 27.

11. Van Eck to Waterson, 10 September 1943, 3/35, vol. 2, MED 22.

12. On 6 September 1939, the South African Parliament declared war on Germany following the British declaration of war on 3 September 1939. See Martin and Orpen, *South African Forces*, vol. 7, pp. 22–23.

13. *Ibid.*, 20, 28.

14. The position of director general of war supplies was created in October 1939 when van der Bijl was appointed. H. J. van der Bijl, "Directorate General of War Supplies: Report on Organization, Principles of Purchase, and Production," 14 August 1940, Papers of the Industrial Manpower Commission, Bc 825, University of Cape Town. In September 1942 the office was expanded to cover both industrial

and military goods and was renamed the director general of supplies. Van der Bijl to Smuts, 7 September 1942, and Smuts to van der Bijl, 12 September 1942, 3/82, MED 24.

15. Martin and Orpen, *South African Forces*, vol. 7, p. 140.

16. From 1936 through 1939 the average annual imports from German-controlled territories were as follows: Belgium, 135,310 tons; France, 15,504 tons; Germany, 71,185 tons. Report on Steel Production, 12 August 1946, 32TC, vol. 2, HEN 450.

17. Minutes, Iscor Board of Directors, 23 January 1941, 509/8, vol. 4B, HEN 3263.

18. Iscor, *Chairman's Address to the Shareholders*, 1944.

19. Van der Bijl to Hofmeyr, 2 January 1940, 3/35, vol. 1, MED 22.

20. Stratten to Labor Council, 28 October 1941, TUCSA, Dc9.12, AH 646, University of the Witwatersrand.

21. Marsh, Greenwood to BTI, 30 April 1945, 32/5/1, vol. 4, RHN 463.

22. *Ibid.* and "Second Report of the Advisory Committee on Post War Readjustment and Development in the Engineering and Chemical Industries, Annexure by the Chairman on the Future Use of D.G.S. Annexe Factories," 3 November 1944, file 511, SEC 105.

23. Usco to Controller of Industrial Manpower, 5 November 1941, and Aerial Bomb Section to Assistant Deputy DGWS, 4 May 1942, COM 2/11, ARB 2003.

24. Memorandum by Internal Auditor, DGS, 29 February 1943, 60/7, SEC 94.

25. Iscor, "Memorandum in Regard to Production and Sales Figures for the Financial Year Ended 30 June 1944" (including figures for 1941–44), 509/8, vol. 7A, HEN 3266.

26. Iscor Memorandum, "Excess War-time Costs," 24 August 1945, 509/3, vol. 5, HEN 3256.

27. "Board of Trade and Industries Investigative Report on the Iron, Steel, and Metallurgical Industries of the Union of South Africa," appendix A, "Reports on Stewarts and Lloyds of South Africa and the Union Steel Corporation," 1944, 32/5/1, vol. 4, RHN 463; General Manager, Standard Bank, Cape Town, to London Board of Directors, 26 January 1945, GMO 3/1/147, Standard Bank Archives.

28. "Board of Trade and Industries Investigative Report on the Iron, Steel, and Metallurgical Industries of the Union of South Africa," appendix A, "Reports on Dunswart Iron and Steel Works, Ltd., Scaw Alloys, and George Stott and Company," 1944, 32/5/1, vol. 4, RHN 463.

29. "VFPC Schedule of Annual Sales of Units of Electricity and Compressed Air," evidence presented to the Industrial and Agricultural Requirements Commission, 24 June 1941, IRC 36, vol. 14, K302; Escom, *Seventh Annual Report*, 1929, and *Seventeenth Annual Report*, 1939; Power Station Notebook, private papers of T. G. Otley noted in Christie, *Electricity, Industry, and Class*, 70; Escom, *Twentieth Annual Report*, 1942.

30. South Africa, *Official Yearbook of the Union of South Africa*, no. 23, 1946.

31. Evidence of A. J. Slater, "Minutes Public Hearing in re Objection by City Council of Pretoria re Grant to Electricity Supply Commission of Greater Rand Extension Licence," 16 May 1947, ECB 28.

32. When regulations covering financial disclosure were changed in 1947, VFPC

reserves jumped from £1,900,000 to £6,900,000. See Christie, *Electricity, Industry, and Class*, 114.

33. *Ibid.*; Escom prices to the VFPC calculated from figures for bulk supply at Witbank and Klip stations in Escom Annual Reports of 1940 to 1945.

34. VFPC memorandum to Board of Trade and Industries, 28 October 1941, 32/5/1, vol. 3, RHN 462.

35. Christie, *Electricity, Industry, and Class*, 114.

36. Escom, *Twenty-third Annual Report*, 1945.

37. Van der Bijl to Hans Pirow, Government Mining Engineer, 29 December 1933, mm68/3, MNW 1136.

38. Van der Bijl to Minister of Mines and Industries, 30 May 1923, mm583/23, MNW 717.

39. Escom to Secretary of Commerce and Industry, 19 April 1943, 508, vol. 1, HEN 3239.

40. Van der Bijl to Smuts, 24 November 1944, 508, vol. 1, HEN 3239.

41. *Ibid.*

42. Before and during the war, ECB chairman van Lingen pushed for greater powers for the board, including control over all municipal electricity supply as well as the investigative powers that Escom held. Joined by the VFPC, the ECB proposed that Escom should be strictly limited to the supply of electricity, while the board should take over all planning and investigation. "Note on the Proposals of the Association of Municipal Electricity Undertakings," 25 May 1945, 403/56, HEN 1819. One day after making this proposal, van Lingen denied van der Bijl's request to expropriate the VFPC. ECB to Secretary of Commerce and Industry, 26 May 1945, 508, vol. 1, HEN 3239. On the earlier criticisms of the SAR see Record of Discussions, 11 March 1938, ECB 72.

43. ECB to Secretary of Commerce and Industry, 14 June 1945, 507, HEN 3221; Secretary of Commerce and Industry to Minister of Commerce and Industry, 27 June 1945, 508, vol. 1, HEN 3239.

44. Phillip Gawith, "Memorandum to Iscor Board Dealing More Specifically with the Results of Visit to United States and United Kingdom," 26 July 1944, 509/8, vol. 7A, HEN 3266; Iscor to Secretary of Commerce and Industries, 14 July 1944, 509/8, vol. 6A, HEN 3265.

45. In applying for a loan from the Standard Bank, Stewarts and Lloyds listed one intended expenditure as the purchase of shares in Vecor "with the object of ensuring an adequate supply of steel for their requirements" from Iscor. See General Manager, Standard Bank, Cape Town, to London Board of Directors, 15 August 1945, GMO 3/1/149, Standard Bank Archives.

46. On the growth in manufacturing output see the *Union Statistics for Fifty Years*, p. S3. Jon Lewis argues that the massive growth in manufacturing activity during the war led to the deskilling of many factory positions and in consequence to certain changes in the work force; namely, that the old craft unions insisted upon whites being placed in the new operative positions. Although this occurred at Iscor, it had less to do with pressure from the craft unions than with the organizational capability of the unskilled and semiskilled white workers to press for such positions and larger issues of control over production and labor. Lewis, *Industrialisation and Trade Union Organization*.

47. Minutes, Iscor Board of Directors, 4 September 1940, 509/8, vol. 4B, HEN 3263.

48. Inspection of Mines and Works by Director Native Labor, 15 February 1940, Assistant Native Commissioner, Pilansberg, to Additional Native Commissioner, Rustenburg, 30 May 1941, 521/408C, NTS 9923.

49. "Thabazimbi: Report of Inspection by Director Native Labour," 15 February 1940, Assistant Native Commissioner, Pilansberg, to Additional Native Commissioner, Rustenburg, 30 May 1941, 521/408C, NTS 9923.

50. Assistant Native Commissioner, Pilansberg, to Additional Native Commissioner, Rustenburg, 30 May 1941, Iscor to Director Native Labor, 19 September 1941, 521/408C, NTS 9923.

51. Jourdan to Iscor Works Manager, Pretoria, 2 April 1942, 521/408C, NTS 9923.

52. Assistant Native Commissioner, Pilansberg, to Additional Native Commissioner, Rustenburg, 30 May 1941, Iscor to Director Native Labor, 19 September 1941, 521/408C, NTS 9923.

53. Assistant Native Commissioner, Pilansberg, to Additional Native Commissioner, Rustenburg, 21 January 1942, 521/408C, NTS 9923.

54. Assistant Native Commissioner, Pilansberg, to Additional Native Commissioner, Rustenburg, 23 January 1942, 521/408C, NTS 9923.

55. *Ibid.*

56. Assistant Native Commissioner, Pilansberg, to Additional Native Commissioner, Rustenburg, 2 February 1944, 521/408C, NTS 9923.

57. Assistant Native Commissioner, Pilansberg, to Additional Native Commissioner, Rustenburg, 23 April 1945, 521/408C, NTS 9923.

58. Assistant Native Commissioner, Pilansberg, to Additional Native Commissioner, Rustenburg, 2 February 1944, 521/408C, NTS 9923.

59. Report of the Shirt Sleeve Committees Appointed by the Conciliation Board, re Jobs to Be Taken over by General Laborers, 15 July 1937, LC 1052/173/2, ARB 571.

60. For similar developments in socialist economies as well as in wartime situations see Burawoy, *Politics of Production*, and Kornai, *Economics of Shortage*.

61. DGS Circular, 1 February 1944, MED 28.

62. In May 1942 Iscor's mechanics threatened to go on strike when their hours were reduced but were persuaded by their union to negotiate with the corporation. Inspector of Labor to Secretary of Labor, 20 May 1942, LC 1058/121, Part 4, ARB 1106.

63. Iscor to Secretary of Commerce and Industries, 9 September 1948, 509/19, HEN 3274.

64. Minutes, Iscor Board of Directors, 23 May 1945, 509/8, vol. 7A, HEN 3266.

65. "Dispute at Iscor," *Star*, 6 June 1941.

66. *Ibid.*; "100 Men in Dispute at Iscor," *Rand Daily Mail*, 7 June 1941.

67. Minutes, Industrial Council for the Iron and Steel Manufacturing and Engineering Industry, Transvaal, 6 June 1941, LC 1058/121/2GII, ARB 1109.

68. Minutes, Iscor Board of Directors, 28 June 1950, 509/8, vol. 10B, HEN 3270.

69. Iscor Labor Agreements, Government Notice No. 912, *Government Gazette*, 21 May 1943, and Government Notice No. 1530, *Government Gazette*, 15 September 1944.

70. Despite the shortage of white artisans, white workers in general were not in especially short supply during the war, due to the voluntary nature of military service in South Africa. Beginning in 1940, the South African military experienced serious problems attracting sufficient numbers of white soldiers. See Martin and Orpen, *South Africa at War*, vol. 7, pp. 72–83.

71. Minister of Commerce and Industries to van der Bijl, July 1934, CI34, MED 8; Tisma Membership, 23 May 1940, LC 1058/121, part 3, ARB 1106.

72. Notes on Conditions of Employment in Works, September 1944, mm 66/19, MNW 1135.

73. Iscor, "Basic Rates of Pay of Journeymen and Value of Allowances and Privileges Expressed as the Value per Hour Worked," c. 1945, Papers of the Industrial Manpower Commission, Bc 825, University of Cape Town.

74. Divisional Inspector of Labor to Secretary of Labor, 3 August 1939, LC 1058/121-4, ARB 1103; SA Non-European Confederation of Iron, Steel, and Metal Workers' Union to Department of Labor, 14 October 1942, LC 1058/121–7, ARB 1103; SA Non-European Confederation of Iron, Steel, and Metal Workers' Union to Chamber of Mines Steel Products, 8 December 1943, LC 1058/121–6, ARB 1103; SA Non-European Confederation of Iron, Steel, and Metal Workers' Union to Department of Labor, 17 January 1945, LC 1058/121–6, ARB 1103.

75. "Besware teen Iscor," *Die Burger*, 12 April 1939; Minutes, Industrial Council for the Iron and Steel Manufacturing and Engineering Industry, Transvaal, 6 June 1941, LC 1058/121/2GII, ARB 1109.

76. Hourly wage rates rose from a prewar figure of 4¼d. to 7¼d. in 1946. Iscor Labor Agreements, Government Notice No. 707, *Government Gazette*, 7 May 1937, Government Notice No. 912, *Government Gazette*, 21 May 1943, Government Notice No. 1530, *Government Gazette*, 15 September 1944, and Government Notice No. 2389, *Government Gazette*, 15 November 1946. Although Iscor was not a party to the 1946 industrial agreement, the corporation accepted many of the terms in the agreement, including wage rates for general laborers.

77. Minutes, Iscor Board of Directors, 27 September 1944, 509/8, vol. 7A, HEN 3266.

78. Posel, *Making of Apartheid*, 34.

79. Paraphrased by VFPC general manager T. G. Otley, Otley to Minister of Mines, 15 January 1943, mm94/13, MNW 1144.

80. Christie, *Electricity, Industry, and Class*, 57.

81. Otley to Minister of Mines, 15 January 1943, mm94/13, MNW 1144.

82. VFPC to Minister of Mines, 19 January 1943, mm94/13, MNW 1144; Memorandum by D. L. Smit, Secretary of Native Affairs, 2 July 1943, 442/280/1, NTS 2225.

83. VFPC to Minister of Mines, 12 January 1944, Memorandum by A. A. Eales, 20 January 1944, mm94/13, MNW 1144; "VFP Natives Threaten to Strike To-day," *Rand Daily Mail*, 21 January 1944.

84. Cable from Minister of Labor, Cape Town, to Department of Labor, Pretoria, 21 January 1944, mm94/13, MNW 1144; Deputy Commissioner, SAP, to Commissioner, SAP, 2 February 1944, 166/332, part 1, NTS 7681.

85. VFPC to Minister of Mines, 31 December 1943, 12 and 26 January 1944, Cable from Minister of Labor, Cape Town, to Department of Labor, Pretoria, 21 January 1944, mm94/13, MNW 1144.

86. Secretary Native Affairs to Minister Native Affairs, 22 January 1944, 166/332, part 1, NTS 7681.

87. Cable from Minister of Labor, Cape Town, to Department of Labor, Pretoria, 21 January 1944, mm94/13, MNW 1144.

88. Secretary Native Affairs to Minister Native Affairs, 22 January 1944, 166/332, part 1, NTS 7681.

89. VFPC to Minister of Mines, 26 January 1944, mm94/13, MNW 1144.

90. The commission recommended that the standard wage for workers at the VFPC should be raised from 12s. per week plus a cost of living allowance of 4s. to 25s. plus a 5s. cost of living allowance. South Africa, *Report of the Witwatersrand Mine Natives' Wages Commission*, 1943, UG21–1944, p. 40.

91. Government Mining Engineer, "Increased Working Costs on Mines," 8 February 1944, mm94/13, MNW 1144.

92. Otley at Interview with Gold Producers Committee, 6 January 1943, Minutes of Meeting between Smuts, Minister of Native Affairs, and Minister of Mines, 7 January 1943, 166/332, part 1, NTS 7681.

93. Minutes of Meeting between Smuts, Minister of Native Affairs, and Minister of Mines, 7 January 1943, 166/332, part 1, NTS 7681.

94. VFPC to Minister of Mines, 22 February 1944, mm94/13, MNW 1144.

95. *Ibid.*

96. Director of Native Labor, Johannesburg, to Secretary of Native Affairs, 27 June 1944, Suspect Staff to Deputy Commissioner, SAP, 10 July 1944, 166/332, part 2, NTS 7681.

97. Minutes of Interview with T. G. Otley, 15 August 1944, 166/332, part 2, NTS 7681.

98. VFPC to Minister of Mines, 26 February 1944, mm94/13, MNW 1144.

99. VFPC to Director of Native Labor, 12 September 1945, and African Gas and Power Workers' Union to VFPC, 24 September 1945, 166/332, part 2, NTS 7681; personal communication to R. Christie from B. Hirson, 7 May 1977, in Christie, *Electricity, Industry, and Class,* 140–41.

100. Otley to Minister of Mines, 26 January 1944, mm94/13, MNW 1144.

101. Vecor to Controller of Industrial Manpower, 22 March 1945, 1612/1/17–6j, ARB 1770.

102. Chief Inspector of Labor to Controller of Manpower, 23 March 1945, 1612/1/17–6j, ARB 1770.

103. At the same time, van Eck was chairman of the Industrial and Agricultural Requirements Commission and the Social and Economic Planning Council, which were also engaged in similar studies of South Africa's long-term economic potential. In 1944 he succeeded van der Bijl as chairman of the IDC. See chapter 6 for a fuller discussion of van Eck and the IDC.

104. Minutes, IDC Board of Directors, 3 November 1943, 506/1/5, vol. 2, HEN 3212; Minutes, IDC Board of Directors, 4, 5 July and 3, 4 October 1945, 506/1/5, vol. 3, HEN 3213.

105. The IDC planned to establish a wool-processing industry in cooperation with the National Wool Growers' Association, but it was never able to obtain the required capital from the association, which had trouble raising it from its members. IDC to Minister of Commerce and Industry, 17 August 1942, 506, vol. 2, HEN

3201. And the IDC also originally planned to establish a cotton-weaving project with Union and Congo, Ltd., a Johannesburg firm, but in 1944 the IDC chairman, H. J. van Eck, advised the board to turn down the private company's proposal as being "uneconomic," and the IDC decided to go it alone. Minutes, IDC Board of Directors, 7 December 1944, 506/1/5, vol. 3, HEN 3213.

106. A. Cornish-Bowden, IDC Technical Adviser, to IDC Managing Director, 14 July 1942, 508/1, SEC 105.

107. Minutes, IDC Board of Directors, 7 December 1944, 506/1/5, vol. 3, HEN 3213.

108. *Union Statistics for Fifty Years*, p. L-3.

Chapter 6: The State Corporations and Apartheid

1. Manufacturing pulled ahead of agriculture much earlier in 1930 and ahead of mining in 1943. See Union of South Africa, *Union Statistics for Fifty Years, 1910–1960* (Pretoria, 1961), pp. A-7, S-3.

2. *Ibid.*, p. L-4.

3. *Ibid.*, p. N-2.

4. Frankel and Herzfeld, "Analysis of the Growth of the National Income," and Oppenheimer, *Future of Industry*.

5. Houghton, *South African Economy*, 181.

6. Oppenheimer, *Future of Industry*, 3, 4.

7. *Union Statistics for Fifty Years*, pp. G-9, G-10.

8. See Posel, *Making of Apartheid*, 48–60, and O'Meara, "The 1946 African Mine Workers' Strike," 163, and *idem*, *Volkskapitalisme*.

9. The Fagan Report was, as Dan O'Meara says, an attempt to be "all things to all men." O'Meara, "The 1946 African Mine Workers' Strike," 163.

10. P. Sauer, "Verslag van die Kleurvraagstuk Kommissie van die Herenigde Nasionale Party," 1947.

11. Quote taken from O'Meara, *Volkskapitalisme*, 111, original in du Plessis, *'n Volk Staan Op*, 104. For a discussion of the various interpretations of apartheid among Afrikaners, see Posel, "Meaning of Apartheid before 1948," 123–39. Also see O'Meara, *Volkskapitalisme*, for another interpretation of the various class interests involved in the formulation of apartheid.

12. O'Meara, *Volkskapitalisme*, 177.

13. In 1940 six textile mills were in operation inside South Africa, producing blankets, rugs, and shawls but only a "very small . . . volume" of flannels, cloth, and wool yarn. See Board of Trade and Industries Report No. 251, "The Secondary Wool Industry," in *Official Journal of the Department of Commerce and Industries*, February 1940.

14. IDC to Secretary of Commerce, 1 and 5 July 1946, 506/1/4, vol. 1, HEN 3205.

15. "Final Analysis of the Textile Industry," annexure 8, 9 November 1950, 123/5/2, vol. 4, RHN 1045.

16. Evidence presented to Board of Trade and Industries by Good Hope Textiles, 27 April 1950, and evidence presented to the Board of Trade and Industries by Fine Wool Products, 1 May 1950, 123/5/2, vol. 4, RHN 1045.

17. IDC Cable, 22 May 1947, 506/1/6, vol. 1, HEN 3221; Minutes, IDC Board of Directors, 14 November 1947, 506/1/5, vol. 5, HEN 3214.

18. "Final Analysis of the Textile Industry," 9 November 1950, 123/5/2, vol. 4, RHN 1045.

19. BTI to Secretary of Commerce, 26 October 1949, 123/5/2, vol. 1, RHN 1044.

20. Minutes, Conciliation Board, Textile Workers' Industrial Union v. Messrs. Fine Wool Products, 4 May 1948, 1052/666, ARB 632.

21. Minutes, IDC Board of Directors, 14 November 1947, 506/1/5, vol. 5, HEN 3214.

22. Evidence presented to Board of Trade and Industries by Fine Wool Products, 1 May 1950, 123/5/2, vol. 4, RHN 1045.

23. South Africa, *Official Year Book of the Union of South Africa, 1956–1957,* p. 214. Tisdell and McDonald, *Economics of Fibre Markets,* 65.

24. Yarn Imports from U.K., 25 October 1949, 123/5/2, vol. 1, RHN 1044.

25. Minutes, IDC Board of Directors, 1 April 1953, 506/1/5, vol. 9, HEN 3216.

26. Cornish-Bowden to van Eck, 14 July 1942, 508/1, SEC 105.

27. Minutes, IDC Board of Directors, 7 December 1944, 506/1/5, vol. 3, HEN 3213.

28. Minutes, IDC Board of Directors, 2 September and 6 October 1943, 506/1/5, vol. 2, HEN 3212.

29. Workers designated as being of "mixed" race, legally termed Coloured in South Africa, were entitled to membership in registered—that is, government recognized—trade unions until 1956, when the Industrial Conciliation Act was amended to provide for separate unions. Minutes, IDC Board of Directors, 11 April 1946, 506/1/5, vol. 3, HEN 3213.

30. A. T. Wanless to J. D. F. Briggs, 20 August and 5 September 1947, A. T. Wanless to S. F. Waterson, 8 September 1947, Ballinger Papers, C2.3.9.15, Library of the University of the Witwatersrand.

31. Textile Workers' Industrial Union to IDC, 9 September 1947, Ballinger Papers, C2.3.9.15, Library of the University of the Witwatersrand.

32. Minutes, IDC Board of Directors, 7 October 1947, 506/1/5, vol. 5, HEN 3214; *Government Gazette,* 7 November 1947.

33. Industrial Conciliation Act No. 36 of 1937, Section 51.

34. Good Hope to Board of Trade and Industries, 3 May 1950, 123/5/2, vol. 3, RHN 1045.

35. Evidence presented to the Board of Trade and Industries by Good Hope Textiles, 27 April 1950, 123/5/2, vol. 4, RHN 1045.

36. Good Hope to Board of Trade and Industries, 3 May 1950, 123/5/2, vol. 3, RHN 1045.

37. Evidence presented to the Board of Trade and Industries by Good Hope Textiles, 27 April 1950, 123/5/2, vol. 4, RHN 1045.

38. Board of Trade and Industries Memorandum re Textile Industry, 11 September 1950, 123/5/2, vol. 4, RHN 1045.

39. Rents ranged from 7s. 6d. to £1 per month for two- and four-room homes plus "a similar charge for services," thus making the overall cost of housing twice that in Temba, the government's other experimental rural township. South Africa, *Official Year Book of the Union of South Africa,* 1950, p. 507.

40. Evidence to BTI from Good Hope, 27 April 1950, 123/5/2, vol. 4, RHN 1045.

41. C Division to Secretary of Labor, 5 February 1952, 1183/12–60, ARB 1587.

42. Chief Clerk C Division to Secretary of Labor, 19 March 1952, 1183/12–60, ARB 1587.

43. Minkley, "'With Shouts of Afrika!'" 71–90. Minkley argues that the strike revealed the growing connection between economic and political repression in the minds of the workers.

44. Minutes, IDC Board of Directors, 5 November 1952, 506/1/5, vol. 9, HEN 3216.

45. *Ibid.*

46. Fine Wool insisted on recognition of the differentiation of wages on an area basis, leading to a breakdown in talks with other manufacturers. Minutes, IDC Board of Directors, 27 January 1948, 506/1/5, vol. 5, HEN 3214; Minutes, Conciliation Board, Textile Workers' Industrial Union v. Messrs. Fine Wool Products, 7 April 1948, 1052/666, ARB 632; Minutes of Meeting between Textile Workers' Union and Fine Wool, 23 February 1950, 1052/833, ARB 655.

47. Textile Workers' Union to Fine Wool, 6 January 1948, Union Statement re Labor Dispute, 16 January 1948, 1052/666, ARB 632.

48. This was the same strategy used by Iscor in dealing with its white operatives during the war. Minutes, Conciliation Board, Textile Workers' Industrial Union v. Messrs. Fine Wool Products, 4 May 1948, 1052/666, ARB 632.

49. Memoranda re Application for Conciliation Board, National Association of Worsted Textile Manufacturers v. Textile Workers' Industrial Union, October 1949, 21 November 1949, C Division to Acting Secretary of Labor, 10 July 1951, 1052/797, ARB 651; C Division to Secretary of Labor, 9 February 1950, 1052/666, ARB 632.

50. Out of a total of 595 wage earners, 352 black workers and an undisclosed number of Coloured females quit the union. Fine Wool to Board of Trade and Industries, 14 March 1950, 123/5/2, vol. 3, RHN 1045; Minutes, Conciliation Board, Textile Workers' Industrial Union v. Messrs. Fine Wool, 8 June 1950, 1052/833, ARB 655.

51. Minutes, Conciliation Board, Textile Workers' Industrial Union v. Messrs. Fine Wool, 8 June 1950, 1052/833, ARB 655.

52. Minutes, Conciliation Board, Textile Workers' Industrial Union v. Messrs. Fine Wool, 16 August 1952, 1052/974, ARB 670.

53. Minutes, Interview with Fine Wool, 1 May 1950, 123/5/2, vol. 4, RHN 1045.

54. Worsted Manufacturers Association to IDC, 8 February 1952, 1052/797, ARB 651.

55. Minutes, IDC Board of Directors, 27 January 1953, 506/1/5, vol. 9, HEN 3216.

56. Minutes, Conciliation Board, Textile Workers' Industrial Union v. Messrs. Fine Wool, 10 December 1952, 1052/974, ARB 670.

57. Minutes, IDC Board of Directors, 7 October 1952, 506/1/5, vol. 9, HEN 3216.

58. Evidence presented to Industrial Legislation Commission by African Textile Workers' Industrial Union, 2 June 1949, Memorandum No. 150, K18.

59. Fine Wool to BTI, 14 March 1950, 123/5/2, vol. 3, RHN 1045; Minutes, BTI Interview with Fine Wool, 1 May 1950, 123/5/2, vol. 4, RHN 1045.

60. Minutes, IDC Board of Directors, 6 September 1949, 506/1/5, vol. 7, HEN 3215.

61. Minutes, IDC Board of Directors, 3 December 1952, 506/1/5, vol. 9, HEN 3216.

62. Analysis of the Textile Industry, 9 November 1950, 123/5/2, vol. 4, RHN 1045.

63. Minutes, IDC Board of Directors, 6 May 1952, 506/1/5, vol. 9, HEN 3216.

64. Minutes, IDC Board of Directors, 1 April 1953, 506/1/5, vol. 9, HEN 3216.

65. The Union Corporation also owned the South African Pulp and Paper Industry (SAPPI) plant on the East Rand, which manufactured pulp from wheat. Minutes, IDC Board of Directors, 8 May 1941, 506/1/5, vol. 1, HEN 3212.

66. Minutes, IDC Board of Directors, 4 May 1948, 506/1/5, vol. 6, HEN 3215.

67. Minutes, IDC Board of Directors, 5 December 1950, 506/1/5, vol. 8, HEN 3216.

68. Minutes, IDC Board of Directors, 5 June 1951, 506/1/5, vol. 9, HEN 3216.

69. Minutes, IDC Board of Directors, 4 May 1948, 506/1/5, vol. 6, HEN 3215; Minutes, IDC Board of Directors, 5 September 1950, 506/1/5, vol. 8, HEN 3216; van Eck to Minister of the Interior, 1 May 1951, 506, vol. 4, HEN 3201.

70. IDC to Controller of Imports, 4 October 1951, 506, vol. 4, HEN 3201; IDC, *Annual Report*, 1970.

71. In particular, steel was needed for three major projects: first, for railway repair and construction postponed since 1929; second, for the development of a major new gold reef in the Orange Free State discovered in 1939; and, third, for housing to relieve the acute local shortage. South Africa, Social and Economic Planning Council, Report No. 10, *Public Works Programme and Policy* (Cape Town, 1946), 33, 71.

72. Commodity Supply Division to Railway Coal and Iron Company, 6 September 1946, and Note by Acting Secretary of Commerce, 28 September 1946, 32, vol. 3, HEN 451.

73. War Supplies, Johannesburg, to High Commissioner, London, August 1946, 32, vol. 3, HEN 451; Monthly Returns on South African Steel Production, 1945–1947, 32, vol. 3, HEN 451; Monthly Returns on South African Steel Production, 1947–1948, 32TC, vol. 3, HEN 450.

74. Iscor's subsidiaries, Usco, Amcor, and Vecor, automatically obtained supplies of steel from Iscor, which were not included in the general sales statistics.

75. Iscor, *Chairman's Address to the Shareholders*, 1947; Iscor to Secretary of Commerce, 27 February 1948, 32, vol. 4, HEN 452.

76. Steel Distribution, 1947–1948, 32/1/9, HEN 456.

77. On the origins of Vecor see chapter 5 and Minutes, Iscor Board of Directors, 17 December 1948, 509/8, vol. 9A, HEN 3268.

78. Evidence presented by Iscor to the Coal Commission, 19 June 1947, vol. 17, K154.

79. In the face of considerable bureaucratic criticism of the extensions, the cabinet had finally decided to provide Iscor with the reduced sum, citing "national issues other than the purely economic ones." Department of Commerce and Indus-

tries Report re Iscor Share Capital, 1946, Iscor Memorandum re Extensions, 8 April 1946, 509/3, vol. 5, HEN 3256; Minutes, Iscor Board of Directors, 8 January 1947, 509/8, vol. 8B, HEN 3267; Minutes, Iscor Board of Directors, 17 December 1948, 509/8, vol. 9A, HEN 3268; Memorandum re Iscor Finances by General Manager, A. M. Hagart, 17 January 1949, 509/25, vol. 2, HEN 3275.

80. The legislation establishing each of the state corporations provided for different types of funding. Escom had been given an initial "start-up" loan by the government but was expected thereafter to obtain funds through the sale of nonvoting stock to the public. Iscor was financed entirely as a private company and obtained money through the sale of voting shares. Loans could be raised only with the approval of the shareholders, and because the government had been forced to buy practically all of the shares, official approval was necessary for the raising of any funds. The IDC was funded entirely through government loans.

81. Minutes, Iscor Board of Directors, 5 February 1947, 509/8, vol. 8B, HEN 3267.

82. Devaluation also served to raise the price of gold exports, helping to ease the balance of payments position. Houghton, *South African Economy*, 181–82.

83. Dan O'Meara argues that this government represented a coalition of interests, including the local petty bourgeoisie and Afrikaner capitalists, who felt overwhelmed by the financial predominance of foreign and mining capital. O'Meara, *Volkskapitalisme*.

84. Minutes, Iscor Board of Directors, 23 June 1948, 509/8, vol. 8A, HEN 3267.

85. See earlier quote above, taken from O'Meara, *Volkskapitalisme*, 111; original in du Plessis, *'n Volk Staan Op*, 104.

86. Undersecretary of Commerce to Secretary of Commerce, 29 June 1948, 509/2, vol. 4, HEN 3252.

87. Van der Bijl private papers, in the possession of Alice Jacobs.

88. The original quote was "Om die posisie in die algemeen te oorweeg." Louw to van der Bijl, 22 July 1948, 509/2, vol. 4, HEN 3252.

89. Secretary of Commerce to Iscor, 8 October 1948, 509/8, vol. 9A, HEN 3268.

90. Theron to Minister of Economic Development, 11 January 1949, 509/25, vol. 2, HEN 3275; Minutes, Iscor Board of Directors, 23 March 1949, 509/8, vol. 9A, HEN 3268; Havenga to Minister of Economic Affairs, 9 December 1949, 509/25, vol. 2, HEN 3275.

91. Iscor to Secretary of Commerce, 3 September 1948, 509/8, vol. 9A, HEN 3268.

92. Alice Jacobs, 23 November 1983.

93. Minutes, Iscor Board of Directors, 24 August 1949, 509/8, vol. 10B, HEN 3270; Professional Adviser to Minister of Economic Affairs, 8 December 1949, 509/25, vol. 2, HEN 3275.

94. Minutes, Iscor Board of Directors, 2 June 1950, 509/8, vol. 10B, HEN 3270.

95. Minutes, Iscor Board of Directors, 27 February 1952, 509/8, vol. 4C, HEN 3263.

96. Sixth Annual Report on Affairs of Iscor to 30 June 1955, 1 March 1956, 509/31, vol. 3, HEN 3277.

97. Secretary of Commerce to Minister of Commerce and Industries, 15 December 1942, 509/3, vol. 4, HEN 3255.

98. Houghton, *South African Economy*, 127.

99. Iscor Memorandum, 8 April 1946, 509/3, vol. 5, HEN 3256.

100. For a history of the South African Iron and Steel Trades Association see Lewis, *Industrialisation and Trade Union Organisation*, 78–87.

101. Industrial Conciliation Act, 1937, Iron, Steel, Engineering, and Metallurgical Industry, Pretoria and Vereeniging, 24 January 1947, Amendments to Agreement published under Government Notice No. 2389, 15 November 1946, 32/4, vol. 1, HEN 459.

102. "Report of the Arbitration Proceedings in Regard to a Dispute between the Yster en Staal Bedryf, Vereeniging, and the Transvaal Iron and Steel Manufacturers Association in Connection with Wages and Other Conditions of Employment at Iscor," 13 April 1949, p. 88, ARB 1058/163–12.

103. Minutes, Iscor Board of Directors, 3 September 1947, 509/8, vol. 8A, HEN 3267; Minutes, Iscor Board of Directors, 22 September 1948, 24 November 1948, 509/8, vol. 9A, HEN 3268.

104. Minutes, Iscor Board of Directors, 26 January 1949, 509/8, vol. 9A, HEN 3268.

105. Minutes, Iscor Board of Directors, 29 June 1949, 509/8, vol. 9A, HEN 3268.

106. Minutes, Iscor Board of Directors, 3 October 1951, 509/8, vol. 4C, HEN 3263.

107. Minutes, Iscor Board of Directors, 27 September, 25 October 1950, 509/8, vol. 10B, HEN 3270.

108. Minutes, Iscor Board of Directors, 27 February 1952, 509/8, vol. 4C, HEN 3263.

109. Report of Year Ended 30 June 1950 on Iscor, 21 March 1951, 509/31, HEN 3277; Sixth Annual Report on Affairs of Iscor to 30 June 1955, 1 March 1956, 509/31, vol. 3, HEN 3277.

110. Report of Year Ended 30 June 1950 on Iscor, 21 March 1951, 509/31, HEN 3277.

111. Iscor, *Annual Report*, 1958, p. 7.

112. Iscor, *Annual Report*, 1959, p. 11.

113. Minutes of Public Hearing re Greater Rand Extension License, 16 May 1947, ECB 28.

114. South Africa, Social and Economic Planning Council, Report No. 11, *Economic Aspects of the Gold Mining Industry* (Pretoria, 1947), 22, 35.

115. South Africa, *Official Year Book of the Union of South Africa*, 1948, 913.

116. Christie, *Electricity, Industry, and Class*, 113–14.

117. Escom Application for Greater Rand Extension License, 8 November 1946, ECB 28.

118. Notes re Power Supply to the Witwatersrand Gold Mines, 31 December 1946, 70/1/2, HEN 564.

119. *Ibid.*

120. R. B. Hagart was the brother of A. M. Hagart, general manager of Iscor at this time.

121. Escom to Secretary of Commerce, 17 March 1948, 508, vol. 1, HEN 3239.

122. Escom to Secretary of the Treasury, 19 April 1948, 508, vol. 1, HEN 3239.

123. Escom to ECB, 14 May 1948, 508/3, vol. 2, HEN 3244.

124. Electricity Supply Commission Annual Returns, 1952, ECB 81/2.

125. Act No. 42 of 1922, clause 9(1).

126. Escom to Secretary of Commerce, 23 March 1948, 508/4, vol. 1, HEN 3246; Escom to Secretary of Commerce, 28 March 1949, 24 March 1950, 28 March 1951, 2 April 1952, 508/4, vol. 1, HEN 3246; Escom to Secretary of Commerce, 25 March 1953, 508/4, vol. 2, HEN 3246.

127. A. M. Jacobs was born in Graaff Reinet in 1886 and studied physics and chemistry at the University of Cape Town. He studied electrical engineering in Germany and worked for a time for Siemens in Berlin and Guggenheim Brothers in New York. His brother, E. L. D. Jacobs, married Alice Buxton, who worked as H. J. van der Bijl's secretary in the 1930s and whose sister, Ethel, later married van der Bijl in 1942. Alice Jacobs produced the only published biography of H. J. van der Bijl, *South African Heritage*.

128. Diary of principal Events re Ulco Supply, 20 January 1949, 507/3/24, HEN 3236.

129. Escom, *Golden Jubilee, 1923–1973*, 32.

130. As Renfrew Christie has pointed out, the number of black workers required by Escom to produce 100 megawatts of electricity fell from 203 in 1969 to 165 by 1977, due to mechanization. See Christie, *Electricity, Industry, and Class*, 181.

131. Minutes, Meeting between Escom and Department of Native Affairs, 17 August 1959, 1555/408C, NTS 9977.

132. Furthermore, Furness pointed out that the stations of the VFPC and the RMPSC operated under the Mines and Works Act, while those of Escom were governed by the Factories Act. In 1950 Escom estimated that the difference in legislation saved the commission £60,000 at the RMPSC stations. Escom to ECB, 14 May 1948, 508/3, vol. 2, HEN 3244; evidence presented by Escom to the Industrial Legislation Commission, 24 November 1950, Memorandum No. 258, K18.

133. Escom to Secretary for Bantu Administration and Development, 2 May 1960, 1555/408C, NTS 9977.

134. South Africa, Social and Economic Planning Council, Report No. 10, *Public Works Programme and Policy* (Cape Town, 1946), 59. Secretary of Commerce to ECB, 3 January 1947, 507/1/3, vol. 1, HEN 3225; Secretary of Commerce to Undersecretary of Commerce, 12 March 1947, ECB Voorsitter (Persoonlik).

135. Jacobs was referring to a scheme to provide electricity to Paul Roux, Fouriesburg, and Clarence in the Orange Free State. Jacobs to Minister of Economic Affairs, 26 January 1950, ECB 33.

136. South Africa, *Official Year Book of the Republic of South Africa*, 1960, 423. Memorandum re Rural Electrification, 11 September 1961, ECB 55/9/3.

137. Escom, *Annual Report*, 1974, Statement 8.

138. During and immediately after the war, other state-funded bodies had been established either by Parliament or through relevant ministries, such as the Fisheries Development Corporation (Act 44 of 1944) and the Council for Scientific and Industrial Research (established in October 1945 as a general government advisory board). However, the only state corporations actively operating in the private economy rather than indirectly supporting industrial development remained Escom, Iscor, and the IDC.

139. Act No. 22 of 1940. Act No. 27 of 1942. IDC to Minister of Commerce and Industries, 19 March 1942, 506/1/4, vol. 1, HEN 3205.

140. By 1953 the IDC had a total of £21,500,000 in loans and investments in companies: £13,000,000 was invested in Sasol and £1,000,000 in Foskor. Schedule of IDC Loans and Share Capital, 7 August 1953, 506/1/4, vol. 5, HEN 3206.

141. The Anglo-Transvaal Investment Company, a mining house, had acquired the South African rights to the German Fischer Tropsch coal-gasification process and in 1937 approached van der Bijl with a proposal. Comparing the importance of the proposition to that of Iscor, he wrote to Smuts, "My own belief is that the production of at least a good proportion of the country's requirements in petrol is as important, from a national point of view, as the production of iron and steel," and he recommended that the government guarantee the issue of £1,000,000 in debentures to get the company started. Van der Bijl to Smuts, 28 June 1937, A842/A, Library of the University of the Witwatersrand. The war did nothing but emphasize the fact that oil was indeed a highly strategic commodity, and Frederick Meyer, a member of the Fuel Advisory Committee, recommended that any company producing oil from coal on a large scale "should be under government control," echoing his earlier recommendations about Iscor. Fourth Interim Report of the Fuel Committee, 6 October 1943, 514/2/5, vol. 1, HEN 3327.

142. IDC to Secretary of Commerce, 14 April 1950, 506/1/4, vol. 2, HEN 3205.

143. Secretary of External Affairs to van Eck, 17 June 1950, 506/1/4, vol. 2, HEN 3205.

144. IDC Memorandum re Sasol, 2 March 1951, 506/1/4, vol. 2, HEN 3205.

145. Secretary of Finance to Secretary of Commerce, December 1951, 506/1/4, vol. 3, HEN 3206.

146. Havenga wrote, "Die versekering van fosfaatvoorrade op 'n langtermyn-basis van groter nasionale belang kan wees as selfs die stigting van Sasol." Memorandum re Foskor, June 1951, 96/1/15, vol. 1, HEN 744.

147. The exact quote was "Nie ekonomies of wenslik." Minutes, Cabinet Meeting re Palaborwa, 26 June 1951, 96/1/15, vol. 1, HEN 744.

Chapter 7: Toward Privatization

1. The state corporations were Escom, Iscor, the IDC, Foskor, Armscor, Soekor, Sasol, Alusaf, and Safmarine. The latter three were turned over to the public, and Iscor was "privatized" in 1990. The South African government was also fighting Communists in Angola and sent troops in 1975 to stamp out the MPLA.

2. South Africa, *White Paper on Industrial Development Strategy in the Republic of South Africa* (Pretoria, 1985), 4.

3. The bulk of expenditures were funded from foreign capital markets and did not actually use 42 percent of South African domestic savings; however, the figure was raised by the commission of inquiry to question the appropriateness of the scale of Escom's expenditures. South Africa, *White Paper on the Report and Recommendations of the Commission of Inquiry into the Supply of Electricity in the Republic of South Africa* (Pretoria, 1984), 10, 15.

4. See *White Paper on Industrial Development Strategy*, 7.

5. *Ibid.*, 3.

6. South Africa, *Official Yearbook*, 1987–1988, 477.

7. Escom, *Annual Report*, 1982.

8. See, for example, Escom's *Annual Report*, 1982, especially statistical tables 5, 6, and 7.

9. South Africa, *White Paper on the Report and Recommendations of the Commission of Inquiry into the Supply of Electricity in the Republic of South Africa* (Pretoria, 1984), 22.

10. "Iscor: Worse is Yet to Come," *Financial Mail*, 7 September 1990, p. 105.

11. United States, *Comprehensive Anti-Apartheid Act of 1986*.

12. "Iscor: Not Better Yet," *Financial Mail*, 13 April 1990, p. 51.

13. "Iscor: Worse than Expected," *Financial Mail*, 8 March 1991, p. 108.

14. "Privatisation: No Stomach for the Fight," *Financial Mail*, 13 April 1990.

15. *Ibid.*

Bibliography

Government Archives

Cape Archives Depot, Cape Town (KABA)

A 583	F. S. Malan Papers
A 608	Fremantle Papers
A 1909	Associated Chambers of Commerce Papers

Central Archives Depot, Pretoria (SABA)

AM	Controller of Agricultural Implements
ARB	Department of Labor
B	Industry Advisory Board
BIS	Advisory Board of Industry and Science
BTI	Board of Trade and Industries
CAC	Central Advisory Committee [Commerce and Industry]
CSD	Commodity Supply Directorate
DGS	Director General of Supplies
ECB	Electricity Control Board
F/FIN	Department of Finance
HEN	Department of Commerce and Industry
ICT	Industries Division, Cape Town
IP	Industrial Section, Pretoria
JUS	Department of Justice
K14	Commission of Enquiry, Base Mineral Industry
K18	Industrial Legislation Commission of Enquiry
K26	Native Economic Commission
K34	Low Grade Ore Commission, 1932
K139	Economic and Wage Commission
K154	Coal Commission
K161	Mining Industry Commission
K302	Industrial and Agricultural Requirements Commission
MED	Minister of Economic Development
MNW	Department of Mines and Industries
NTS	Department of Native Affairs
RHN	Board of Trade and Industries

S	Scientific and Technical Committee
SAS	South African Railways
SC	Iron and Steel Control
SEC	Social and Economic Planning Council
STA	Scientific and Technical Adviser

Transvaal Archives Depot, Pretoria (TABA)

A1	Smuts Papers
C33	Transvaal Customs and Industries Commission
C40	Power Companies Commission
CS	Colonial Secretary
CT	Colonial Treasurer
GOV	Governor-General
LA	Legislative Assembly
LEG CO	Legislative Council
LTG	Lieutenant Governor
MGP	Military Governor, Pretoria
SNA	Secretary of Native Affairs
SS	State Secretary

Other Archives and Library Collections

Barclays Bank Archives

NBSA	Minutes, Board of Directors

Hoover Institute

S. H. Frankel Papers

Institute of Contemporary History, Bloemfontein (INCH)

PV 23	Tom Naudé Collection
PV 90	Papers of C. W. Malan
PV 108	Oswald Pirow Collection
PV 346	F. W. Beyers Collection

Parliamentary Library, Cape Town

Ann 339–1920	Memorandum of Agreement between Minister of Railways and Pretoria Iron Mines Ltd.
Ann 340–1920	Deed of Indemnity, Pretoria Iron Mines
Ann 705–1920	Subsidiary Agreement between Minister of Railways and Pretoria Iron Mines Ltd.
Ann 370–1924	Report of Committee upon an Economic Policy for the Union
Ann 203–1927	Gutehoffnungshutte Report
Ann 243–1927	Memorandum on Gutehoffnungshutte Report
Ann 26–1930	Numbers of European Males Engaged in Principal Urban Centers
Ann 330–1931	Special Report on the Purchase of Iscor Debentures
Ann 665–1934	Agreement between SAR and Iscor

Ann 866–1937	Basis of Steel Prices
Ann 53–1938	Report of the Vereeniging Location Riots, 1937
Ann 330–1938	Steel Prices
Ann 47–1943	Report of the Interdepartmental Committee on the Social, Health, and Economic Conditions of Urban Natives
Ann 607–1944	Basis of Steel Prices

Standard Bank Archives

| GMO | General Manager Reports |
| INSP | Inspector's Reports |

University of Cape Town

| Bc294 | Patrick Duncan Papers |
| Bc825 | Papers of the Industrial Manpower Commission |

University of the Witwatersrand

A842/A	J. C. Smuts Papers
A1269F	Central South African Railways
AH646	Tucsa Papers
AH1008	Records of the Iron Moulders' Society
A410	Ballinger Papers

Private Papers

Papers of H. J. van der Bijl, in the possession of Alice Jacobs and Marion Marsh

Official Publications

Imperial Blue Books

> Report on Trade, Commerce, and the Gold Mining Industry of the SAR, 1897
> Report of the Transvaal Concessions Commission, 1901

Union of South Africa

> Union Statistics for Fifty Years, 1910–1960
> Official Year Book of the Union of South Africa, editions covering 1910–1960

Board of Trade and Industries Reports
No. 7	Iron and Steel Industries, 1922
No. 251	Secondary Wool Industry, 1940
No. 282	Manufacturing Industries, 1945
No. 286	Iron, Steel, Engineering, and Metallurgical Industries, 1946
No. 311	Iron, Steel, Engineering, and Metallurgical Industries, 1948

Commissions of Enquiry
UG1–1918	State Mining Commission, 1916–1918
UG34–1920	Low Grade Mines Commission, 1920
UG33–1921	Coal Commission, 1921

UG14–1926   Economic and Wages Commission, 1925
UG16–1932   Low Grade Ore Commission, 1930
UG37–1935   Industrial Legislation Commission, 1935
UG33–1940   Industrial and Agricultural Requirements Commission,
                 1940–1941
UG49–1940   "   "   "
UG40–1941   "   "   "
UG27–1940   Rural Industries Commission, 1940
UG21–1944   Witwatersrand Mine Natives' Wages Commission, 1943
WPG–84   Supply of Electricity
WPG–85   Industrial Development Strategy
WPG–87   Privatization and Deregulation

Electricity Supply Commission
    Annual Reports, 1923–1960
    Establishment of an Undertaking at Cape Town, 1924
    Establishment of an Undertaking at Witbank, 1925
    Supply of Electricity from Colenso Power Station, 1925
    Establishment of an Electrical Undertaking at Durban, 1926
    Acquisition of an Electrical Undertaking at Colenso, 1927
    Establishment of an Electrical Undertaking at Sabie, 1927
    Establishment of an Electrical Undertaking on the Witwatersrand, 1934
    Establishment of an Electrical Undertaking at Brakfontein, 1939
    Electrical Undertaking at East London, 1948
    *Twenty-five Years: Record of the Origin, Progress, and Achievements of Escom,
        1923–1948*
    Golden Jubilee, 1923–1973
    A Leadership Corporate Profile, 1986

House of Assembly
    Debates of the House of Assembly as reported in the *Cape Times*, 1915–1923
    Debates of the House of Assembly, 1914, 1924–1950
    Parliamentary Register, 1910–1961

Industrial Development Corporation
    Director's Reports and Accounts, 1946–1960
    The IDC: Its Work and Influence, 1940–1965
    *1940–1970: Thirty Years On . . . The Story of the Founding and Growth of the
        IDC*, 1971
    Nywerheid-ontwikkelingskorporasie van Suid Afrika Beperk: Finansiele
        Inligting bykomig tot die verslag van die Hoofrekenmeester, 1978

Iron and Steel Corporation
    Director's Reports and Balance Sheets, 1931–1960
    A Brief History and Description of the Iscor Works [pre-1934]
    *The South African Iron and Steel Corporation and Its Subsidiary and
        Associated Companies*, 1936
    A Few Facts about Iscor, 1936
    Staal in Suid-Afrika, 1928–1953

The South African Iron and Steel Industry, 1975
Steel in South Africa [n.d.]

Select Committee Reports
SC9–12   The Scrap Iron Agreement, 1912
SC2–19   The Rand Mines Power Supply Company Water Supply Bill,
                  1919
SC5B–20   Memorandum of Agreement between Minister of Railways
                  and Pretoria Iron Mines, 1920
SC7–22   The Electricity Bill, 1922
SC5–27   The Iron and Steel Industry Bill, 1927
SC1–28   The Iron and Steel Industry Bill, 1928

Social and Economic Planning Council Reports
Report No. 1   Re-Employment, Reconstruction, and the Council's Status,
                  1942
Report No. 2   Social Security, Social Services, and the National Income,
                  1944
Report No. 3   Aspects of Public Service Organization and Employment,
                  1944
Report No. 4   The Future of Farming in South Africa, 1945
Report No. 5   Regional and Town Planning, 1944
Report No. 6   Social and Economic Statistics in the Union, 1944
Report No. 7   Taxation and Fiscal Policy, 1945
Report No. 8   Local Government Functions and Finances, 1945
Report No. 9   Native Reserves and Their Place in the Economy of the
                  Union of South Africa, 1946
Report No. 10   Public Works Programme and Policy, 1946
Report No. 11   Economic Aspects of the Gold Mining Industry, 1947

Published Works

Adam, Heribert, and Hermann Giliomee, Ethnic Power Mobilized: Can South
    Africa Change? (New Haven, 1979).
American Iron and Steel Institute, The Making of Steel (New York, 1964).
Amsden, Alice, Asia's Next Giant: South Korea and Late Industrialization (New
    York and Oxford, 1989).
Arndt, E. H. D., Banking and Currency Development in South Africa, 1652–1927
    (Cape Town and Johannesburg, 1928).
Batstone, Eric, Anthony Ferner, and Michael Terry, Consent and Efficiency:
    Labour Relations and Management Strategy in the State Enterprise (Oxford,
    1984).
Bosman, G. C. R., The Industrialization of South Africa (Rotterdam, 1938).
Botha, D. J. J., "On Tariff Policy: The Formative Years," South African Journal of
    Economics 41:4 (December 1973): 321–55.
Bozzoli, Belinda, "Capital and the State in South Africa," Review of African
    Political Economy 11 (January–April 1978): 40–50.
———, The Political Nature of a Ruling Class: Capital and Ideology in South
    Africa, 1890–1933 (London, 1981).

Braverman, Harry, *Labor and Monopoly Capital: The Degradation of Work in the Twentieth Century* (New York, 1974).

Bundy, Colin, *The Rise and Fall of the South African Peasantry* (Berkeley and Los Angeles, 1979).

Burawoy, Michael, *The Politics of Production: Factory Regimes under Capitalism and Socialism* (London, 1985).

Cardoso, Fernando Henrique, "Dependency and Development in Latin America," *New Left Review* 74 (1972): 83–95.

———, and Enzo Faletto, *Dependency and Development in Latin America* (Berkeley, 1979).

Cartwright, A. P., *The Dynamite Company: The Story of African Explosives and Chemical Industries Limited* (Cape Town, 1964).

———, *The Corner House: The Early History of Johannesburg* (Johannesburg, 1965).

Christie, Renfrew, *Electricity, Industry, and Class in South Africa* (Albany, 1984).

———, "Antiquated Industrialization: A Comment on William Martin's 'The Making of an Industrial South Africa'," and "Propaganda, Reality, and Uneven Development: A Rejoinder to Bill Martin," *International Journal of African Historical Studies* 24:3 (1991): 589–608, 619–20.

Clarke, Simon, "Capital, Fractions of Capital, and the State: 'Neo-Marxist' Analysis of the South African State," *Capital and Class* 5 (1978): 32–75.

Cooper, Frederick, *On the African Waterfront: Urban Disorder and the Transformation of Work in Colonial Mombasa* (New Haven, 1987).

Davenport, T. R. H., *South Africa: A Modern History* (Toronto, 1991).

Davies, Robert, *Capital, State, and White Labour in South Africa, 1900–1960: An Historical Materialist Analysis of Class Formation and Class Relations* (Brighton, 1979).

———, David Kaplan, Mike Morris, and Dan O'Meara, "Class Struggle and the Periodisation of the State in South Africa," *Review of African Political Economy* 7 (1976): 4–30.

de Kiewiet, C. W., *A History of South Africa: Social and Economic* (Oxford, 1957).

de Kock, Gerhard, *A History of the South African Reserve Bank, 1920–1952* (Pretoria, 1954).

de Kock, J. ed., *Dictionary of South African Biography* (Cape Town, 1968).

Delius, Peter, *The Land Belongs to Us: The Pedi Polity, the Boers, and the British in the Nineteenth-Century Transvaal* (Johannesburg, 1983).

Denoon, Donald. "'Capitalist Influence' and the Transvaal Government during the Crown Colony Period, 1900–1906," *Historical Journal* 11:2 (1968): 301–31.

———, *A Grand Illusion: The Failure of Imperial Policy in the Transvaal Colony during the Period of Reconstruction, 1900–1905* (London, 1973).

Doxey, G. V., *The Industrial Colour Bar in South Africa* (Cape Town, 1961).

Dubow, Saul, *Racial Segregation and the Origins of Apartheid in South Africa, 1919–1936* (New York, 1989).

du Plessis, E. P., *'n Volk Staan Op: Die Ekonomiese Volkskongres en Daarna* (Cape Town, 1964).

du Toit, André, and Hermann Giliomee, eds., *Afrikaner Political Thought: Analysis and Documents* (Berkeley, 1983).

Evans, Peter, *Dependent Development: The Alliance of Multinational, State, and Local Capital in Brazil* (Princeton, 1979).

Feldman, Gerald, D., *Iron and Steel in the German Inflation, 1916–1923* (Princeton, 1977).

Fine, Ben, "Scaling the Commanding Heights of Public Enterprise Economics," *Cambridge Journal of Economics* 14 (1990): 127–42.

Frankel, S. Herbert, *Capital Investment in Africa: Its Course and Effects* (London, 1938).

——, and H. Herzfeld, "An Analysis of the Growth of the National Income of the Union in the Period of Prosperity before the War," *South African Journal of Economics* 12:1 (June 1944): 112–38.

Franzsen, D. G., *Economic Growth and Stability in a Developing Economy: Some Aspects of the Union's Post-War Experience* (Pretoria, 1960).

Fraser, M., and A. Jeeves, eds. *All That Glittered: Selected Correspondence of Lionel Phillips, 1890–1914* (Cape Town, 1977).

Freer, Pamela, *South Africa to 1990: Growing to Survive*, Economist Intelligence Unit Special Report No. 239 (London, 1986).

Freund, Bill, "The Social Character of Secondary Industry in South Africa, 1915–1945 (With Special Reference to the Witwatersrand)," in Alan Mabin, ed., *Organisation and Economic Change: Southern African Studies*, volume 5 (Johannesburg, 1989).

Garson, N. G., "Het Volk: The Botha-Smuts Party in the Transvaal, 1904–1911," *Historical Journal* 9:1 (1966): 101–32.

Gerschenkron, Alexander, *Economic Backwardness in Historical Perspective* (Cambridge, Mass., 1962).

Gordon, C. T., *The Growth of Boer Opposition to Kruger, 1890–1895* (Cape Town, 1970).

Greenberg, Stanley, *Race and State in Capitalist Development: Comparative Perspectives* (New Haven, 1980).

Hancock, W. K., *Smuts, Volume 1: The Sanguine Years* (Cambridge, U.K., 1962), and *Smuts, Volume 2: The Fields of Force* (Cambridge, U.K., 1968).

Henderson, W. O., *The State and the Industrial Revolution in Prussia, 1740–1870* (Liverpool, 1967).

Henry, J. A., *The First Hundred Years of the Standard Bank* (London, 1963).

Hindson, Doug, *Pass Controls and the Urban African Proletariat* (Johannesburg, 1987).

Hobson, J. A., *The War in South Africa: Its Causes and Effects* (London, 1900).

Holland, Stuart, ed., *The State as Entrepreneur* (London, 1972).

Houghton, D. Hobart, *The South African Economy* (Cape Town, 1973).

——, and Jenifer Dagut, *Source Material on the South African Economy, 1860–1870, Volume 1: 1860–1899* (Cape Town, 1972).

Hughes, Thomas P., *Networks of Power: Electrification in Western Society, 1880–1930* (Baltimore, 1983).

Iliffe, John, Book review of Christopher Saunders, *The Making of the South African Past*, and Kenneth Smith, *The Changing Past*, in *Social Dynamics* 15:1 (1989): 143–45.

Innes, Duncan, and Martin Plaut, "Class Struggle and the State," *Review of African Political Economy* 11 (1979): 51–61.

——, *Anglo-American and the Rise of Modern South Africa* (New York, 1984).

Jacobs, Alice, *South African Heritage: A Biography of H. J. van der Bijl* (Pietermaritzburg, 1948).

Jeeves, Alan H., *Migrant Labour in South Africa's Mining Economy: The Struggle for the Gold Mines' Labour Supply, 1890–1920* (Johannesburg, 1985).

Johnstone, Frederick, *Class, Race, and Gold: A Study of Class Relations and Racial Discrimination in South Africa* (London, 1976).

Jones, Leroy P., ed., *Public Enterprise in Less-Developed Countries* (New York, 1982).

Kaplan, Dave, and Mike Morris, "Labour Policy in a State Corporation: A Case Study of the South African Iron and Steel Corporation," *South African Labour Bulletin* 2:6 (1976): 21–33 and 2:8 (1976): 2–21.

Keegan, Timothy, *Rural Transformations in Industrializing South Africa* (Johannesburg, 1986).

Kooy, M., and H. M. Robertson, "The South African Board of Trade and Industries: The South African Customs Tariff and the Development of South African Industries," *South African Journal of Economics* 34:3 (December 1966): 205–24.

Kornai, Janos, *The Economics of Shortage* (New York, 1980).

Kruger, D. W., *South African Parties and Policies, 1910–1960* (London, 1960).

Kubicek, Robert V., *Economic Imperialism in Theory and Practice: The Case of South African Gold Mining Finance, 1886–1914* (Durham, 1979).

Laux, Jeanne, and Maureen Molot, *State Capitalism: Public Enterprise in Canada* (Ithaca and London, 1988).

LeMay, G. H. L., *British Supremacy in South Africa, 1899–1907* (Oxford, 1965).

Lewis, Jon, *Industrialisation and Trade Union Organisation in South Africa, 1924–1955: The Rise and Fall of the South African Trades and Labour Council* (Cambridge, U.K., 1984).

Lim, Hyun-Chin, *Dependent Development in Korea, 1963–1979* (Seoul, 1986).

Lipton, Merle, *Capitalism and Apartheid: South Africa, 1910–1984* (Totowa, N.J., 1985).

Lonsdale, John, "From Colony to Industrial State: South African Historiography as Seen from England," *Social Dynamics* 9:1 (1983): 67–83.

Maier, Charles S., *Recasting Bourgeois Europe: Stabilization in France, Germany, and Italy in the Decade after World War I* (Princeton, 1981).

Marais, J. S., *The Fall of Kruger's Republic* (Oxford, 1961).

Marks, Shula, *Reluctant Rebellion: The 1906–1908 Disturbances in Natal* (Oxford, 1970).

——, and Stanley Trapido, "Lord Milner and the South African State," *History Workshop* 8 (Fall 1979): 50–80.

——, eds., *The Politics of Race, Class, and Nationalism in Twentieth-Century South Africa* (London, 1987).

Martin, H. J., and Neil D. Orpen, *South African Forces, World War II, Volume 7: South Africa at War: Military and Industrial Organization and Operations in Connection with the Conduct of the War, 1939–1945* (Cape Town, 1979).

Martin, William, "The Making of an Industrial South Africa," *International Journal of African Historical Studies* 23:1 (1990): 59–85.

——, "Developmentalism: The Pernicious Illusion. A Response to Renfrew Christie's 'Antiquated Industrialization'," *International Journal of African Historical Studies* 24:3 (1991): 609–17.

Mawby, A. A., "Capital, Government, and Politics in the Transvaal, 1900–1907: A Revision and Reversion," *Historical Journal* 17:2 (1974): 367–415.

Mendelsohn, Richard, *Sammy Marks: 'The Uncrowned King of the Transvaal'* (Cape Town, 1991).

Minkley, Gary, "'With Shouts of Afrika!': The 1952 Textile Strike at Good Hope Textiles, King William's Town," *Social Dynamics* 16:2 (1990): 71–90.

Morris, Mike, "The Development of Capitalism in South African Agriculture," *Economy and Society* 5:3 (1976): 293–343.

Nattrass, Nicoli, "Wages, Profits, and Apartheid" (PhD dissertation, University of Oxford, 1990).

Neumark, S. Daniel, *Economic Influences on the South African Frontier, 1652–1836* (Stanford, 1957).

O'Donnell, Guillermo, *Modernization and Bureaucratic Authoritarianism* (Berkeley, 1973).

O'Meara, Dan, "The 1946 African Mine Workers' Strike and the Political Economy of South Africa," *Journal of Commonwealth and Comparative Politics* 13:2 (July 1975): 146–73.

———, *Volkskapitalisme: Class, Capital, and Ideology in the Development of Afrikaner Nationalism, 1934–1948* (Johannesburg, 1983).

Oppenheimer, H. F. *The Future of Industry in South Africa* (Johannesburg, 1950).

Posel, Deborah, "The Meaning of Apartheid before 1948: Conflicting Interests and Forces within the Afrikaner Nationalist Alliance," *Journal of Southern African Studies* 14:1 (1987): 123–39.

———, *The Making of Apartheid, 1948–1961: Conflict and Compromise* (Oxford, 1991).

Richards, C. S., *The Iron and Steel Industry in South Africa* (Johannesburg, 1940).

———, "The Growth of Government in South Africa since Union," *South African Journal of Economics* 25:4 (September 1957): 239–63.

Richardson, Peter, and Jean Jacques Van-Helten, "The Gold Mining Industry in the Transvaal, 1886–1899," in Peter Warwick, ed., *The South African War: The Anglo-Boer War, 1899-1902* (London, 1980).

Rueschemeyer, Dietrich, and Peter B. Evans, "The State and Economic Transformation: Toward an Analysis of the Conditions Underlying Effective Intervention," in Evans, Rueschemeyer, and Theda Skocpol, eds., *Bringing the State Back In* (New York, 1985).

Schumann, C. G. W., "Business Cycles in South Africa, 1910–1933," *South African Journal of Economics* 2:2 (June 1934): 130–59.

Seidman, Ann, and Neva Seidman, *South Africa and U.S. Multinational Corporations* (Westport, Conn., 1977).

Seidman, Gay Wilcox, "Labor Movements in Newly Industrialized Countries: South Africa and Brazil," Ph.D. dissertation, University of California at Berkeley, 1990.

Simons, H. J. and R. E., *Class and Colour in South Africa* (Middlesex, 1969).

Smith, Thomas C., *Political Change and Industrial Development in Japan: Government Enterprise, 1868–1880* (Stanford, 1955).

Stadler, A. W., "The Party System in South Africa, 1910–1948," Ph.D. dissertation, University of the Witwatersrand, Johannesburg, 1970.

Thompson, Leonard, *The Unification of South Africa, 1902–1910* (Oxford, 1960).

Tisdell, C. A., and P. W. McDonald, *Economics of Fibre Markets: Price Fluctuations and Economic Interdependence between Man-Made Fibres, Wool, and Other Natural Fibres* (Newcastle, 1977).

Trapido, Stanley, "Reflections on Land, Office, and Wealth in the South African

Republic, 1850–1900," in Shula Marks and Anthony Atmore, eds., *Economy and Society in Pre-Industrial South Africa* (London, 1980).

————, "Landlord and Tenant in a Colonial Economy: The Transvaal, 1880–1910," *Journal of Southern African Studies* 5:1 (1978): 26–58.

Tsurumi, E. Patricia, *Factory Girls: Women in the Thread Mills of Meiji Japan* (Princeton, 1990).

van den Heever, C. M., *General J. B. M. Hertzog* (Johannesburg, 1946).

van der Bijl, H. J., *The Thermionic Vacuum Tube and Its Applications* (New York, 1920).

van der Poel, Jean, *Railway and Customs Policies in South Africa, 1885–1910* (London, 1933).

————, ed. *Selections from the Smuts Papers, Volume 5: 1919–1934, Volume 6: 1934–1945 and Volume 7: 1945–1950* (Cambridge, U.K., 1973).

Van-Helten, J. J., "German Capital, the Netherlands Railway Company, and the Political Economy of the Transvaal, 1886–1900," *Journal of African History* 19:3 (1978): 369–90.

van Onselen, Charles, *Studies in the Social and Economic History of the Witwatersrand, 1886–1914, Volume 1: New Babylon* (Johannesburg, 1982).

Wade, Robert, *Governing the Market: Economic Theory and the Role of Government in East Asian Industrialization* (Princeton, 1990).

Wagner, Roger, "Zoutpansberg: The Dynamics of a Hunting Frontier, 1848–1867," in Shula Marks and Anthony Atmore, eds., *Economy and Society in Pre-Industrial South Africa* (London, 1980), pp. 327–37.

Walker, Eric, *A History of Southern Africa* (London, 1957).

Walstedt, Bertil, *State Manufacturing Enterprise in a Mixed Economy: The Turkish Case* (Baltimore, 1980).

Webster, E., *Cast in a Racial Mould: Labour Process and Trade Unionism in the Foundries* (Johannesburg, 1985).

Wilson, Ernest J., "Contested Terrain: A Comparative and Theoretical Reassessment of State-Owned Enterprise in Africa," *Journal of Commonwealth and Comparative Politics* 21:1 (March 1984): 4–27.

Wilson, Francis, *Labour in the South African Gold Mines, 1911–1969* (Cambridge, U.K., 1972).

Wilson, Monica, and Leonard Thompson, eds., *The Oxford History of South Africa, Volume 1: South Africa to 1870* (New York, 1969).

Wolpe, Harold, "Capitalism and Cheap Labour Power in South Africa: From Segregation to Apartheid," *Economy and Society* 1:4 (1972): 425–56.

Yudelman, David, *The Emergence of Modern South Africa: State, Capital, and the Incorporation of Organized Labour on the South African Gold Fields, 1902–1939* (Westport, Conn., 1983).

Index